JAN SMUTS

and his
International Contemporaries

JAN SMUTS

and his
International Contemporaries
O. Geyser

COVOS DAY
Johannesburg & London

By the same author:
Die Ou Hooggeregshofgebou: Afrikaanse uitgawe, Kaapstad, 1958
The Old Supreme Court Building, English edition, Johannesburg, 1982
The Native Policy of Theophilus Shepstone, Johannesburg, 1969
The Nationalist Party, Volume 1, 1914 – 1924, Co-editor, Cape Town, 1975
Détente in Southern Africa, Bloemfontein, 1977
BJ Vorster Select Speeches, Bloemfontein, 1977
Watershed for South Africa, London, 1961. Durban, 1983

Copyright © O. Geyser, 2001

Published by Covos Day, 2001
Oak Tree House, Tamarisk Avenue,
PO Box 6996, Weltevredenpark 1715, Gauteng, Republic of South Africa
E-mail: covos@global.co.za

Cover design and lay-out: HRH Graphics, Centurion, South Africa
Email: j.design@mweb.co.za

Printed and bound by United Litho

ISBN 1-919-87410-0

TO ERIKA

*JAN SMUTS, THAT WONDERFUL MAN, WITH HIS
IMMENSE, PROFOUND MIND, AND HIS EYE WATCHING
FROM A DISTANCE THE WHOLE PANORAMA OF
EUROPEAN AFFAIRS.*

WINSTON CHURCHILL

CONTENTS

Foreword viii

Introduction: In a Class of His Own xiii

1. Cecil John Rhodes 1

2. Alfred Milner 23

3. Henry Campbell-Bannerman 51

4. David Lloyd George 73

5. Winston Churchill 95

6. Mahatma Gandhi 115

7. Eamon de Valera 139

8. The Windsors 161

9. Charles de Gaulle 185

10. Adolf Hitler 203

Select Bibliography 226

Index 236

FOREWORD

The life of Jan Christiaan Smuts has interested, even fascinated, scholars, world statesmen, kings and queens and numerous leading figures in national and international politics for almost half a century. After finishing his law studies at Christ's College, Cambridge, he unsuccessfully applied for a post as lecturer in philosophy at the South African College, Cape Town. "One cannot help speculating," wrote Professor W.K. Hancock, "about the difference it would have made to the history of South Africa (and other countries) if Smuts had settled at the age of 25 in quiet academic groves."

Smuts was an extremely versatile person who was interested in law, philosophy, botany, politics, literature and much more. He pioneered in philosophy with his book *Holism and Evolution*. The University of Hamburg in Germany once asked Smuts permission to publish his *Holism and Evolution* for use in Spain and South America. Before the Second World War, Smuts' *Holism* was translated into German, but it was banned by the Nazis during the War. In November 1945 Smuts wrote to Margaret Gillett that, according to Professor Adolf Mayer-Abich, *Holism* was once more taught in the university and that interest in the subject was increasing on the Continent all the time. "But I don't wish to give permission for the Spanish translation," Smuts wrote, "as so much of the scientific part is really obsolete. The advance of physics and biology in the last 20 years has really been phenomenal, and my early chapters read like pre-scientific. I wish I could find time to write my second volume, and let the first become antiquarian as it is practically antiquated." This is a very good example of Smuts' scientific approach to his interest in philosophy.

At one stage he was a world authority on grasses. A fellow student once predicted "that there was not a post in the British Empire that Smuts might not win if God Almighty spared him." Smuts played a decisive and leading role in two world wars; he was a factor to be reckoned with at the peace negotiations in Paris after the First World War and he was the architect of the

British Commonwealth of Nations. In Britain he was the confidant of two successive kings and Sir Winston Churchill. Smuts also played a most important role during the Second World War, *inter alia*, as highly respected adviser to King George VI and Sir Winston Churchill.

During his lifetime Smuts had many honours bestowed on him abroad: 27 honorary doctorates, 26 national decorations and the freedom of 17 cities and towns. He was chancellor of the universities of Cape Town and Cambridge and rector of St Andrews. Smuts became a most controversial figure nationally as well as internationally. As politician and statesman he was honoured and scorned; as philosopher and ecologist few recognised his value.

My personal interest in Jan Smuts resulted from my interest in, and consequent research on, the British Commonwealth of Nations. The transformation from British Empire to British Commonwealth of Nations after the First World War and the ultimate development of the latter, is a fascinating period in world history. The role that Smuts played in all of this is undoubtedly of immense significance for South Africa. Professor Nicholas Mansergh refers to Smuts' role in the Commonwealth as "the strangest of all Commonwealth careers". After the Second World War Smuts saw the development of the Commonwealth into a structure that did not conform to his vision for the Commonwealth. He was strongly opposed to India remaining in the Commonwealth after she became a republic in 1947. He rejected a dual loyalty outright. He believed that as a member of the Commonwealth absolute loyalty should be exclusive to the British monarch as leader of the Commonwealth. To Smuts this new, and to a certain extent unexpected, development in the Commonwealth was certainly a traumatic experience. He once wrote: "I am a firm believer in the Commonwealth, not only for its own sake and that of South Africa, but as the first tentative beginnings of great things for the future of the World."

For many years I was of the opinion that there was really no place for another biography on Smuts. However, it gradually became clear to me that more in-depth studies of Smuts may prove fruitful. I therefore decided to investigate his contact with several leading international political contemporaries. I decided to include Cecil John Rhodes in spite of the fact that he was not a politician of international stature at the time, but simply because he actually unintentionally, but radically, diverted Smuts' interest in and vision of South African politics from supporting Rhodes' imperialism to supporting Paul Kruger's republicanism. At this time Rhodes was prime minister of the Cape Colony. The obvious question is: how did Smuts influence international politics through his contact with these contemporaries and what was the nature of the relationships he personally had with them? He knew them all well and some of them were even close friends.

Although Smuts never met Rhodes and Adolf Hitler in person, both of them nevertheless had an interesting impact on his life. On returning from Cambridge, Smuts idealised Rhodes's political vision for South Africa and Africa as a whole. It all fitted in well with his *holism*. But when Rhodes' involvement in the Jameson Raid was revealed, he simply commented: "It was hero worship pure and simple." Smuts' letters to colleagues and friends in England and the United States regarding Hitler make interesting reading matter. Until shortly before the outbreak of the Second World War he did not condemn Hitler outright. "Hitler," he wrote, "is personally friendly towards the British Empire." Smuts asked for an understanding of Hitler and urged British political leaders to negotiate with him. To a great extent Smuts' contact and dealings with his contemporaries reveal his personality in a most extraordinary way.

I am deeply indebted to the staff of a great number of academic and research institutions, abroad and in South Africa, who assisted me during the long period of research. First of all I would like to acknowledge the gracious permission of Her Majesty the Queen to consult relevant research material in the Royal Archives at Windsor Castle, in preparation of this manuscript. Lady Sheila de Bellaigue, registrar of the Royal Archives, and her staff, was most helpful during my visit to the Royal Archives. Father Ignatius Fennessey, OFM, Franciscan Library, Killiney, Ireland, assisted me considerably in consulting the Eamon de Valera papers housed in the Library. I would also like to acknowledge the assistance of the staff of the following academic and research institutions: Institute of Commonwealth Studies, University of London; Centre of African Studies, University of London; Imperial War Museum, London; British Museum, London; Collindale Press Library, London; Commonwealth Society Library, Cambridge; Public Record Offices, London, Edinburgh and Dublin; National State Archives, Dublin. In South Africa: State Archives, Pretoria; Jagger Library, University of Cape Town; Sasol Library, Free State University, Bloemfontein.

I want to extend my sincere gratitude to our daughter, Dr Astrid Geyser-Jankielsohn, for her assistance on the computer. I do appreciate her patience and understanding when confronted by a computer illiterate. I am deeply indebted to my wife Erika, who has been my companion for more than three decades, not only in marriage, but also in research. For this reason I gratefully dedicate this book to her.

O. GEYSER
BLOEMFONTEIN, 2001

Jan Smuts as a young man. (Cape Archives Repository)

INTRODUCTION

In a Class of His Own

When Jan Christiaan Smuts was born on 24 May 1870, on the birthday of Queen Victoria, no one could have predicted his future fame. The infant was described as a "sickly, rickety child". To those close to him he was "an unprepossessing lad showing no signs of promise". His parents were most concerned and looked pityingly at him as he wandered about the farm or looked after the cattle and the sheep. "He is a poor and unhealthy youngster," said his father, "a queer fellow without much intelligence ..."[1] This "sickly, rickety child" was to become prime minister of South Africa twice: from 3 September 1919 to 30 June 1924 and once again from 5 September 1939 to 3 June 1948—the only South African premier to be prime minister twice in different periods. His insight into world affairs and his exceptional intellectual abilities gave him a prominent place in the councils of the world, and no one else before or since has placed South Africa internationally as he did. But it also made him one of the most controversial statesmen of his time.

During the First World War Smuts was the only non-Commonwealth prime minister to become a member of Lloyd George's Imperial War Cabinet and later the only non-British politician to become a member of the British War Cabinet. It was General Louis Botha's choice to divert Lloyd George's invitation to sit on the Imperial War Cabinet to his more able and competent deputy. This eventually proved to be a very wise decision. Smuts' versatility was of such a nature that Lloyd George used him for a great variety of purposes.

"I had no time for anything but work," he remarked afterwards. "There was no end to the work they wanted me to do. I have never worked so hard in my life. My hair became white. My brother, at 60, has hardly a white hair. My hair was nearly white at 50."[2]

And they also needed Smuts in the United States. Lord Northcliffe urged Lloyd George to send Smuts on a special envoy to convince the Americans of the effectiveness of the British war effort. "As to big men," said Northcliffe, "the only big military man who could help here (in America) is Smuts."[3]

Smuts played a prominent role at the peace negotiations in Paris after the First World War. Although his old reserve was still very much part of him, he was much more accessible than he had been in South Africa. A colleague referred to him as "a wise and sagacious counselor and a good friend". Throughout the peace negotiations he was cool, calm and collected.

"Nearly every one I have met has asked me to be certain to meet Smuts," wrote President Wilson's envoy, Colonel House, in his journal on 13 November 1917. "He has grown to be the lion of the hour.... He is one of the few men I have met in the government who does not feel tired. He's alert, energetic, and forceful."[4] Smuts' counsel was sought world-wide. Today, his statue stands in Parliament Square, London, the only Commonwealth leader there.

Jan Smuts was born on the family farm Bovenplaats, near Riebeeck West, a remote little village in the Cape Colony. He was barely six years old when the family moved to the farm Klipfontein, approximately 19 kilometres from Riebeeck West. He was the second son of his parents, Jacobus Abraham Smuts and Catharina Petronella, or Cato, as she was affectionately known to relations and friends. His father, later elected to represent Malmesbury in the Colonial Parliament in Cape Town, was referred to as "a pillar of his church" and his mother as "a fine and learned lady".[5] Cato's brother, Boudewyn de Vries, studied for six years at the Theological Faculty at Utrecht in Holland. He became the local Dutch Reformed minister at Riebeeck West. He was referred to as one of the liberal-minded Dutch Reformed ministers in the Cape Colony. As a young boy Smuts witnessed, in their home, numerous discussions on current political affairs. The establishing of British Imperialism after the annexation of the Transvaal in 1877 by Sir Theophilus Shepstone certainly did not pass unnoticed by the Smuts' at Klipfontein. All this undoubtedly had a great and, to a certain extent, decisive influence on Smuts' life.

Smuts attended the school of the renowned Mr T.C. Stoffberg in Riebeeck West. Only after the death of his elder brother was Smuts given the chance, at the age of 12, to attend school. It was the custom at the time for the eldest son to receive an education and that he should then become a minister of the Dutch Reformed Church. As the second eldest son, Smuts was thus destined to work on the farm. Mr Stoffberg later said that "Jan Smuts was one of the most brilliant pupils he had ever taught and the hardest-working boy he had ever met."[6] After spending four years at Riebeeck West, Smuts passed the examination, which entitled him to enter a matriculation class at any college with ease. He ultimately enrolled at the Victoria College, Stellenbosch. In those early years his interest was in subjects as diverse as botany, philosophy and literature. As far as the latter was concerned, he especially enjoyed the works of Shelley, Keats, Shakespeare and Walt Whitman.[7] Of the six professors under whom he studied at Victoria College, three had come from Edinburgh University, Scotland. Whenever he had occasion in later life to visit Scotland, Smuts enjoyed telling his audiences that he owed his education to Scotsmen.[8] In 1891 Smuts took his degree in science and literature at Stellenbosch and received honours in both. He was a brilliant scholar. Having won the Ebden Scholarship, he decided to go to Cambridge to study law. To the intense disappointment of his parents, Smuts had long since abandoned the idea of becoming a minister of the Dutch Reformed Church.

Victoria College was a wonderful experience for Smuts. The academic world was unlocked to him by most able professors. Hancock wrote: "Victoria College, Stellenbosch, stamped its enduring imprint upon the mind of Smuts." Smuts took no part in the usual sports and games. He exercised instead by taking long solitary walks in the mountains. And then, shortly after his 17th birthday, he fell in love with Sybella Margaretha (Isie) Krige. She was six months younger than Smuts. Isie was pretty and charming with immense energy, mental as well as physical. German *lieder* became their favourites. Isie had fallen in love with German literature and was determined to make the young Smuts a Goethe lover. And he on his part wanted to make her a Shelley worshipper. For her 17th birthday, on 22 December 1887, he wrote Isie a special letter. Among other things he wrote the following:

*Need I tell you what sympathy I feel for you on this, your
17th birthday? No, you know I have more than mere words
can express. Some wishes I have expressed in verse ... some
aspirations which I know accord with your own.... May I
add more? It is that we may be faithful to each other, that
our mutual love may be pure and unselfish, that in
whatever relation and circumstances we may be, it may
grow from more to more, and if possible, never be
dissolved; that we may be bound together in Soul and
Spirit by a holy and true love. People generally have but few
chosen friends; so you needn't be surprised when I tell you I
have only two on earth, you being one of them: and you are
the only one to whom I feel myself drawn by every tie of
sentiment and nature.*[9]

Smuts and Isie had much in common. Both were "quiet and
reserved and both were fond of botany, English and German
literature, and other intellectual pursuits".[10]

Smuts, Isie and daughter
Susanna Johanna (Santa).
(Smuts House Museum)

At Cambridge Smuts was
registered as a student at
Christ's College. Student life had
no or little meaning for him. He
had time for nothing but work.
His academic achievements were
remarkable. In one of the issues
of the *Cape Times* in 1894 a
friend wrote: "Smuts' success is
unprecedented in Cambridge
annals. He took parts I & II of the
Law Tripos at the same time and
was placed first in the first class
of each, and has been awarded
the George Long prize in Roman
Law and Jurisprudence, a prize
only awarded in cases of special
merit...."[11] In the Faculty of Law,
the year 1894 became known as
"Smuts' year". After passing the

necessary examinations with distinction, Smuts was admitted to the Middle Temple in London. In December 1894, it was reported in South African newspapers that "the council of Legal Education awarded Smuts, J.C. a special prize of £50 for the best examination in Constitutional Law (English and Colonial) and Legal History". It was undoubtedly an amazing series of successes. In England Smuts could have had a distinguished career in law. He was offered a professorship at Christ's College. But he was longing to get back to South Africa and consequently declined this exceptional honour for one so young. "To remain in Cambridge," wrote Hancock, "to enjoy the comforts and cultivation of a Combination Room, to achieve eminence in the academic study of Law—these were the prospects which now opened out before him. He was committed in heart and mind both to the world of philosophy and to the world of South African politics."[12]

While at Cambridge Smuts was less self-contained. He nevertheless remained a serious young man throughout. His reserved nature was undoubtedly a major stumbling-block in making friends on the campus. One person, who knew him well in those days, spoke of him as a young man with "a pale face and white hair, conspicuous in the university library on hot afternoons when all the under-graduate world was at play."[13] But there was also another reason for not making friends. There were those who invited him and would very much have liked to befriend this young man with the "unusual mental powers". Smuts never returned the invitations, because he could simply not afford to return their hospitality. "He had to spend the whole of his first winter," wrote Hancock, "shivering in the cold and damp of Cambridge because he could not afford to buy himself woolen underwear."[14] This situation was due mainly to a bank failure with his Ebden Scholarship.

It is interesting to note that Smuts' reserved nature was not a stumbling-block at all in forming solid relationships with his lecturers. He was most probably far more mature and more interested in and inclined to intellectual and scientifically directed conversation. In the correspondence between him and his lecturers, especially those in law, one discovers a mutual respect as well as a degree of affinity towards each other. Smuts had hardly any friends in his own age group. In Cambridge he befriended two Indian Muslims, who later became prominent personalities in their own country. And then there was the South African trio, F.S. Malan, N.J. de Wet and L. Krause, who remained his devoted friends during years of political turmoil and strain in South Africa. It was in their company that Smuts regularly attended services at the Presbyterian Church in Cambridge. After the service, in the evening, they usually had a meal together. Professor J.I. Marais, Professor of Theology at Stellenbosch, appreciated Smuts' attendance of services in the Presbyterian Church. His three friends invited him on several occasions to accompany them on one of their regular outings by train to London. Eventually they succeeded in persuading Smuts to accompany them. Somehow they lost him in London between Liverpool Station and Putney. Smuts was at Liverpool Station at the appointed time to meet his friends for the return journey to Cambridge. He told his astonished friends that he enjoyed every minute of the day ... in the library of the Middle Temple!

Smuts' successes at Cambridge did not compensate for being away from home. Yet England in general and Cambridge in particular left their mark. "I owe my education and some of the greatest pleasures of life," he later said, "to England, to its great literature and its profound thinkers."[15] Professor Marais felt reason to warn him that an "Anglicised Afrikaner is as disgusting a creature as an Anglicised Scotsman".[16] In the light of events in the years to come it might seem to have made the warning superfluous. But Smuts was adamant as regards his *Afrikanerskap*. "I am an Afrikaner and my soul is with my people," he once said. "In no person's breast does the flame of dedication burn higher than mine."[17]

Smuts sailed for home in June 1895. Arriving in South Africa he settled in Cape Town, "determined to carve out a legal career for himself". He was called to the Cape bar and began to practice as a junior barrister. Although a fair amount of work did come his way in the beginning, the number of his clients gradually diminished. "Despite his sparkling intellect and his thorough knowledge of law," wrote Crafford, "success was denied him, for he was lacking in qualities the possession of which brought dozens of briefs to his mental inferiors."[18] It was clear that Smuts could not apply his knowledge effectively to the realities of life. At this time he also applied unsuccessfully for a lectureship in law at the South African College in Cape Town in March 1896.[19] Smuts periodically attended sessions of the Old Cape Parliament as a reporter. At first he was only "mildly interested" in the proceedings. Gradually "the conviction grew within him that his future lay not in the legal but in the political world"[20]—a decision which later proved to be of tremendous significance for South Africa in particular and for the British Empire and later the British Commonwealth.

Misplaced trust in Cecil John Rhodes, prime minister of the Cape Colony, lead to Smuts' decision to migrate to the Transvaal. Rhodes and his co-conspirators' plans to overthrow the Kruger government were exposed when the Jameson Raid, destined to invade the Transvaal, went terribly wrong. Smuts could no longer give his trust to Rhodes. He consequently realised that there was no longer a future for him in the Cape. He received Transvaal citizenship as a burgher of the second class, thus renouncing his British nationality of his own accord. Smuts became a member of the Johannesburg bar and, in 1898, at the extremely young age of 28, he was appointed state attorney under President Paul Kruger.[21] He was later promoted to Kruger's assistant secretary of state. Smuts assisted Kruger in his negotiations with the British high commissioner in South Africa, Lord Alfred Milner, regarding the *Uitlander* problem in the Transvaal,[22] which eventually resulted in the Anglo-Boer War.

Smuts became Kruger's right-hand man in his negotiations with Milner in an attempt to prevent war between the Transvaal and Britian. Smuts realised that Milner was not interested in peace at all. He wanted war and nothing else in order to incorporate Transvaal into the British Empire. While Milner gradually developed a high regard for the abilities of the young attorney general of the Transvaal, Smuts held Milner's arrogance in high contempt. He referred to the British high commissioner as one of "the academic nobodies who fancy themselves great imperial statesmen".[23] Smuts regarded the Anglo-Boer War as an injustice imposed by Britain on the peoples of the two Boer republics. On 4 January 1902 Smuts wrote an open letter to W.T. Stead:

> *It would be idle for me to pretend that I have any extra sympathy for the British people after the cruel wrongs and irreparable injuries which have been heaped upon my people.... And it is to me saddening to think that a nation which has done so much for human liberty and thought should now turn back on all its most sacred traditions and deliberately perpetrate a crime in South Africa which has probably no parallel in the history of the world. It really seems to me as if it cannot be the same people which I learnt to know years ago, as if it is no longer itself or master of its actions, as if it is possessed by some malignant demonic influence which is impelling it ever farther under its despotic sway. My hope and prayer is that it may be rid of this demon of Jingoism or Imperialism or whatever else you call it, and that an end may be made to all those horrors and sufferings in South Africa which no one who has not seen them will ever understand. Let it however be as God wills. To my dying day I shall remain thankful that it has been permitted to me to see a picture of human constancy, of silent and uncomplaining endurance, of heroic battling for the highest and noblest ideal of man, and of perfect trust in God, such as perhaps the modern world has no parallel for.*[24]

Lord Moran, personal physician to Winston Churchill, once wrote of Smuts: "It appears that this solitary, austere Boer with his biblical background lives in a world of his own."[25] And Sir Philip Magnus once referred to Smuts as: "An extremely quick worker, aided by a phenomenal memory which had in early life been almost photographic."[26] In a less flattering way G.H. Galpin wrote: "In the southern hemisphere the greatest Englishman is an Afrikaner...General Smuts."[27] J.P. Mackintosh refers to Smuts as a "shrewd and hard Afrikaner".[28] With Smuts' *holism* in mind Professor T.J. Haarhoff, a South African academic, wrote: "Life to him was an expanding creative force, something more than the addition of arts, and not confined to the strait waistcoat dogma."[29] Another South African, the well-known South African author Alan Paton, wrote of Smuts: "His name was on all men's lips, even those who hated him.... One could hate a man and say that he counted for nothing, but one did not say that of Smuts. Not even his other most bitter opponents, the communists, ever underrated him."[30] And Paton himself was a fierce critic of Smuts!

The Smuts figure also evoked response on a more personal level. John Colville, private secretary to Winston Churchill during the Second World War, refers to an incident during the War when Smuts came to London accompanied by his son Japie. They were to stay at *Chequers,* the official country residence of British prime ministers. At the appropriate time Smuts invited Colville and Japie to join him in his favourite hobby—walking. He had planned to walk quite a distance to Beacon Hill in the Chilterns. Soon, Colville and Japie discovered that they could not keep up the same speed as the 75-year-old field marshal. "Finally," he records in his diary, "Japie sat down. His father was, he said, a wonderful man, but he was totally out of touch with the modern technological age. He still had old-fashioned interests such as philosophy and wild flowers. And, he added bitterly, hill-climbing."[31] It is in incidents like these that the mysticism of Smuts lay. Different people looked at Smuts from different angles and different backgrounds. All researchers in due course encounter extreme difficulty in analysing Smuts' complex personality.

Smuts was not always the self-contained and serious

Smuts and infant Japie, 1907.
(Central Archives Repository)

man most people characterised him to be. At times he could surprise his family, friends and colleagues with unexpected leisurely behaviour. There was the day when he left the buildings of Parliament in Cape Town after a hectic and tiresome debate. Coming out of the building he saw some boys playing marbles. His interest and curiosity was immediately aroused. He stepped up to the boys: "No! No! This is not the way to shoot when playing marbles." He went down on one knee and showed the astonished boys how to do the trick. This was the unpredictable Smuts at his best.

Smuts was often accused of having no time for "small talk". This was not true. From time to time he had the need to escape from the tensions of public life and spend some time with friends in a relaxed atmosphere. But there was a condition to it: the conversation had to be almost exclusively in his own field of interest. Nevertheless there were times when he could relax in full. This was usually after a day in natural surroundings— especially after mountain-climbing. After this severe exercise, which could last a whole day, he permitted himself a glass of cold beer, which he always enjoyed. At some occasions he also enjoyed a whisky. And then, on their arrival home, he would first think of the comfort of his companions. "Get yourselves a beer," he would invite them, "or perhaps a brandy, if you prefer that."[32]

An important facet of Smuts' complex personality was undoubtedly his versatility. His many-sided personality was one of his most important characteristics. Naturally it attracted worldwide attention and from people from all spheres of life. His versatility actually formed the basis of his personality, which dominated his life throughout. Add to this his exceptional intellect and it becomes clear why his fellow-students at Victoria College, in particular a student called Carel van Zyl, prophesied: "There was not a post in the British Empire that Smuts might not win if God Almighty spared him."[33] In spite of the fact that he entered politics at a relatively early stage of his life, his intellectual abilities and academic achievements brought him worldwide recognition. Professor Hancock refers to Smuts' years at Cambridge as the "golden period"[34] in his life and Professor Mansergh wrote of his "firsts and prizes all the way".[35] In 1936 Albert Einstein, during his visit to Columbia University in the United States, told John Phillips that Smuts was one of only eleven men at that time who truly understood his theories of Relativity.[36] In this respect it is interesting to note that Einstein later said that Eamon de Valera was one of only nine in the world who truly understood his theories of Relativity![37] And in an appreciation Lord Todd, master of Christ's College, Cambridge, wrote in 1970: "Christ's College where he (Smuts) studied, has more than 500 years of history behind it, but I am sure that out of all our members past and present, we would choose three as truly outstanding—John Milton, Charles Darwin, and Jan Smuts."[38] The following unfriendly and sarcastic description was written of Smuts:

> *Yes, he was a wonderful man, he is a wonderful botanist, the botanists think he is a wonderful soldier, the soldiers think he is a wonderful philosopher, the philosophers think he is a wonderful world reformer, the word reformers think he is a wonderful politician.*[39]

In spite of the fact that this sounded a bit unkind it nevertheless typifies the extraordinary many-sided personality of Smuts. Smuts became absorbed in the works of Shelley, Keats, Shakespeare, Whitman, Emily Brontë, Goethe and Schiller. They were his favourite writers. He had loved poetry ever since first reading Shelley's *Prometheus Unbound*.[40] And then there was his great interest in law, philosophy, botany, archaeology, the classics and various related fields. He lost himself from time to time in these interests, when he could escape from his hectic political program. "Throughout his life," wrote Hancock, "he pursued poetry, philosophy, botany, archaeology and all his other interests during the time available to him after he had taken the measure of his day's work."[41] He once wrote to Margaret Gillett:

> *Most nights I go to bed with some botany book. My work is now too much to permit of philosophy at that late hour. But botany is like a sweet opiate, expelling the day's interests and pre-occupations.*[42]

Smuts' love for the natural world developed in the early days of his youth. It remained a determining factor throughout his life—"it took shape in his thought, speech and writing". Smuts once wrote: "Her genetic fibres run through all our being. Our physical organs connect us with millions of years of her history. Our minds are full of memorial paths to human experience."[43] Hancock describes Smuts' love for the natural world and its creatures in a very striking way, which seems to be the foundation of his later academic interest: " … a thrill of delight ran through him at the sight and sound and touch of the familiar near-by things. He shouted to the beasts and birds, talked to the little creatures in the crevices of the rocks, played with the pebbles and 'made love to the plants'."[44] It was on his father's farm that the young Smuts "began to grow not only in body but in spirit". He wandered regularly around the farm with old Adam, a farm labourer, "who loved his master's children and loved teaching them the exciting little things of country life."[45] Adam taught him where to dig for edible roots, where to look for tortoises, how to seek shelter against the elements of the weather and how to keep warm in front of a roaring fire. In later life it was these recollections that he cherished most. It was in nature that he found peace for his impetuous mind. It was in nature, Smuts once said, that he felt near to his Creator. In this respect he wrote:

The emotional appeal of Nature is tremendous. Sometimes more than one can bear. For the overwrought mind there is no peace like Nature. For the wounded spirit there is no healing like hers. Some of my deepest emotional experiences have come to me on the many nights I have spent under the African sky.[46]

Anthony Trowbridge wrote that Smuts and Francis of Assisi must have had something in common regarding his "perception of the co-ordination of all the kingdoms, vegetable, animal and human".[47]

Foremost in his love for nature lay his interest in botany. At a certain stage he was the leading international expert on grasses. Smuts was once in the company of a well-known American botanist and a South African botanist, Professor

Hancock from the University of Natal in Pietermaritzburg. The three of them were on a day excursion to the Royal National Park in the Drakensberg in Natal. The American botanist, who was a woman, asked Professor Hancock—she was not aware of the expert and specialised knowledge of Smuts—to identify specific grasses she had observed during their excursion. Naturally the professor decided to leave the explaining and identification to the expert. Smuts, as usual, was most willing to respond to the request. To the astonishment of the American lady Smuts not only identified the various types of grasses, but even explained and analysed in detail the genealogy and the ecology of the grasses. The American botanist was extremely surprised to hear this scientific explanation from a general. "How is it," she asked Smuts hesitatingly, "that I am learning all this not from the Professor but from you, a general?"[48] With a twinkle in his blue eyes, Smuts responded immediately: "But my dear lady, I am only a general in my spare time."[49]

It was frequently said that Smuts had little time for people. "It would be truer," wrote Hancock, "to say that he had little time for many people but a great deal of time for some people."[50] Smuts' friendships were rarely exclusive relationships between only two people. His friendships usually reached out and developed until a variety of people, with whom he was friendly, discovered that they were unconsciously bound together in a complex pattern. Emily Hobhouse, Olive Schreiner and Margaret Clarke, later Gillett, can inter alia be mentioned in this regard. Margaret Clarke, whom Smuts met in South Africa as an assistant to Emily Hobhouse, informed him that she was to become engaged to a Cambridge contemporary, Arthur Gillett. She wrote: "I don't know how much you would like him, but I believe Mrs Smuts would like him very much, and I know he would like you both. He is not as clever as you, and it is not his lot in life to be a statesman."[51] In years to come Smuts and Arthur Gillett thoroughly enjoyed each other's company. "Each man thought the other a splendid fellow," wrote Hancock, "and Mrs Gillett found cause before long to chide Smuts for addressing all his letters to her husband rather than to her. 'After all, she had known him first!'"[52] In 1911 the Gillett's first son was born. Not surprisingly they named him Jan.

There were a few other friends with whom Smuts shared some of his intimate thoughts. Among his lecturer friends was W.J. Wolstenholme. Wolstenholme decided to become a Congregational minister but in time he abandoned this idea. Hancock describes him as a "lapsed Christian who retained his Christian conscience".[53] Wolstenholme operated mainly on the fringe of academic activities in Cambridge. He lectured in German on a restricted scale. It is interesting to note that this "valetudinarian and semi-recluse" played a most important role in the forming of Smuts' personality in the years at Cambridge. As a bachelor Wolstenholme led a hermit's life and withdrew to his extensive and representative library. He read extensively over a wide spectrum, especially in philosophy, economy and sociology. He often dreamed of the *magnus opus* he so much wanted to write, but for which he had neither the mental strength nor the perseverance. Being a bachelor with such a retiring personality it must have been special to him that a brilliant and bright young man like Smuts should enjoy his company. "The relationship between this strangely assorted pair," wrote Hancock, "was charming and just a little comical: Smuts so full of enthusiasm, drive and the itch for system-building: Wolstenholme so tired, so timid, so submissive to his own sad conception of a planless, purposeless, morally indifferent universe."[54]

Then there was Louis Botha who was most probably one of Smuts' closest friends over many years. He had a high regard for Botha. Botha was the diplomat and Smuts the mastermind. Botha respected Smuts' abilities and consulted him on all matters. When he sent Smuts to London in March 1917 to represent South Africa at the Imperial Conference, he wrote to Mrs Smuts:

Yes, Mrs Smuts, the friendship between Jannie and me is an unbreakable bond, which will persist throughout our lives. We have never had an irreparable difference which could not be resolved, and there was never a difference which, having been resolved, left a feeling behind, and that is why I love him as much as and more than my own brother. We have gone through deep waters together, and even through mud, to save our people, and although there are many who only want to curse us, there never were two people who have worked harder and more honestly for our people and who have done more than Jannie and I.[55]

People in general used to refer to Botha and Smuts as "Ou Baas and Klein Baas". After his death, Botha was succeeded by Smuts as prime minister of the Union of South Africa. On hearing the news of Botha's death Smuts was deeply saddened. "I am now prime minister," he wrote to Margaret Gillett on 6 September 1919, "but my heart is not in the thing and only an overwhelming disaster brought me there. Botha's loss to this country is quite irreparable. His was just the role which I temperamentally could not play, and you know how necessary that role is in the world. I shall do my best without being sanguine about success."[56]

There was also Professor Charles Murray from the Theological Seminary at Stellenbosch with whom Smuts made an early contact. He wrote to Professor Murray as a 16-year-old lad to inquire about the set-up for intended students at Victoria College:

Allow me the honour of your reading and answering these few lines. I intend coming to Stellenbosch in July next, and, having heard that you take an exceptionally great interest in the youth, I trust you will favour me by keeping your eye upon me and helping me with your kindly advice. Moreover, as I shall be a perfect stranger there, and, as you know, such a place, where a large puerile elements exists, affords fair scope for moral, and what is more important, religious temptation which, if yielded to, will eclipse alike the expectations of my parents and the intentions of myself, a real friend will prove a lasting blessing for me. For of what use will a mind, enlarged and refined in all possible ways, be to me, if my religion be a deserted pilot and morality a wreck?[57]

And then there was another theologian at Stellenbosch. Hancock describes Professor J.I. Marais, who was later regarded as Smuts' mentor, as "an Afrikaner of Huguenot stock and a man of true scholarship, saintliness and humanity".[58] It was Professor Marais who came to Smuts' assistance a year or two later when Smuts was confronted with a severe crisis in his career. Marais had, during Smuts' years at Victoria College and Christ's College, a really special formative influence on him. Marais had a basic trust in Smuts and he held Smuts in very high regard. He was very pleased when he learned that Smuts was attending sermons at the Presbyterian Church in Cambridge in the company of fellow students from South Africa. After four years at Cambridge, Smuts decided to move back to South Africa. He moved to the Transvaal after a short stay in Cape Town. Marais was extremely upset with Smuts' decision. "Are you going to the Tranvaal?" he wrote to Smuts. "I had so wished that you would stay among us. We need leaders. But who can interfere if your calling is there and not here? God be merciful to our poor country. I mourn for it. We have no leaders of *character*.... God knows that I have sometimes hoped that you were the man chosen by God."[59]

During his years as a student at Victoria College he also befriended Johannes du Plessis who later became professor in Mission Science at the Theological Seminary at Stellenbosch. In the late '30s, after a visit to Du Plessis' widow in Stellenbosch, Smuts wrote: "You will remember him as the man who was excommunicated by the Dutch Reformed Church because he did not believe in verbal inspiration. He was a fine scholar and noble spirit and dear companion of my youth."[60] The way in which the Dutch Reformed Church treated Du Plessis affected Smuts deeply and he found it difficult to come to terms with this severe intolerance shown by the Church. He could not understand how and why fellow Christians and colleagues could treat a refined character and an extremely gifted scholar in the way Du Plessis was treated. He was after all a leading figure in the Dutch Reformed Church. It is not clear how this influenced Smuts' attitude towards the Church—the Dutch Reformed Church in particular.

Smuts cannot be described as religious in the true sense of the word, especially in the Afrikaner religious tradition, but he was undoubtedly a believer. Many of his pronouncements are proof of this. Notwithstanding Wolstenholme's influence, the idea of God was continually in Smuts' mind. At Cambridge he once wrote: "God is at the beginning, God is at the end, but is He always between these limits?"[61] During this time Smuts was "persistently in search of a philosophy which would reconcile the universe of scientific mechanism with the universe of value and purpose."[62] His criticism of the Dutch Reformed Church undoubtedly contributed to the attacks the Church launched on him from time to time. He told two young ministers from the Dutch Reformed Church that he could not have written his book—*Holism and Evolution*—without being a believer. In May 1907 Patrick Duncan, colonial secretary of the Transvaal, said that Smuts was "disliked as a free-thinker by the Predikante".[63]

Smuts and Churchill had a long and exceptional friendship that stretched over a period of almost 50 years. Churchill said to Heaton Nicholls, the current South African high commissioner to the Court of St James, that he and Smuts were "like two old lovebirds, moulting together on a perch but still able to peck".[64] In Britain Smuts was regarded most highly. "General Smuts' reputation," wrote John Colville, "stood high, not only with Churchill, but with all parties in the Cabinet, with the leaders of the armed forces and with informed opinion throughout the Commonwealth and Empire."[65] He was referred to as "Downing Street's Prince Charming". But it was Churchill in particular who held Smuts in high regard as friend and adviser. "Foremost in Churchill's esteem was General Smuts," wrote Colville, "whom he easily persuaded the King to create a Field Marshal. No active statesman, apart from Churchill, had longer practical experience."[66] On the other hand Smuts once said of Churchill: "Mr Churchill slept when he was working and worked when he wanted to be sleeping."[67] This was another example of the free association between Smuts and Churchill.

It is a well-known fact that Smuts had close links with members of the British monarchy—the House of Windsor. It was an association that originated during the reign of King George V and Queen Mary, through to King George VI and Queen Elizabeth and their two daughters, the princesses

Elizabeth and Margaret. Due to the King's interference and influence Smuts played an all-important and decisive role in Lloyd George's negotiations in 1921 with Eamon de Valera regarding Irish independence. The King frequently sought Smuts' advice on this matter while he was in London for the Imperial Conference of 1921. And during the Second World War it was his son George VI who consulted Smuts on various occasions.

In the active politics of the day Smuts hardly had any advisers. "As a matter of fact," he once wrote to Margaret Gillett, "I am so busy these days that I can find little time for consulting my colleagues."[68] Major Piet van der Byl, a War Cabinet colleague of Smuts during the Second World War, wrote in his autobiograhy that Smuts hardly ever consulted his colleagues. "With all his colossal brain and outstanding qualities of leadership," Van der Byl wrote, "he never seemed to have learnt by experience."[69] In 1924, after Smuts' party was defeated in a by-election in the Wakkerstroom constituency, Smuts called for a general election without consulting anybody in the party. He was cautioned by his senior colleagues that his government was very unpopular with the electorate and that it could turn out disastrous for the prime minister at the polls. There was even the possibility that Smuts could lose his parliamentary seat, Pretoria West, in the proposed general election. The South African Party was defeated by General J.B.M. Hertzog's National Party and Smuts lost his parliamentary seat! He was offered the unopposed constituency of Standerton. Smuts held this seat until his surprised defeat in the general election of May 1948.

There was one political adviser whom Smuts held in high regard over a long period. He was Louis Esselen, chief secretary of the South African Party. On Esselen's death Smuts said: "To me the passing of Louis Esselen comes as a very heavy personal blow. Our association dates from the South African War and through all the wars and politics since those far-off events. He was a very close personal friend and we worked together as comrades through all the crises of our times. Never a truer friend, never one more unselfish, more devoted, more dependable than Louis Esselen. Whether it was war or politics, or the simple affairs of daily life, he was a companion beyond compare. So he served Louis Botha, so he served me through fair and stormy weather … the soul of loyalty and devotion."[70] Hancocks mentions that friends meant more to Smuts than books: "They are all dropping off one by one."[71] As a key figure in the party Smuts used to discuss, in detail, the most important political issues of the day with Esselen. Any of Smuts' instructions to Cabinet ministers went through Esselen and it is known that Esselen initiated many of these instructions. Esselen was in fact the "Power-behind-the-throne".

Nevertheless, as Lord Harlech, British high commissioner to South Africa, referred to Smuts in one of his regular *communiques* to the British prime minister: "Smuts' own weakness is extreme tenderness for old friends and colleagues in past struggles and a reluctance to try out new men."[72] This characteristic of Smuts was, according to Harlech, the reason why his Cabinet was stuffed with "a terrible lot of old dead wood". He refers to Stuttaford, Clarkson and Stallard as three "elderly backward-looking men who are administratively weak and cut no ice in the country"; Deneys Reitz, "charming but completely idle"; Harry Lawrence "has little innate mental capacity and finds even his departmental work a burden"; Hofmeyr, "a narrow Gladstonian liberal of a very donnish type, with little human personality". Another remark by Harlech in one of his *communiques* throws interesting light on Smuts as a politician. "He is an extrovert," wrote Harlech, "while his colleagues are introverts for whom the Union alone is sufficiently full of problems and difficulties without launching into thought on wider African and still less world problems."

It was at Cambridge that Smuts became increasingly interested in philosophy. But at Cambridge he received no assistance from the specialists in philosophy. No wonder that the conversations between him and Wolstenholme were dominated by philosophical discussions. He unsuccessfully applied to attend the lectures of Professor James Ward. Professor Ward was hesitant to admit a "dilettante from the Law School" to the world of philosophy.[73] About 30 years later Smuts received a letter "in considerable perturbation" from the Cambridge professor. Someone told him that Smuts reacted critically to his book, *The Realm of Ends*. With a clear conscience Smuts could supply him with a reassuring answer. "It is odd," wrote Hancock, "to think of the Cambridge professor seeking reassurance from the pupil he had turned away."[74] It is interesting to note that Wolstenholme discouraged Smuts from exploring philosophy. He was convinced that Smuts' "philosophic quest was bound to end in failure". He encouraged Smuts rather to give preference to history writing and to become involved in politics. Smuts was convinced that philosophy and politics were totally complementary to each other. And when Smuts submitted his manuscript, *An Inquiry into the Whole,* in March 1912 to Wolstenholme, the latter was not impressed at all.

He wrote to Smuts that it was a "matter of wonderment" that a man "so overloaded by political burdens could manage to produce any work of philosophy at all".[75] Wolstenholme pleaded with Smuts not to "rush it into print". "Don't go before the public," he hurriedly advised Smuts, "before you have the best and ripest of which you are capable to put before them."[76] Smuts was not demoralised by Wolstenholme's negative response. He continued exploiting philosophy enthusiastically in all its facets. Regarding Wolstenholme's negative attitude towards Smuts' exploitation of philosophy and especially the concept of *holism,* Hancock wrote:

> *If Wolstenholme could have lived into the mid-twentieth century, he would have found the ideas of his friend amazingly and (from his own point of view) disconcertingly alive. In Cambridge, to which Smuts and Wolstenholme both belonged, all kinds of people— theologians, astronomers, geneticists ... had become infected, whether they knew it or not, by the holistic virus.*[77]

Many years later Smuts wrote to Margaret Gillett regarding his pursuit of philosophy. He informed her that he had received a letter from the Hamburg University asking his consent to publish his *Holism* in Spanish for use in Spain and South America. Before the Second World War, Smuts' *Holism and Evolution* was translated into German but it was banned by the

Nazis during the War. Smuts wrote that, according to Professor Adolf Mayer-Abich, *Holism* was once more taught in the university and that interest in the subject was increasing on the Continent all the time. "But I don't wish to give permission for the Spanish translation," Smuts wrote, "as so much of the scientific part is really obsolete. The advance of physics and biology in the last 20 years has really been phenomenal, and my early chapters read like pre-scientific. I wish I could find time to write my second volume, and let the first become antiquarian as it is practically antiquated."[78] This is a very good example of Smuts' scientific approach to his interest in philosophy. It was by now more than a mere lay interest. Smuts realised that an interest based on scientific methods would be necessary if he wanted to make a contribution in the field of philosophy. With this in mind he once wrote:

> *I have today a clearer vision of what holism means than I had twelve years ago, just as the effort of 1925 was an advance on that of 1910. If I could retire to the Bush for six months at least I could do some real thinking. The philosophical implications of the idea have given me a good deal of trouble during the last few years. I believe the key to religion is to be found along holistic lines, but the subject is full of pitfalls, and one hesitates to write about it.*[79]

Smuts was one of the main architects of the British Commonwealth. After the First World War he drafted a preliminary *Constitution of the British Commonwealth* to be discussed at the forthcoming Constitutional Conference of 1921.[80] With the development of nationalism in the British dominions and the British colonies, Smuts was convinced that it was of absolute necessity that the British Empire be transformed into a Commonwealth. To him the Empire had reached the stage of "adapt or die". He initially opposed Milner and his *Round Table* reformers who were opting for a federation.[81] On receiving the draft constitution from Smuts, L.S Amery, secretary of state for dominion affairs, wrote to him:

I have read your draft memorandum with the greatest interest and with complete agreement on the main points. Working separately it seems that we have both arrived at more or less identical conclusions, not only on questions of principle but also of actual machinery, and that is at any rate not unhopeful as to the feasibility of what we advocate.

I entirely agree with you that it is desirable not only to secure at the forthcoming constitutional conference certain general declarations of constitutional right, as Duncan Hall suggests, but also to frame the draft of those declarations now at the present prime minister's conference and have it in circulation during the next twelve months, in order to focus public opinion in the Empire. While we do not want anything in the nature of a fixed or written constitution for the British Commonwealth, we do want a general agreement and public understanding on fundamentals, and not always to be questioning these afresh or pulling our institutions up by the roots. The suggested declarations would have that desired effect and the process of constitutional evolution would then go on both as between the different parts of the Empire, and in each part of the Empire severally, without further questioning of the underlying fabric.[82]

The rise, development and consolidation of the British Commonwealth provided the opportunity for several statesmen to play important roles in international politics—something that they otherwise would not have been able to do. Without the rise of the Commonwealth they would not have been able to exert any decisive influence on international affairs. Smuts was one of these statesmen to whom the rise and development of the Commonwealth offered exceptional opportunities for making his influence clearly felt. The role that Smuts played in transforming the British Empire into the British Commonwealth and in the subsequent development of the Commonwealth after the First World War was of such importance that many years later Mansergh referred to Smuts' political career as the "strangest of all Commonwealth careers".[83]

Smuts' role in establishing and developing the British Commonwealth has been described by some historians as an all-important and dominant one. The role that he played internationally in this process has, however, rather been over-emphasised from time to time. Yet the insight he revealed at different international conferences was brilliant throughout. With his very first appearance at an Imperial Conference he already succeeded in focusing attention upon himself. It is interesting to note that not one of Smuts' biographers has mentioned his appearance at this conference, which was held in London in July 1909 to discuss the defence of the Empire. Smuts was one of the Transvaal representatives at the conference and whereas all the other representatives from South Africa were wary about voicing their opinions on the eve of the Union, this was not the case with Smuts. He delivered two lengthy speeches, which in every way constituted an important contribution. This was his first appearance at an international gathering of this nature and it must undoubtedly have been quite a unique experience for Smuts. "The experience," wrote Duncan Hall, "may well have led him to formulate in his own mind the clear-cut conception of the Commonwealth, which he revealed in a conversation a year later."[84] Very few politicians had made such an impression on the international scene as Smuts had done. It seemed as if he had a special flair for grasping the essence of any matter discussed at a conference, the ability to summarise salient points tersely and then to give clear direction to the discussions.

His speeches as a member first of the Imperial and later of the British War Cabinet during the First World War suggested that he was trying to establish a link between the Commonwealth of Nations, which was already in the process of developing, and the League of Nations, which was beginning to take shape on paper. He believed that in the process of linking these two organisations together, he would be able to play a vital role. Many others shared this belief and consequently his ability and his potential as a statesman of international stature was very highly rated. His becoming a member of the British War Cabinet was not only in the interests of South Africa, but altogether of wider significance. Smuts firmly believed that he was actively serving humanity as a whole.

In the solution of the problems that confronted him, he depended upon his remarkable intellect. His active brain and restless nature recognised no bounds and he never hesitated to advance one scheme after another, so covering a wide field. Unfortunately these schemes, as far as the actual results were concerned, frequently reflected a certain measure of impetuosity. Duncan Hall was quite correct when he wrote: "He (Smuts) sometimes lets his foresighted vision of 'human advance' blind him to the dangers lurking ahead."[85] And Lord Moran feared "that his arrogance will (would) trip him up".[86]

Ultimately Smuts' interest in the Commonwealth led to rejection by his own people. He was criticised as being a traitor to South Africa and accused of being more interested in Britain's affairs and its welfare than in that of South Africa and its people. Mansergh wrote in this respect:

In the deeper sense Smuts never 'fell away'. But at times he did become dangerously insensitive to some of the innermost aspirations of his own people. He neglected language, he was unwise, if even more unlucky, in his reaction to the 1914 rebellion and, preoccupied with Commonwealth and world affairs in London, he so lost touch with the source of his own being as to regret that he had not stood in 1918 as a candidate for the British House of Commons. Was the price of increasing absorption in the idea and the possibilities of Commonwealth to be detachment from his own Afrikaner people? This was a suspicion, and far more than a suspicion, on the part of many, who found no satisfaction in the spectacle of a Boer general finding fulfillment as a 'handy-man of Empire'.[87]

It was argued from time to time that one of the main reasons for Smuts' controversy as an Afrikaner, was his commitment to bringing Afrikaner and English together. He said in 1935:

I have played the game by both Afrikaans- and English-speaking South Africans. I have done my best to stand by both impartially. If a man like me who has done what I have done in the affairs of South Africa is not to be trusted

*any more, then I do not know who is to be trusted. They are
shaking the very foundation, which reflects not so much on
me, but on the whole of South Africa and the people of
South Africa.*[88]

In the first general election after the Second World War Smuts
suffered the same fate as Winston Churchill in Britain. In May
1948 Smuts was defeated at the polls by Dr D.F. Malan's
Nationalist Party.

There remained an intriguing facet of Smuts' very complex
personality, which still needed to be investigated in depth. Smuts
never hesitated to deliver commentary, to give advice and to solve
difficult problems. Even when he was completely ignorant
regarding the political intrigue unfolding behind the scenes in
Southern Africa towards the end of the 19th century, he did not
hesitate to barge in. It seemed as if he always wanted to be in the
centre of things. Was there perhaps an anxiety to gain personally?
And later he tried to solve
the Irish question overnight.
He continually offended the
French during the First and
Second World War and in
particular Charles de Gaulle.
Is there in this regard a
possible thread that runs
through Smuts' life?

*Smuts and his close friend and
confidant Louis Esselen.* (Central
Archives Repository)

1. F.S. Crafford, *Jan Smuts. A Biography,* 5.
2. *Ibid.,* 143.
3. *Ibid.,* 142.
4. *Ibid.*
5. W.K. Hancock, *Smuts, I. The Sanguine Years, 1870 – 1919,* 5, 7.
6. *Ibid.,* 11.
7. S.B. Spies, *et al* (eds), *Jan Smuts. Memoirs of the Boer War,* 11.
8. Hancock, 1, 19.
9. *Ibid.,* 17.
10. Crafford, 11.
11. *Ibid.,* 13.
12. Hancock, 1, 46.
13. Crafford, 13.
14. Hancock, 35.
15. Smuts Papers, Volume I, 4 January 1902, 463.
16. Nicholas Mansergh, *The Commonwealth Experience,* 371.
17. Anthony Trowbridge, *Holism and Evolution, 1926 – 1986, in Veldtrust,* December 1986.
18. Hancock, 1, 13.
19. *Ibid.*
20. Hancock, 1, 35.
21. D.W. Kruger, *Paul Kruger,* Volume II, 1883 – 1904, 172.
22. Spies, 85.
23. Mansergh, 371.
24. Smuts Papers, Volume I, 4 January 1902, 463.
25. Lord Moran, *Winston Churchill. The Struggle for Survival, 1940 – 1965,* 52.
26. Philip Magnus, *Smuts.* In Lord Longford, *et al, The History Makers,* 150.
27. G.H. Galpin, *There are no South Africans,* 395.
28. J.P. Mackintosh (ed), *British Prime Ministers in the Twentieth Century,* 23.
29. T.J. Haarhoff, *Smuts the Humanist,* 36.
30. Alan Paton, *Hofmeyr,* 258.
31. John Colville, *Footprints in Time. Memories,* 128.
32. Piet Meiring, *Generaal Jan Smuts en Brandewyn.* In André P. Brink, *Heildronk,* 35.

33. Hancock, 1, 31.
34. *Ibid., 83.*
35. Mansergh, 371.
36. Trowbridge, 16.
37. Tim Pat Coogan, *De Valera. Long Fellow, Long Shadow*, 35.
38. Trowbridge, 16.
39. *Die Beeld,* 24 May1970.
40. Crafford, 12.
41. Hancock, 45.
42. Smuts Papers, Volume V, 4 April 1933.
43. Trowbridge, 17.
44. Hancock, 1, 10.
45. Crafford, 5. See also Hancock, 1, 8 – 9.
46. Trowbridge, 16 – 17.
47. *Ibid.,* 17.
48. *Ibid.,* 14.
49. Trowbridge, 14.
50. Hancock, 1, 281 – 282.
51. *Ibid.,* 287.
52. *Ibid.*
53. *Ibid.,* 44.
54. *Ibid.*
55. *Ibid.,* 549.
56. Smuts Papers, Volume V, 6 September 1919, 5.
57. Smuts Papers, Volume I, 12 June 1866, 4.
58. Hancock, 1, 20.
59. *Ibid.,* 62.
60. Hancock, 304 – 305.
61. *Ibid.,* 45.
62. *Ibid.*
63. Austen Chamberlain, *Politics from Inside. An Epistolary Chronicle, 1906 – 1914,* 78.
64. Martin Gilbert, *Road to Victory. Winston Churchill, 1941 – 1945,* 1149.
65. John Colville, *The Fringes of Power. Downing Street Diaries.* Volume One, *1939 – October, 1941,* 319.
66. *Ibid.,* 397.
67. *Ibid.*
68. Smuts Papers, Volume VII, 9 November 1945, 19.

69. Piet van der Byl, *The Shadows Lenghten,* 63.
70. Crafford, X.
71. W.J. Hancock, *Smuts, 2. Fields of Force, 1919 – 1950,* 525.
72. PREM: 4/44/1, Office of the High Commissioner, Pretoria. *Harlech to British Prime Minister, London, 2 October 1941.*
73. Hancock, 1, 39.
74. *Ibid.,* 39 – 40.
75. *Ibid.,* 290.
76. *Ibid.*
77. *Ibid.,* 305.
78. Smuts Papers, Volume VII, 9 November 1945, 20.
79. Smuts Papers, Volume VI, 29 June 1936, 49.
80. Smuts Papers, Volume V, 65 – 77. See also D.O. 114/65, X/1 9233: *Principal Changes in Constitutional Forms Relating to the Dominions, 1910 – 1935.*
81. O. Geyser, *Watershed for South Africa. London 1961,* 7 – 8. See also Hancock, 1, 427.
82. Smuts Papers, Volume V, 20 June 1921, 78. See also D.O. 117/33, X1/ 8945, *Amery to Smuts,* 20 June 1921.
83. Mansergh, 370.
84. H. Duncan Hall, *Commonwealth. A History of the British Commonwealth of Nations,* 37.
85. *Ibid.,* 273.
86. Moran, 52.
87. Mansergh, 373.
88. Trowbridge, 14.

Jan Smuts, 1939. (Central Archives Repository)

Cecil John Rhodes. (Cape Archives Repository)

1

Cecil John Rhodes

"It was hero worship pure and simple."
J.C. Smuts (Hancock, *Smuts*, 1, 59)

"Keep your eye on that young fellow Smuts."
C.J. Rhodes (Crafford, *Jan Smuts*, 12)

Smuts and Rhodes never met in person. They were only once indirectly in contact when Rhodes visited Stellenbosch in 1888. Rhodes went to Stellenbosch, the seat of Afrikaner learning at the time, to address the young Afrikaner students at Victoria College on graduation day.[1] After Rhodes had finished his speech the head student stepped on to the platform. He was a slender youth of 18. In contrast to his youthful appearance he seemed to be extremely serious. His arrogant bearing would appear a more solid characteristic in his later life. There were also the signs of the expressed humility of a scholar. His personality, lacking the warmth of emotional power, impressed more than it attracted.[2] In his expression of thanks to the speaker on his address, Smuts spoke on Pan-Africanism.[3] At first Rhodes looked extremely bored,[4] but gradually he became interested in what Smuts had to say on

1

this topic. Smuts spoke on a topic "dearest to the heart of the visitor".[5] In spite of an initial shyness, Smuts spoke in well-formed phrases. His deeply reflected thoughts "were expressed in a sonorous and flexible voice cleverly employed to bring out intended oratorical effects".[6] Afterwards Rhodes inquired after the name of the young man: Jan Christiaan Smuts, he was told, aged 18, the son of a Cape farmer. Later Rhodes told Jan Hofmeyr, leader of the Afrikaner Bond, "Keep your eye on that young fellow Smuts!"[7] John X. Merriman, a leading political figure in Cape politics, remarked to Jacobus Smuts as they listened to the head student thanking Rhodes: "Jannie will be the first man in South Africa."[8] More than 20 years later Merriman, in his own right "the greatest parliamentary orator in South Africa",[9] remembered with admiration this speech in a letter to Smuts.[10]

Rhodes was prime minister of the Cape Colony because of the support of the Afrikaner Bond. In spite of their different backgrounds and political philosophies, a special relationship developed between Rhodes and Hofmeyr based on Cape politics.[11] Hofmeyr, in strange contrast to Paul Kruger, was more sympathetically inclined to many of Rhodes' ideas. For years he had been an intimate friend and political ally to Rhodes. It seemed that both men had, each in his own way, the interest of the Cape Colony in particular and that of South Africa in mind.[12] Hofmeyr's friendship with Rhodes dated from the time of Rhodes' renunciation of "selfish imperialism". He confessed: "I was a rabid Jingo once. I am no longer.... The imperial factor must be eliminated."[13] This was a friendship that rested on very insecure foundations. The question to ask in this regard is: Was Rhodes using Hofmeyr or was Hofmeyr using him? Hofmeyr's political *modus operandi* was to work actively behind the scenes. This led to Merriman nicknaming him "The Mole". Nevertheless Hofmeyr had his political strategy in place. J.G. Lockhart wrote:

> *While no government could survive for long without the passive support of the Bond, for most of his political life Hofmeyr carefully avoided the responsibilities of office. He would be kingmaker, not king, ensuring by the votes he*

> *controlled that any government in office followed a policy*
> *congenial to the Dutch.*[14]

Rhodes was undoubtedly an "inveterate opportunist". In spite of his open declaration, his ultimate ambitions in Africa and the imperial dreams of the "powerful British coterie of Conservative leaders of the Chamberlain School were almost identical".[15] A common interest, regarding what they called *Colonialism* or *Colonial Home Rule*, actually prompted the ostensibly singular friendship between Rhodes and Hofmeyr. Their common goal was "the union of Dutch and British into one South African nation, with a common feeling of South African nationhood" and to quote Rhodes, "the government of South Africa by the people of South Africa with the imperial tie for defence".[16] In April 1893, however, Merriman and two of his political colleagues withdrew from the Cape government. Rhodes consequently reshuffled his ministry and won the election of 1894. Hofmeyr resigned his seat in Parliament for health reasons.

"In 1895, when Hofmeyr retired from Parliament," wrote Lockhart, "Rhodes lost his most valued supporter and most shrewd adviser. It is a fair conjecture that if Hofmeyr had still been at his elbow, the disaster of the Jameson Raid would never have befallen."[17] Hofmeyr nevertheless retained his hold over the Bond and the Bond retained its faith in Rhodes.

In an attempt to secure the support of the Bond, Rhodes gave way to many of Hofmeyr's demands. He gave, *inter alia,* way to religious school education, to the cancellation of all Sunday train services and to a disenfranchisement of "raw natives". In return Hofmeyr had to vote with the Bond against notions disagreeable to Rhodes—such as an export tax on diamonds. This was one of Rhodes' many means of vengeance.[18] The Bond was mainly a farmers' party. It is therefore understandable why it had a zeal for the free importation of everything except competitive foodstuffs. Rhodes, being exceptionally cunning in political manipulation, knew perfectly well how to exploit all this to his own political advantage. He planned for moderate agricultural protection and for the possibility of an expanding market on the Rand goldfields. This was of course subject to

Rhodes' concession for a railways and customs union. Native policy could have been a stumbling-block. In the Bond there existed some diversity of opinion with regards to the Native policy.[19] There was general unconcern as far as doctrine went. Basic political and economic factors, which could easily have developed into serious stumbling blocks, were amicably solved between Rhodes and the Bond. The Franchise Act of 1892 quietly settled the political question. On the economic front there was a common desire to have a labour market in the "neighbourhood of his (every farmer's) own farm, just as Rhodes wanted it in Kimberley".[20]

Hofmeyr's ambition to achieve equality between the Dutch and English languages was completely acceptable to Rhodes. Rhodes was in those days an adherent of the Cape Dutch. In this regard he said: "I like the Dutch. I like their homely courtesy and their tenacity of purpose, and we have always got on very well together."[21] Hofmeyr once said of the relationship between him and Rhodes:

> *I remember about the time we were introduced, the Transvaal war broke out, and Mr Rhodes—perhaps as it behoved him—was all against the Boers and Transvaal independence. I was on the other side. But when the war was over we had a talk with one another, and I said to Mr Rhodes, 'It is an awful pity the war broke out'. I was surprised when Mr Rhodes said, 'No, it is not. I have quite changed my opinion. It is a good thing. It has made Englishmen respect Dutchmen and made them respect one another.' Well, when an Englishman could speak like that to a Dutchman, they are not far from making common cause with one another.*[22]

In 1892 Rhodes helped Hofmeyr bring the Dutch language nearer to equality with English in the schools of the Cape Colony. The two of them had much more in common than they actually realised. They were also in complete harmony in their approach to colonialism. To them it meant, at the time, completely the opposite of what it came to mean half a century later. For them it did not mean imperial domination but the "elimination of the imperial factor". It did not mean subordination to an outside foreign power, but rather "the vigorous assertion of local and national interests".[23]

Rhodes and Hofmeyr were both active in extending the local interest of South Africa. This was the main reason why Hofmeyr tolerated, and consequently approved, Rhodes' economic and territorial expansion in the north. At first Hofmeyr doubted the wisdom of expanding northwards in the direction of the Transvaal. He initially doubted the "wisdom of policies which showed every appearance of stealing a march upon the northern Boers and hemming them in".[24] He was willing to work with them at any time in an "equal partnership" promoting the common interest of South Africa as a whole. But it became increasingly more difficult to do so. Firstly, there was no definition of the "common good". Secondly, since the goldmines of the Rand had brought wealth and power to the Transvaal, the leaders found themselves in a position where they had stronger bargaining powers. This of course had a direct influence on the policies of South Africa. If ever the leaders of the Transvaal were looking in the direction of a united South Africa, it would certainly be according to their own *modus operandi*—most probably in the direction of "a domination of the old ways over the new ways".[25] Naturally, in this situation, the Boers would dominate the rest. This of course was just the opposite of that which Hofmeyr had set his heart on. Hofmeyr believed that eventually a new leadership would take over in the Transvaal and that with time and patience everything would come right. What he did not realise was that Rhodes was running out of patience. By the end of 1894 Rhodes was a very sick man. Time had become a decisive factor. Rhodes had begun a race against an early death with so much still to be done. "His self-control began to give way," wrote Denys Rhoodie, "and his patience was reaching a breaking point. A spirit of adventure distorted his outlook and judgement—the Kruger government had to go at all costs."[26]

On his return to South Africa, after four years in Cambridge, Smuts supported without reservation the ideals of Rhodes and Hofmeyr concerning "a common feeling of South African nationhood". He probably heard Hofmeyr referring to the alliance between Rhodes and the Bond as "magically sealed". But Smuts did not understand Cape politics—let alone the alliance between Rhodes and Hofmeyr. To him the political set-up at the Cape did not seem to have changed much from the time of his departure for Cambridge four years ago. Without second thoughts Smuts became a member of the Afrikaner Bond. "In comparison with Hofmeyr," Hancock wrote, "Smuts of course knew practically nothing either about Rhodes or any of the other important persons whose plans or plots were shaping the history of his country."[27] Within a few weeks of his return, Smuts published an article in which he discussed confidently the recent session of the Cape Assembly. It seemed as if he had been present from the very beginning to report its proceedings.[28] His ambitions were awakened as his knowledge of South African politics grew and he started identifying himself with political life at the Cape. Gradually it became clear that he visualised a great future for himself in a united South Africa as envisaged by Rhodes and Hofmeyr. William Clomer wrote that Smuts "admired Rhodes both for being so like and so unlike himself".[29] The "isolationism" of Kruger did not appeal to him. On the other hand, the "big ideas of Rhodes held for him a peculiar fascination".[30]

"Dreaming with boyish ardour of a sub-continental federation," wrote Sir Philip Magnus, "Smuts publicly attacked the selfish Boer nationalism of Paul Kruger, president of the Transvaal."[31]

Smuts continued writing articles in English and Dutch for leading Cape newspapers. He, *inter alia,* severely criticised the Transvaal government's employment of Hollanders in preference to South Africans. In an article on Johannesburg, he made mention of its "colossal materialism which is destined to play a great part in South Africa".[32] He also attacked Dr Thomas Muir, superintendent of education for the Cape Colony, in the newspaper *Ons Land,* for importing his departmental officials from England and Scotland instead of employing educated South Africans. There seemed to be a driving force behind Smuts encouraging him to portray his opinion on a variety of political issues at the time. Consequently he wrote articles on a variety of contemporary subjects such as immigration, the native problem and many more. From time to time he attended sessions of the Old Cape Parliament as a reporter. Gradually his interest in active politics developed into a reality. For the future of the Cape Colony and for the future of South Africa as a whole, the solidarity between Cape Dutch and Cape English, as he envisaged it, was of the utmost importance.[33] At that stage it appeared secure to him. Smuts was convinced that it was ties of interest and of sentiment that joined Rhodes and the Afrikaner Bond. Smuts examined, and ultimately rejected, Kruger's claim to leadership in South Africa. He saw with increasing excitement the possibility of vast expansion into the hinterland of Africa. He probably asked himself if there was the slightest possibility that he could get involved in this most exciting political venture. Smuts started to take all this for granted. And then, most unexpectedly, Smuts received a note from Hofmeyr. He was cordially requested to come at his earliest convenience to the headquarters of the Bond in Cape Town. Needless to say, Smuts was surprised and extremely thrilled. Was this his first solid step in entering active politics? It was quite normal that Smuts had his own personal idea of what it could be all about. But he could not have been absolutely sure. Without any delay and with great expectations he left for the headquarters of the Afrikaner Bond.[34]

Olive Schreiner, the eminent South African writer and author of *The Story of an African Farm*, and her husband, Samuel Cronwright, warned Smuts from time to time against Rhodes. Olive Schreiner was once an admiring friend of Rhodes. It is interesting to note that she was initially "perpetually torn between contempt and admiration" for him. When she first met Rhodes, around 1890, she said she felt "a kind of mysterious affinity with him". She added that:

He is even higher and nobler than I expected; but our friends are so different (that) we could never become close friends. He spoke to me more lovingly and sympathetically of 'An African Farm' than anyone has ever done.[35]

Olive Schreiner later became one of Rhodes' most bitter antagonists. Due to the deterioration of Olive's health, the

Cronwrights settled in Kimberley. They challenged Rhodes in his own stronghold of Kimberley. They were, in their own way, formidable enemies whom Rhodes could simply not ignore. Olive Schreiner had a great and influential standing with a large reading public "throughout the English-speaking world", and her husband was a "prickly and pertinacious radical".[36] The couple had written a paper on the political situation of South Africa. They accused Rhodes of "misleading or seducing the Afrikaner Bond". According to them, Rhodes was making the Bond an instrument of his "capitalist plots" in the north.[37] In the paper they clearly hinted at collusion between Rhodes and the Rand *Uitlanders*—an attempt to overthrow Kruger's government in the Transvaal.[38] The Cronwright-Schreiners made an appeal to all South Africans to take a stand and join forces against Rhodes. Cronwright initially read the paper to the *Literary Society of Kimberley* and subsequently he and his wife published it as a pamphlet under joint authorship. It stands to reason that Olive Schreiner had a major part in compiling the paper.

Olive Schreiner, 1897. (Cape Archives Repository)

After all the criticism they had piled on Rhodes, Olive Schreiner, even after opposing Rhodes' native policy, especially over the Stropp Bill in 1894, declared that "she still believed in his greatness".[39] Even after the Jameson Raid, she still refused to write articles attacking and condemning him. But in her book, *Trooper Peter Halket of Mashonaland,* she attacked Rhodes mercilessly. She even rejoiced in the hatred felt for him by the Boers in

1899. In the light of all this Rhodes had no choice but to protect his prestige and secure his political future.

Until then, Smuts had made himself well acquainted with the leaders of the Bond. Rhodes and Hofmeyr remembered that he had lauded the Rhodes–Hofmeyr combination in his numerous press articles. In the light of the Cronwright-Schreiner attack on Rhodes, Hofmeyr found it appropriate to remind Rhodes of the young man he had encountered in Stellenbosch in 1888 at Victoria Colleges' graduation ceremony. It was time to utilise the special talents of this young man who subscribed to the Rhodes–Hofmeyr alliance, and who was furthermore a member of the Afrikaner Bond. When he arrived at the headquarters of the Bond, Hofmeyr informed Smuts that he had a message from Rhodes. He requested Smuts' assistance. Hofmeyr told Smuts that Rhodes was very upset by Olive Schreiner's and her husband's criticism in Kimberley. Furthermore he told Smuts that it was he (Hofmeyr) who had suggested to Rhodes that he (Smuts) should be sent to Kimberley to neutralise the criticism of Rhodes' political opponents. Rhodes consequently asked Hofmeyr to get in touch with Smuts. Would he go?[40] Smuts was not only willing to go, but in fact extremely eager to undertake such a task. He regarded it as a chance of a lifetime! "Here," wrote Crafford, "was his chance at last. It was a heaven-sent opportunity."[41] Smuts prepared his address to the *De Beers Mines Political and Debating Society* on the subject of *The Political Situation*.

Smuts did not really understand what Rhodes had actually asked him to do. Was Smuts, in spite of all his qualities, really qualified to do this? At this stage Smuts knew so little about political manipulation and those involved. The retiring high commissioner, Sir Henry Loch, had submitted certain proposals 12 months earlier to the colonial secretary in London for a possible *Uitlander* rising in Johannesburg.[42] He suggested that the uprising be supported by a military incursion from the Bechuanaland Protectorate. The new high commissioner, Sir Herculus Robinson, "returning to South Africa (was) well acquainted with him and well disposed towards him".[43] The new colonial secretary in London, Joseph Chamberlain, was also a closed book to Smuts. Smuts knew nothing about

President Paul Kruger and his ministers. The same applied for Charles Leonard, Lionel Phillips and the other leaders of the *Uitlanders*. He had never been north of the Vaal River, or even the Orange River! Smuts was completely ignorant of the political intrigue gradually unfolding behind the scenes in Southern Africa. The stage was set for political drama of the highest order.

The president and the secretary of the *De Beers Mines Political and Debating Society* were commissioned to meet Smuts at the Kimberley railway station. To their astonishment they approached "a pale-faced, blue-eyed, ridiculously thin and tall young man 'without hair on his face', who looked no more than seventeen".[44] They had expected Jan Christiaan Smuts, the 25-year-old Cape Town advocate with a list of distinguished academic achievements from Victoria College, Stellenbosch, and Christ's College, Cambridge, to look rather different.

On the evening of 29 October 1895 Smuts found himself on the platform of the Kimberley Town Hall. The town's newspaper reported the next day that the audience had been "large, representative and enthusiastic."[45] Crafford wrote that the "hall was packed."[46] Cronwright, however, said that the hall was only half full and the speech was a failure. When the mayor introduced the speaker to the 2 000-odd people, they were at first amused. What could this "insignificant-looking bit of a lad … tell them about the political situation that they did not already know"?[47] But very soon they fell under the spell of the oratorical power of this "bit of a lad"! In spite of the fact that Smuts did not tell them anything new in his speech of two hours, he kept their attention throughout. It was clear that the people disagreed with almost everything he had to say. They also realised that the majority of his statements were far removed from the actual basic facts.[48] But they nevertheless listened attentively.

Smuts wrote his Kimberley speech in the same way that he compiled his essays. He soon realised that he was speaking over the heads of Kimberley's miners, clerks and shopkeepers. He had to adjust considerably. "The speech," wrote Hancock, "as reported is long, wordy and more commonplace in its imagery than was customary with him. Still, it possessed clarity of design and purpose."[49] Smuts told his audience that the most important political issue, to be handled with extreme wisdom and with great care, was the race problem. The two fundamental problems at issue were, firstly, the consolidation of the white race and, secondly, white policy towards the other races.[50] He continued:

> *At the southern corner of a vast continent, peopled [by] over 100 000 000 barbarians, about half a million whites have taken up a position, with a view not only to working out their own destiny, but also of using that position as a basis for lifting up and opening up that vast dead-weight of immemorial barbarism and animal savagery to the light and blessing of ordered civilisation. Unless the white race closes it ranks in this country, its position will soon become untenable in the face of that overwhelming majority of prolific barbarism.*[51]

Smuts argued that material forces alone could never draw the two white peoples together. It was essential that the "sentiment of nationality" should cooperate with them in all aspects. The sentiment to which he referred had already "found its first powerful expression" in the Afrikaner Bond. It had reached, according to Smuts, a higher stage in the Bond's partnership with Rhodes.

To convince his audience of the extreme necessity of bringing together the Dutch and English speakers, he pointed out several negative developments should the attempt of Rhodes and Hofmeyr fail. What would the ultimate consequences be, Smuts asked, if the "new capitalistic society" in Kimberley should find them entrenched by an unyielding Afrikanerdom?[52] What would the consequences be if a foreign power, for instance Germany, who had already established itself in South West Africa, involved itself in South African affairs?[53] Or perhaps the South African Republic would indulge in a northward expansion into Central Africa?[54] All this could, according to Smuts, lead to a situation in which the rivalries of the great European Powers could be "sucked and drawn into the very heart of South Africa".[55] Smuts emphasised that there could be no greater danger than this for the future of the white people. "From this danger," Smuts continued his argument, "Rhodes has delivered us by his northward march. It was the march of South African nationhood."[56]

Smuts defended Rhodes' policies on every front. After dealing with corruption charges and moderate agricultural protection,[57] he concentrated mainly on the native policy of Rhodes. It was clear that, although Kimberley enthusiastically supported certain sections of the policy, there were other sections they had certain reservations on. Smuts made it very clear to his audience that the white people of South Africa had "duties to perform" as well as "rights to assert" and "interests to defend". "I for one," he said, "consider the position of the white race in South Africa one of gravest responsibility and difficulty. They must be the guardians of their own safety and development ... at the same time they are the trustees for the coloured races. The situation is unique."[58] He consequently dealt with the democratic principle in a situation which, seen in perspective, was undoubtedly unique. He pointed out that the democratic principal had never been applied in any part of the world without qualification. He referred to Britain, which still had the House of Lords and ultimately no universal suffrage in the true sense of the word. In New Zealand, Smuts pointed out, they found it fit to have differential franchise for the Maories. It was only in the United States that the democratic principle really came into effect—but not without a certain degree of pretence—"the law conceded democratic equality but physical force took it away".[59] Smuts continued:

> *I mention these facts, simply to remind you that the question of the application of advanced political principles to any people, or part of a people, is not an abstract, but a very practical question, to be decided on the facts of each individual case.... Now the mistake that has been made in the past is to assume that the full and entire democratic formula applied to our South African racial conditions. Mr Saul Soloman and others looked upon the abstract political or religious formula of universal equality as a safe rule of practical politics. I am afraid they were wrong.*

> *Their theory would have been inapplicable to civilised*
> *Europe; a fortiori, it was inapplicable to barbarous Africa.*
> *And I think one of the most conspicuous advances we have*
> *made in Cape politics during the last decade or more*
> *consists precisely in recognising that they were wrong ...*
> *that we have come down from the Utopian cloudland of*
> *abstract theory; and that now for the first time we are in a*
> *position to consider our great racial problem on its*
> *merits.*[60]

Smuts proclaimed himself an "empiricist" as far as native policy was concerned. "Dogmas of equality and of inequality" and of "unity and of separateness" were repugnant to him.[61] The situation that had been created by history, and the needs that arose from this situation, was his starting point. He argued that the power was in the hands of the white people and that they should be allowed to exercise it "in a spirit of responsibility and prudence". Smuts warned against abusing power by oppressing the natives. This could lead to a dangerous situation. The whites would allow their own civilisation to be affected if they permitted natives "to sink into degradation". Hancock wrote: "As in his student days, it was the 'browning' of the white man's character, not merely of his skin, that Smuts feared."[62] Smuts was convinced that the natives at their stage of development "must receive differential treatment under the law of the land". He realised that an appreciable number of natives were advancing beyond that stage of development and it was therefore a process that the law of the land should recognise.

The speech contributed greatly and most effectively to widespread acknowledgement of a rising young politician. Smuts received numerous letters of congratulations, *inter alia,* from the attorney general of the Cape Colony, W.P. Schreiner—the brother of Olive Schreiner. He welcomed Smuts' exposure of the "mischievous fallacy" that "abstract democratic principles were applicable to the complex racial situation of South Africa". Olive Schreiner naturally took the opposite view regarding the "major premise underlying the whole speech, namely, the trustworthiness of Rhodes". Her husband applauded the honesty and sincerity of the speaker, but rejected Smuts' arguments. He added: "He doesn't know Rhodes."[63] It is interesting to note that, at the very moment that Smuts was asked by Hofmeyr to go to Kimberley on Rhodes' behalf, the latter was secretly scheming to bring about what the Schreiners had predicted.[64]

It had become abundantly clear to Rhodes by the end of 1894 that it was extremely urgent to overthrow the Boer regime in the Transvaal. "Previously," wrote Rhoodie, "Rhodes had been content to realise his ambitious dream of a federated South Africa by way of a gradual, peaceful unification on an economic basis. Now, however, his approach (has) changed radically."[65] Rhodes accused Kruger of being utterly irreconcilable. According to the Cape prime minister there were "ten more years of mischief in him". "We cannot wait till he disappears," Rhodes maintained. "South Africa is developing too rapidly. Something must be done to place the control of the Transvaal in the hands of a more progressive ruler than Oom Paul."[66] Rhodes disapproved of Sir Henry Loch's suggestion of an *Uitlander Demonstration* during the latter's visit to the Transvaal. "Rhodes wanted to promote his own kind of imperialism, and his egotism would never have permitted him to become a mere accomplice in the furtherance of British imperialism."[67]

The plot to topple Kruger's government in the Transvaal, however, went terribly wrong. Rhodes was to strike at Kruger shortly after Smuts' return from Kimberley. He secretly imported arms into the Transvaal in order to equip his fellow *Uitlander* conspirators. He despatched Dr Leander Starr Jameson and a strong detachment of armed men to Pitsani, near the border of the Transvaal. The troops were to invade the republic and, assisted by the *Uitlander's* revolt, overthrow the Boer government. After one or two skirmishes the raiders surrendered ingloriously to General Piet Cronjé at Doornkop. "Dr Jameson, I have the honour to meet you," said the Boer general ironically.[68] The Jameson Raid was a total failure and the end of Rhodes' political career was on the horizon. In Kimberley, the Cronwright-Schreiners responded: "What will Smuts say now?"[69] The reaction varied on Rhodes' involvement in the Jameson Raid. Before looking at the various reactions it is important to note the analysis of Rhodes' character by Lockhart:

> *He (Rhodes) lived, in fact, in a dream world in which everything would come right in the end, however improbable it might seem, thanks to his genius. He hated to be brought down to earth by smaller minds. These were the psychological marks of a mentality that was in some respects conspicuously childish.*

There were other marks of it as well. One was his curiously undeveloped handwriting that sprawled vast and scarcely legibly across the notepaper—sometimes barely a dozen words to the page. The language and thoughts of his letters were often no less childish and they evoked a corresponding quality in the replies of some of those to whom he wrote.[70]

Hofmeyr, close friend and political ally of Rhodes, one in vision for an united South Africa, was extremely shocked when he learned about Rhodes' involvement in the Jameson Raid:

> *I had the feeling as if my wife had deceived me with my best friend ... Rhodes imagines himself a young king, the equal of the Almighty ... perhaps a Clive and Warren.*[71]

The reaction of John X. Merriman was of special significance. He also, being an old friend, turned his back on Rhodes in disgust:

> *The raid was not only wrong in its inception, but it is the deceit and treachery which accompanied it that I object to; and the raid has put Mr Kruger in his old position and rehabilitated him in the civilised world: that is the pity of it, and for that we have to thank Mr Rhodes ... I do say, Mr Rhodes is unworthy of the trust of the country!*[72]

The place given to the *Uitlanders* as an important instrument in the raid was certainly not honourable. Eric Walker, the South African historian, wrote in this respect: "Schreiner knew that even Rhodes held them to be 'cosmopolitan and trustworthy', and Milner had no high opinion of them. Some of his friends were even less charitable."[73]

Smuts was of course devastated when the news of the Jameson Raid reach him on New Year's Day, 1896. Never in his life had he suffered a shock of this kind. He was on holiday at the family farm, Klipfontein, during the raid. Smuts found it difficult to believe Rhodes' complicity.[74] This was the man whom he idealised. He defended his policies and now he had been deceived! "We are weary of the past," a heartsick Smuts wrote, "we are weary of our own errors and the errors of Downing Street, old, new and newer; and our prayer now is that we may be left alone to redeem ourselves."[75]

For Smuts the worst was that while he was defending Rhodes in his articles and on the platform in Kimberley, Rhodes had pretended to cooperate with Afrikanerdom in the interests of the Commonwealth and had thus grossly betrayed him. Naturally, all hopes had now been shattered. He had visualised a proud future for himself, but now this would never materialise. "He felt," wrote Crafford, "miserable, deeply humiliated, and angry. Rhodes had made a fool of him. His fellow Afrikaners would look scornfully at him and ridicule him. They would never forgive him for singing Rhodes' praises in Kimberley."[76]

Smuts found it extremely difficult to come to terms with what Rhodes had done to him as a person and to Afrikanerdom in general. The enormity of Rhodes' betrayal of trust completely overwhelmed Smuts. He could not forget what he called the Englishman's "treacherous duplicity".[77] He gradually discovered that Rhodes had nevertheless become an obsession with him. In spite of all that had happened the image of Rhodes did not diminish. In essence, Rhodes was still "the man with great and inspiring ideas, the image of the colossus astride a continent."[78] Smuts did not realise that in time to come he, Jan Smuts, would be called *Rhodes Redivivus*. But for now "he felt himself to be in the quicksands."[79] He was desperately searching for a path to follow, but this evaded him for the present. Above all, he had to define his stance towards Rhodes. At first Smuts refrained from criticising Rhodes publicly. He admitted that Rhodes appeared to be guilty of conspiracy, but it would be wise to wait a while. "Some people," wrote Hancock, "were inciting the Afrikaner Bond to declare immediate war upon Rhodes. But the Bond would do better to maintain a watchful neutrality until the facts became clear."[80] It did not take Smuts too long to make up his mind. On 14 January he appeared, together with Merriman, on an anti-Rhodes platform in Philadelphia, near Malmesbury. By now it was abundantly clear to him that Rhodes had betrayed his trust. By betraying his trust Rhodes had "destroyed the whole fabric of policy which he, Smuts, had expounded so confidently a few months back at Kimberley."[81] Was there any alternative? "He could," wrote Hancock, "see no alternative that satisfied his reason; but his emotions told him that Jingoism was incorrigible, that 'blood is thicker than water', that Afrikaners must rally to each other across the frontiers to defend their language, their tradition and their destiny as a free people."[82]

Smuts could no longer trust Rhodes. In spite of all that had happened, he could not bring himself to vilify Rhodes. Smuts still, even after the local committee of inquiry established beyond doubt that Rhodes had betrayed his trust as prime minister of the Cape Colony, looked upon Rhodes in "lament for fallen greatness".[83] Could this all have been a "cry from the heart"?[84]

There now dawned a difficult period of decision-making for Smuts. In his mind's eye he had seen himself already as a leading and influential Cape politician working towards a unified South Africa, together with political colossi such as Cecil John Rhodes and Jan Hofmeyer. "In the course of 1896," Smuts confessed, "it became so clear to me that the British connection was harmful to South Africa's best interest that I feared my further position as a Cape politician would be a false one. I therefore left the old colony for good and settled in the Transvaal."[85]

---

1. Felix Gross, *Rhodes of Africa,* 198. F.S. Crafford, *Jan Smuts. A Biography,* 12.

2. Gross, 198. W.K. Hancock, *Smuts, I. The Sanguine Years, 1870 – 1919,* 31.
3. Gross, 198. Hancock, 1, 31.
4. Gross, 198.
5. Crafford, 12.
6. Gross, 198. Kenneth Ingham, *Jan Christian Smuts. The Conscience of a South African,* 5.
7. Gross, 198. Crafford, 12.
8. Crafford, 12.
9. Hancock, 1, 31.
10. *Ibid.*
11. Hancock, 1, 52 – 54.
12. *Ibid.*
13. Crafford, 21.
14. J.G. Lockhart, *et al, Rhodes,* 85.
15. Crafford, 21.
16. *Ibid.,* 19.
17. Lockhart, *et al,* 201.
18. Gross, 198.
19. Hancock, 1, 52.
20. *Ibid.,* 52. Lockhart, 199.
21. Lockhart, 85.
22. *Ibid.,* 86 – 87.
23. Hancock, 1, 53.
24. *Ibid.*
25. *Ibid.*
26. Denys Rhoodie, *Conspirators in Conflict. A Study of the Johannesburg Reform Committee and its role in the conspiracy against the South African Republic,* 15.
27. Hancock, 1, 53.
28. *Ibid.,* 51.
29. William Clomer, *Cecil Rhodes,* 20.
30. Crafford, 19.
31. Philip Magnus, *Smuts,* in Lord Longford, *et al,* (eds), *The History Makers,* 142.
32. *Ibid.,* 14.
33. Hancock, 1, 52.
34. Crafford, 15.
35. Lockhart, 20.

36. Hancock, 1, 55.
37. *Ibid.*
38. Crafford, 20.
39. Lockhart, 20.
40. Crafford, 20. Ingham, 13.
41. Crafford, 20.
42. Rhoodie, 15 – 17.
43. Hancock, 1, 53.
44. Gross, 257.
45. Hancock, 1, 55.
46. Crafford, 20.
47. Gross, 258.
48. *Ibid.*
49. Hancock, 1, 55.
50. *Ibid.* Ingham, 13 – 14.
51. Hancock, 1, 55 – 6.
52. *Ibid.*, 56.
53. *Ibid.*
54. D.W. Kruger, *The Making of a Nation. The History of the Union of South Africa,* 15.
55. Hancock, 1, 56.
56. *Ibid.* Ingham, 14.
57. Hancock, 1, 56.
58. *Ibid.*, 56 – 57. Ingham, 14.
59. Hancock., 1, 57.
60. *Ibid.*
61. *Ibid.*
62. *Ibid.*
63. *Ibid.*, 58.
64. Crafford, 21.
65. Rhoodie, 14.
66. *Ibid.*, 17.
67. *Ibid.*, 16.
68. Crafford, 21. Walter, Nimcocks, *Milners Young Men. The "kindergarten" in Edwardian Imperial Affairs,* 5.
69. Hancock, 1, 58.
70. Lockhart, 26 – 27.
71. Gross, 295.
72. *Ibid.*, 292.

73. Eric A. Walker, *W.P. Schreiner. A South African,* 139.
74. Crafford, 22.
75. Neil Hepburn, *Smuts: Prophet of the new Empire.* In *The British Empire,* Volume 7, Part 75, 58.
76. Crafford, 22.
77. *Ibid.,* 23.
78. *Ibid.*
79. Hancock, 1, 58.
80. *Ibid.,* 59.
81. *Ibid.*
82. *Ibid.*
83. *Ibid.* Thomas Pakenham, *The Boer War,* 21 – 22.
84. Hancock, 1, 59.
85. Ingham, 16.

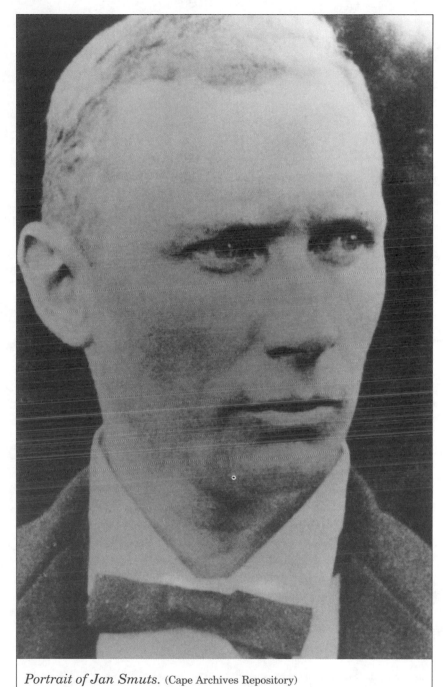

Portrait of Jan Smuts. (Cape Archives Repository)

Sir Alfred Milner, high commissioner. (Cape Archives Repository)

2

Alfred Milner

"Milner is as sweet as honey, but there is something in
his very intelligent eyes which tells me that he is a
very dangerous man."
J.C. Smuts (Smuts Papers, 1, 90)

"Kruger's brilliant State Attorney."
Alfred Milner (Milner Papers, 1, 409)

The new British high commissioner for South Africa, Lord
Alfred Milner, landed in Cape Town in May 1897. The
appointment of Milner in South Africa confirmed all Jan
Smuts' fears about British policy towards South Africa.[1] "The
announcement," wrote Walter Nimocks, "of Milner's appointment as governor of the Cape Colony and high commissioner for
South Africa, was released in February 1897. To the average
Englishman Milner's name meant nothing, but among those
who knew him and were aware of his ability the announcement
was well received."[2] Although Milner was born in Germany, his
parents were of British descent. He came to South Africa with
outstanding credentials. He was well known for his excellent
experience in good and effective administration. After receiving

his early education on the Continent he became a distinguished law scholar at Balliol College, Oxford. After completing his studies, Milner was admitted to the bar in 1881. He is said to have obtained from Oxford "her peculiar gift of dry and impervious arrogance".[3]

Milner initially decided on a career in journalism. His devotion and ardour for imperialism and social reform was already visible at an early stage in his career as a journalist.[4] In 1887 he was appointed official private secretary to G.T. Goschen, the chancellor of the exchequer. Two years later, on Goschen's recommendation, Milner was promoted to the position of director-general of military finances in Egypt.[5] In 1892 he returned to England as chairman of the board for inland revenue.[6] Egypt was undoubtedly a job well done! Eventually his competence, thoroughness and prestige paid off. He was appointed to the post of high commissioner in South Africa. Whitehall considered him, without question, a suitable choice for this high post in the Empire. In the Colonial Office, Joseph Chamberlain was sure that they had made the right choice.

Joseph Chamberlain. (Transvaal Archives Repository)

Milner's highest priority was the consolidation of the British Empire. He was of the opinion that "South Africa is (was) ... the weakest link in the imperial chain ... ." He was determined to put this straight in order to secure the stability and the unity of the Empire, even if it meant "crush(ing) Afrikanerdom". At the same time Milner was well aware of "the tremendous responsibility which rests upon the man, who is called upon to try and preserve it from snapping ... ."[7] Milner was an outspoken and convinced Imperialist. Crafford points out: "(His) appointment to the high position in South Africa was a calamitous one. He came to South Africa fully resolved to 'crush Afrikanerdom'. Nor did he scruple to say so."[8] He had an ungovernable desire to expand and fully establish the British Empire to the outskirts of the globe. In the Empire's race against competing countries, Milner regarded closer political and economic ties within the Empire of the utmost importance. British universal supremacy and the advantages coupled with it formed the basis of his political philosophy.[9] It was therefore crucial to Milner that South Africa was not lost to the Empire. "He had been sent out to South Africa," wrote Sarah Gertrude Millen, "to continue the policy interrupted by the Raid ... Rhodes' policy, Chamberlain's policy ... of making a whole thing of South Africa: making it safe for South Africans and safe for England ... safe against Germany and great against the future."[10]

Milner was widely respected by the leaders of both political parties in Britain. Nimocks wrote:

In choosing Milner, Salisbury and Chamberlain selected an administrator rather than a politician. Political circles in London were filled with men whose careers would have been advanced by such an appointment. But instead of making a choice from that group the Prime Minister and the Colonial Secretary offered this important post to a forty three year old bureaucrat with many political connections, but no desire to use whatever reputation he might earn in South Africa as a steppingstone to important political positions in Great Britain.[11]

Chamberlain instructed Milner to act with great caution in South Africa. When Milner landed in Cape Town he seemed to be in full accord with Chamberlain's wishes.[12] Chamberlain pointed out to Milner that the Jameson Raid had put the British government in a very thorny situation. Therefore only "flagrant aggression" by the Boers would justify a war with the Transvaal. Milner kept this in mind. Trouble could erupt in the Cape Colony and the British people could eventually find this unacceptable. The colonial secretary pointed out that time was on the side of the British and it would therefore be wise "to play a waiting game".

Although this was extremely difficult for Milner, he initially obeyed instructions. In the meantime his ear was constantly on the ground and he was fully prepared to gain information prior to taking action. His attitude towards the Transvaal, however, was that of finding fault wherever he could. He was more interested in what the critics of the Transvaal had to say than the defenders. He wanted to hear that the whole of South Africa could be administered with great success as an integral part of the British Empire.[13] Milner always judged societies by their administrative efficiency. In applying this criterion to the Transvaal he came to the conclusion that the Transvaal was in urgent need of reform. Realising that the chance to reform was very slim, he informed Chamberlain in 1898 that Britain's interest in South Africa would be best served on all fronts by declaring war on the Transvaal.[14] Without delay Chamberlain made it very clear to Milner that there was no change in his original instructions. It was quite understandable that Chamberlain could hardly, at that stage, take any risks. The dilemma of the disastrous Jameson Raid was still fresh in the minds of those in White Hall. "He had survived," wrote Ingham, "the parliamentary inquiry into the raid only by dextrous manipulation of the commission's proceedings and he could run no more risks. Above all he was fully aware that there would be no enthusiasm in Britain for war with the Republic."[15]

Milner showed exemplary restraint for approximately nine months. It is abundantly clear that this went totally against the grain of Milner's temperament and conviction. He was a man who wanted things to be done. His political testament, which he wrote in his old age, clearly reflects his character in this respect:

CREDO. Key to my position.
I am a Nationalist and not a cosmopolitan ... I am a British (indeed primarily an English) Nationalist. If I am also an Imperialist, it is because the destiny of the English race, owing to its insular position and long supremacy at sea, has been to strike roots in different parts of the world. I

am an Imperialist and not a Little Englander because I am a British Race Patriot.... The British State must follow the race, must comprehend it, wherever it settles in appreciable numbers as an independent community. If the swarms constantly being thrown off by the parent hive are lost to the State, the State is irreparably weakened. We cannot afford to part with so much of our best blood. We have already parted with much of it, to form the millions of another separate but fortunately friendly State. We cannot suffer a repetition of the process.[16]

There was a widespread feeling amongst Afrikaners as well as Englishmen that the utmost must be done to prevent war between Britain and the Transvaal. They were thinking of the consequences of such a war not only on the Transvaal but also on the rest of South Africa. "Do endeavour, my dear brother," wrote William Schreiner, the prime minister of the Cape Colony since the defeat of Rhodes' party in 1898, to Smuts, "to secure reasonable concessions. If you have done that it will be an immense service to South Africa. Imagine the joy with which Rhodes and Co. would welcome the fact, if the president and *Raad* should be stung into an attitude of refusing to do what is reasonable...."[17] From Jan Hofmeyr, Smuts received a shower of cabled advice: "Time for pouring oil on stormy waters and not on fire. Do not delay ... situation is serious and time precious." Hofmeyr also sent Smuts a warning: "Cherish no illusion about Colony." Hofmeyr wanted to make it very clear to Smuts that he should not expect the

Jan Smuts as state attorney.
(Cape Archives Repository)

Cape Afrikaners to "rush *en masse* to arms" should hostilities break out between Britain and the Transvaal. It should also be kept in mind that "most of them know nothing about the bearing of arms".[18]

To the relief of Sir William Butler, commander-in-chief in South Africa, it was announced that Kruger and Milner were to meet in Bloemfontein in an attempt to settle their differences regarding the *Uitlander* problem. Although Sir William distrusted Milner, as he distrusted Rhodes and his satellites on the Rand, he still hoped against all hope that the Bloemfontein Conference would turn out to be successful. "All political questions in South Africa," said Sir William, "and nearly all the information sent from Cape Town to England, are now being worked by ... a colossal syndicate for the spread of systematic misrepresentation."[19] The Bloemfontein Conference commenced on 31 May 1899 and ended on 5 June. The conference was not a success. Milner arrived at the conference with a large representative team to assist him in the negotiations with the president of the Transvaal. Two members of the Executive Council, two officials, and Jan Christiaan Smuts accompanied Kruger.[20] "In the last critical months," wrote Spies, "Smuts had been Kruger's chief minister; he, rather than the state secretary, F.W. Reitz, had been chosen by the president to be his adviser at the Bloemfontein Conference and thereafter; it is not too much to say that in all but name, Smuts had become state secretary."[21]

Milner had decided beforehand to concentrate on the thorny franchise question in the Transvaal. The franchise consequently occupied most of the delegates' time. Right from the start Milner made far-reaching demands. He insisted on immediate concessions. It was crystal clear to all that if Kruger should grant these concessions to Milner it would be suicide for the Transvaal. Smuts intervened and urgently advised Kruger to make "concessions" to Milner. The president yielded. But the high commissioner made it clear that he was not prepared to bargain. "He had stated what he wanted," wrote Crafford. "Nothing else would satisfy him."[22]

Smuts hurriedly drew up a "complete reform bill". He had of course Kruger's consent to do this. *Uitlanders* would be granted the franchise seven years after their arrival in the Transvaal. It was, taking into consideration the special circumstances, from the British point of view, a considerable concession made by Kruger. Milner, however, was not interested in Smuts' document. He had made up his mind and if the Boers did not do what they were told, he was prepared to "break off the negotiations".

Smuts, seated next to Kruger, was infuriated by Milner's rudeness and proud, detestable conduct. The only conclusion reached by everybody was that Milner's attitude "was decidedly provocative". It was with extreme difficulty that Smuts succeeded in giving his full attention to the work of the conference. "But Smuts pulled himself together," wrote Crafford. "He was Kruger's mainstay. It was his duty to steer clear of personalities."[23] Although Kruger made further concessions, Milner remained adamant. He would only be satisfied with that which he had demanded in the beginning ... or nothing!

When Kruger finally realised that there was nothing further to achieve, he said with great emotion: "I understood from His Excellency's arguments that if I do not give the whole management of my land and government to strangers there is nothing to be done ... I am not ready to hand over my country to strangers."[24] It was Kruger's viewpoint throughout the duration of the conference that he would give "everything, everything, everything" for peace. But if "they touch my independence, I shall resist."[25] As Kruger spoke these words, Smuts was sitting beside him, "a pale and intense young man," wrote Crafford, "with unflinching light-blue eyes, staring coldly and ruthlessly at Milner in whom he found more than his match in arrogance and whose attitude had aroused in him a burning resentment."[26] He had to exercise extreme self-discipline to hold himself in check at Milner's scornful treatment of the president, himself and his colleagues. Milner and Smuts were destined to meet again in the very near future.

"If there was one man," wrote Gertrude Millin, "who was not, in Colonel Reitz's words, spoiling for a fight, and had no desire for a rupture, it was Smuts. They said of Smuts in those days ... the Dutch said it ... that if something were still needed finally to ensure the coming of war it was Smuts' over-eagerness for peace."[27] Arriving back in Pretoria after the Bloemfontein Conference, Smuts said to Pieter Grobler, Kruger's nephew and secretary, at the railway station: "It is absolutely clear to me that Milner is planning for war." Lord Oliver, a well-known author at the time, was convinced that Milner's attitude and consequent hostilities were the outcome of "his determination to round off the Empire before it was too late".[28] Smuts had now entered into negotiations with Conyngham Greene, the British agent in Pretoria. This was a desperate personal effort to avoid war.[29] On 25 August Smuts finally wrote to Greene:

> *The terms of a settlement as contained in a formal note of this Government, dated 19th August, were very carefully considered, and I do not believe that there is the slightest chance that these terms will be altered or amplified. Your decision will therefore have to be arrived at on these terms as they stand.*[30]

Smuts was still struggling with the overwhelming question: Was Chamberlain really determined to re-annex the Transvaal, regardless of public opinion? Was there ultimately to be war? And then he felt, "the sooner the better". He struggled to keep control of his feelings: "Our *volk*, throughout South Africa, must be baptised with the baptism of blood and fire before they can be admitted among the great peoples of the world." And he was convinced that they would win. "Either we shall be exterminated or we shall fight our way out ... and when I think of the great fighting qualities that our people possess, I cannot see why we should be exterminated."[31] Only when Smuts' bid was rejected by Chamberlain personally did the Transvaal state attorney start preparing for war. He now believed that war was inevitable.[32] Smuts prepared a memorandum that provided the Transvaal government with a blueprint for political, economic and military action in the coming war.[33] It is interesting to note that up to the outbreak of the War, Smuts' only contact with military matters had been his membership as a student of the militia at Stellenbosch. Nevertheless his greatest wish, during the first months of the War, was to be in the operational area.[34] Neither the Smuts–Greene discussions, nor any further communications with the representatives of the British government had any effect on the growing tension. Milner, without any concrete proof, sent a cable dated 31 August to White Hall that stated: "British South Africa was prepared for extreme measures." This was very far from the truth. And Cecil John Rhodes, who was in England at that time, cynically remarked to some friends: "Three years ago I made a raid and everybody said I was wrong. Now the Queen's government are [is] preparing another raid, and everybody says they are right." Referring to the British flag, he later said, "[It] is the greatest commercial asset.... We are not going to war for the amusement of royal families as in the past, but we mean practical business."[35]

On 2 September Chamberlain broke off diplomatic relations with the Kruger government. Soon after this announcement large numbers of troops landed in Natal. They immediately started taking up positions on the borders of that colony.[36] The Transvaal government had to act. Without delay Smuts drafted an ultimatum, which was despatched to the British government on 9 October.[37] It requested "an immediate withdrawal of Her Majesty's forces." Kruger had no option. He certainly would have been a traitor to his people if he had not launched the ultimatum. A fortnight previously, when matters became critical, the editor of one of New York's leading newspapers had cabled the Transvaal government to ask "if they would put up a fight if necessary?" Replying on behalf of Kruger, Smuts said: "Yes. It will be a fight that will stagger humanity."[38] On 4 September 1899, in a secret memorandum to the Transvaal executive, he wrote:

> *South Africa stands on the eve of a frightful blood-bath out of which our people will come ... either as ... hewers of wood and drawers of water for a hated race, or as victors, founders of a United South Africa, of one of the great empires of the world ... an Afrikaner republic in South Africa stretching from Table Bay to the Zambezi.*[39]

The War commenced on 11 October, and the Orange Free State decided to fulfil her treaty obligations. They declared themselves an ally of the Transvaal. The nations of the world were interested spectators as the two republics indulged in an epic struggle which was, to say the least, a most uneven struggle. "On one side there fought," wrote Crafford, "the greatest, wealthiest, and most powerful Empire the eye of man had ever seen, commanding inexhaustible resources; on the other hand, a mere handful of untrained farmers amounting to ... men, women and children all told ... less than Birmingham's population at the time."[40]

The War lasted for two-and-a-half years. Both sides had to pay a high price. This price was especially high on the side of the two Boer republics. The women and children in the concentration camps suffered and those who were forced to leave the farms wandered unsheltered in the veld. The first peace talks were held in Middelburg in February 1901 and were followed later by the Pretoria Conference in May 1902, which ultimately led to Vereeniging later that month. When the Pretoria Conference began in May 1902, Colonel Ian Hamilton allowed his thoughts to go back to the Bloemfontein Conference held three years before. He found, according to Pakenham, "his insights dramatically confirmed". He asked himself why the Bloemfontein Conference had failed. Suddenly it became clear to him that it failed solely because of Milner's attitude. The inevitable result, "under the circumstances", had been "this bloody war".[41] Hamilton believed that the War was "providential", because of the need to confirm imperial supremacy over all South Africa. "But the time has now come when we want quite another sort of winding-up to the palaver."[42] Colonel Henry Rawlinson was equally hostile towards Milner's policy. He was rightly convinced that this was a policy to drag out the War, in an attempt to impose on the Cape Crown Colony government. "I am inclined to think," he said, "that we shall not be able to make Milner 'King' of South Africa."[43] Hamilton's as well as Rawlinson's views undoubtedly reflected, to a great extent, the personal view of their chief. It was of great significance to try and unravel why there was such a deep gulf between their views and those of Milner.

Hamilton realised not only why Milner was trying to block the peace talks, but also why he wished to destroy the Boers as a political force in order to benefit the 'Loyalists' in all spheres of the South African political set-up. This filled Hamilton with disgust and he just could not accept it. In January he warned Winston Churchill that real Loyalists were "preciously scarce" ... except in so far as "loyalty is a South African political expression, meaning anti-Dutch". A month later he told Churchill:

Do let us profit by our experience when we smashed the Zulus for the Boers, and not repeat the mistake by annihilating the Boers for the Jew burghers. You have no idea what arrogant insolent devils you will discover as soon as Mr Boer has lost his mauser. If one could only keep a tame commando in perpetuity striking distance of the mines, all would go as merry as wedding bells. Otherwise your great government will find itself rather vulgarly snubbed as soon as you wish to interfere in the smallest degree with the Chamber of Mines pretention to run the whole of Africa for its own particular advantage.[44]

Churchill agreed. "He had 'very little admiration' for the Cape Loyalists or for the *Uitlanders* of the Transvaal," writes Pakenham. "The Boers, not they, must be 'the rock' on which the British position must be founded. On their part, it was a 'shrewd' move of the Boers to pre-empt the Loyalists."[45]

On 15 May the national delegates arrived in Vereeniging, 80 kilometres south of Pretoria, for the peace negotiations. The Boer commandos, scattered all over the two republics, selected the delegates. The 60 delegates chose a five-man negotiation team: Generals Botha and De la Rey, State Attorney Smuts for the Transvaal, and Judge Hertzog and General De Wet for the Orange Free State.[46] The peace terms, if agreed upon, still had to be ratified by the delegates in Vereeniging. The negotiation team had not been given plenary powers. It also had to be ratified by the British Cabinet in London.[47] The team suggested that Smuts have an informal talk with Kitchener and Milner. Milner now had the chance of a *pis aller*—to restore the talks to the Middelburg line of February 1901.[48] The three men worked out a draft for the introduction to the surrender terms. The Boer leaders were recognised as "acting as the government of the South African Republic" and "acting as the government of the Orange Free State"—two governments officially abolished by the British nearly two years earlier.[49] They were to agree in return that the burghers would recognise King Edward VII "as their lawful sovereign".[50] A sub-committee would draw up the details of the peace agreement. This would then be submitted for discussion and ratification. "At this stage," wrote Pakenham, "De Wet exploded. It was he and Steyn who had long been recognised as the main obstacles to a peace conference (and thus Milner's principal remaining hope of a breakdown)."[51] De Wet spoke clearly for Steyn as well, who was at that stage too ill to go to Pretoria.

Eventually the two lawyers, Smuts and Hertzog, were left to wrestle with Milner and his legal adviser, Sir Richard Solomon, attorney general of the Cape. Pakenham wrote that the negotiations ran smoothly once De Wet was out of the way. At long last the draft agreement was submitted to the full committee. The text of the draft was cabled to London. The possibility of an agreement increased dramatically and with it Milner's total frustration. To Chamberlain he despatched on the 21st a last comment—"over-my-dead-body". Negotiations had "taken a turn for the worse". The Boers were making "preposterous proposals". He was himself "in a weak position, as Kitchener did not always support him even in the presence of the Boers". If Kitchener sent them "strange proposals", then he begged the Cabinet to block them. He was of the opinion that should the peace talks in Vereeniging break up, the Boers would "surrender left and right". "The men here," Milner argued, "are either anxious to upset negotiations or bluffing, in reliance on our weakness, probably the latter."[52]

Due to international response and the influence of public opinion in Britain, Milner realised that he could not hope for much from Chamberlain. The German kaiser, to the dismay of Milner, had sent his uncle, the king, a cable *en clair* on 2 May. He congratulated him on offering "most liberal" terms and "fervently hoping [hoped]" the Boers would accept them. Chamberlain made it abundantly clear to Milner in January

Lord Kitchener. (Transvaal Archives Repository)

that the Middelburg terms were still on the table. Any hope for Milner's policy of fighting the War "to the bitter end" would depend on Steyn and De Wet.[53]

The text from South Africa was handed to the Colonial Office on 22 May. They thought the terms were not "preposterous" at all. To a certain extent they were actually surprised. The following day Chamberlain met with the permanent secretary to discuss the changes in the terms, if any, to be ultimately recommended to the Cabinet. He then received Milner's private cable denouncing the new terms —especially the "detestable" Clause II (£3 million to cover their enemies' war debts). Chamberlain cabled back, testily: "There should be some argument more cogent than the money cost to justify it, and would you go so far as to wreck agreement at this stage upon this question?"[54]

The Cabinet discussed the new terms on 23 May. In general, they were pleased with them. In any case, it was an improvement on Middelburg. The Cabinet did, however, compromise with Milner on certain clauses. Salisbury's Cabinet left Kitchener's new terms as they were originally received. Milner, therefore, failed to jeopardise the terms. The Cabinet wanted the text to be put to the Boer delegates in Vereeniging without delay. The text was cabled back to South Africa on 27 May. There was still, albeit, a very slim chance of blocking the agreement, which could result in a gain for Milner. The Cabinet had agreed to allow the Boers only time for a simple 'yes' or 'no'.[55]

In their situation the Boer delegates could hardly vote 'no'. The suffering of the women and children had demoralised the commandos. Pakenham points out that it was not the sufferings of the women and children in the concentration camps that was the decisive factor for the Boers, but rather the state of those who had been left in the veld and were refused, according to Kitchener's latest policy, admittance to these camps. "The women were in a most pitiable state," Botha was quoted as saying, "now that the lines of the blockhouses had been extended in all directions over the country. Sometimes the commandos had to break through the lines and leave the women alone.... "[56] The Transvaal was now threatened from two sides. The natives were stirring, and the women and children were vulnerable at a time when their menfolk were least able to protect them. No support at all could be expected from the Cape Colony. There was not the slightest possibility of an Afrikaner rising there. It was therefore clear that the "Boer cause must stand or fall by virtue of what could be achieved in the republics."[57] Judge Hertzog's strongest argument for peace was that "some of their own people had turned against them, and were fighting in the ranks of the enemy."[58] These were the so-called joiners. Botha himself declared the condition of the whole country "hopeless". "The English people," wrote Hancock, "were getting sick of the war and prominent persons were urging their government to come to terms with the Boers; the foreign peoples were becoming ever more embittered against the English because of the terrible conditions in the refugee camps."[59] And Smuts said at this stage: "This fearful state of things has undoubtedly touched the conscience of the English public.... Perhaps God's will is that through our ill-treated women and children a decisive end should be made to this war."[60]

Botha once again raised the issue of people demanding that the leaders fight to "the bitter end". He pointed out that nobody could really tell where that bitter end was. "Is it there," Botha asked, "where every man is either buried or banished? Do not let us regard a period of universal burial as the bitter end."[61] Acting President Schalk Burger, and even General de la Rey, agreed. "Fight to the bitter end?" asked De la Rey. "Do you say that? But has the bitter end not come?"[62]

Soon after 2 pm on Saturday, 31 May 1902, the 60 delegates in Vereeniging voted. An overwhelming majority was in favour of Kitchener's peace. The peace agreement was signed in Kitchener's headquarters in Pretoria. Kitchener and Milner met the representatives of the two republics on arrival. The latter looked "grey and ill". Schalk Burger signed for the Transvaal and De Wet for the Orange Free State. Kitchener signed last.

Smuts wrote to his wife, who was at that time in Pietermaritzburg and under doctor's surveillance for an illness difficult to diagnose:

> *The tragedy is over. The curtain falls over the Boers as British subjects, and the plucky little Republics are no more. Peace was signed last night at Pretoria.... So we shall start afresh, working along the lines opened by the new conditions. I accept my fate ... that is the only manly course left.*[63]

Smuts played an important role in drafting the terms of the peace settlement. The clause relating to the possible granting of the franchise to black men in the Transvaal and the Orange Free State was eventually redrafted by Smuts and in its new form accepted by the British government. It meant that the governments of the Transvaal and the Orange Free State would decide "on the vital issue of voting rights for blacks in their territories" and not the British government.[64]

Milner did not feel like celebrating. In his heart he must have felt that he had lost. Throughout the process he had hated the prospect of "the war ending with a written document containing conditions and pledges that would restrict the freedom of British action."[65] The possibility of masterminding the "great game for mastery" in South Africa had slipped through his fingers. Three years before, when he decided to instigate war between Britain and the Transvaal he had not been too hopeful. But what Milner simply could not accept was that Kitchener had thrown the game away when victory was not far away. This was really too much to bear. "All that he could say," wrote Pakenham, "was that he had prevented a disastrous peace being signed. He had stopped Kitchener from putting a date to the restoration of self-government. That was the vital thing."[66] Milner was satisfied that he had bought time for himself and his *kindergarten*. It would be their ultimate goal to build up the gold industry as a functional basis in order to launch all their reforms. This would result in bringing into the Transvaal, according to Milner, the much-needed "new blood". He wanted settlers for the Rand and for the farms—"united, loyal, imperial-minded British settlers by the thousand, drawing on loans offered by Wernher–Beit."[67]

Milner had expressed himself more frankly in a letter written a few weeks previously to Hanbury Williams who had been transferred on promotion to the Colonial Office. "I attach the greatest importance of all," he wrote, "to the increase in the British population. British and Dutch have to live here on equal terms. If, ten years hence, there are three men of British race to two of Dutch, the country will be safe and prosperous. If there are three of Dutch to two of British, we shall have perpetual difficulty."[68]

In addition to being British high commissioner in South Africa, Alfred Milner now became governor of the two conquered republics and his headquarters were in Johannesburg. He took over the administration of the newly-formed Transvaal and Orange River Colony. His new responsibility included launching and directing reconstruction in the broadest sense of the word. From the start it was clear to Milner that Johannesburg, the heart of the mining industry and South Africa's largest centre of population, was crucial to his reconstruction program. "A great Johannesburg," he said in 1902, "great in intelligence, in cultivation, in public spirit—means a British Transvaal."[69] In this venture he was to be assisted by his famous *Balliol Kindergarten,* a group of young university graduates from Oxford.[70] They generally proved themselves to be extremely able. They contributed much to what is usually regarded as the special achievements of Milner in South Africa.[71] Among these young men were John Buchan and Patrick Duncan, who later became respectively governor general of Canada and South Africa; Lionel Curtis, Geoffrey Dawson, and Philip Kerr, the latter later became Lord

Lothian. Referring to Milner's political strategies in South Africa, Hancock wrote:

> *Milner's military calculations had been proved wrong. His political calculations were now to be tested by events. He held in his hand the entire power for which Kruger and Rhodes had contended; yet not quite so firmly as he would have wished. In the former Boer republics his rule was as near absolute as the Crown Colony system permitted ...*"[72]

The new regime's ultimate goal was "a federated British South Africa in a federated British Empire with an Imperial Parliament in Britain directing its destinies from afar."[73] Smuts, of course, never had any enthusiasm for any form of federation and he was bound to oppose this vigorously for many years to come. Milner and his aides were to be disillusioned by the growing colonial nationalism, which was destined to radically change the character of the old imperialism. Milner was soon to learn that all his efforts to Anglicise the Boers in the true sense of the word were doomed from the start. Milner's educational policy, *inter alia*, infuriated the Afrikaners. "Dutch should only be used to teach English," Milner said, "and English to teach everything else."[74] What all this eventually resulted in was simply to "stir up extreme resentment and to precipitate a fresh outbreak of Afrikaner nationalism. Smuts and Hertzog ultimately turned out to be the foremost opponents of Milner and Milnerism."[75]

It was extremely difficult for Smuts to come to terms with the fact that Milner and his *kindergarten* now occupied the positions which he and his colleagues had been forced to vacate. "One lives here," he wrote to John X. Merriman, who had succeeded Jameson as prime minister of the Cape, "in an atmosphere which is entirely devoid of culture, and is frankly materialistic in the worst sense."[76] He also wrote to Emily Hobhouse. Although Smuts wrote to her mainly about the Chinese labour the Transvaal government was considering introducing, he could nevertheless not restrain himself from pouring out his frustrations as regards the political developments in the Transvaal:

> *You must not blame me too much for sitting still and doing nothing. There is a strong desire in me and in all of us to do something; but what? There seems to be nothing in common between our ideals of public policy and those of the authorities. We think that government must be for the greatest good of the greatest number; they think that the mining industry must be saved at all costs. And it cannot and will not be saved, for the major part of it is bogus and a sham....*
>
> *I see the day coming when British South Africa will appeal to the Dutch to save them from the consequences of their insane policy of today. And I fear—I sometimes fear with an agony bitterer than death—that the 'Dutch' will no more be there to save them or South Africa. For the Dutch too are being undermined and demoralised by disaster and despair and God only knows how far this process will yet be allowed to go on.*[77]

This letter caused a stir in political and journalistic circles. Seldom had a statesman so young written a letter of this kind. Smuts was now 34. Miss Hobhouse, who was at the time very anti-British, handed the letter to *The Times* without consulting Smuts. She meant no harm. The letter was published in *The Times* of 15 March 1904. "Smuts wrote," said Gertrude Millin, "at the age of thirty-four, like a young man betrayed at his first encounter with life...."[78] The letter damaged him at that stage of his political career. He later said that he was sorry that the letter was published, because he would have expressed himself "more cautiously had I known it would be published".[79]

According to Hancock a legend had grown up that Smuts "relapsed under Milner's rule into embitterment, ennui and despair."[80] If this was the case, it has never really been established. Smuts blamed Milner for all the misfortunes. "An almost unreasonable bitterness," wrote Crafford, "begotten of his thwarted ambition, tortured him. And Milner epitomised those forces of oppression which shackled him—Milner the satrap, whose hauteur invariably infuriated him and whose arrival in Africa had spelled ruin to Afrikanerdom in general and Jan Smuts in particular. Milner was his arch-enemy. He and what he stood for must be destroyed."[81]

Gradually Botha's moderate influence once again made itself felt on Smuts. Mansergh aptly refers to Botha as "a man of wiser counsel though not comparable intellectual attainments as Smuts."[82] It was at this stage that Smuts' idea of undoing and neutralising Milnerism started taking shape in a specific plan of action. During the lengthy talks between Smuts and Botha, the two stable-mates eventually decided that a secure future for South Africa could only, for a start, be accomplished within the British Empire. "Behind the Commonwealth and international statesman," wrote Hancock, "there remained the man conditioned by his experience. During the Boer War Smuts knew enough to know that there was an England other than the country of Rhodes, Chamberlain and the nineteenth century."[83]

Botha always had a soothing influence on the restless Smuts. When Botha assured Smuts on his return from Europe that the self-government, which Kitchener had all but promised the ex-republics, must inevitably come, he once again started dreaming about the future.[84] Botha, De Wet and De la Rey had just returned from Europe where they had launched a campaign to collect money for reconstruction purposes in the Transvaal and the Orange River Colony. They also had the opportunity to speak to leading British politicians. Once again all the possible schemes for the future started taking shape in Smuts' head. With these evolving schemes he would be able, so he assumed, to expedite the installing of self-government and thus bring about the downfall of Milner.

Self-government alone, however, was not Smuts' ultimate goal. He was already looking beyond self-government—at heart he was still the disciple of Cecil John Rhodes. In Vereeniging, Smuts said to the Reverend Kestell, chaplain to Steyn and De Wet: "The idea of the *imperium* grips me. It is something wonderful."[85] He was envisaging a united South Africa stretching from Cape Agulhas to the Limpopo and beyond—a nation in its own right, but still within the Empire. Smuts stated in his public appearances that the war of freedom "had been fought for 'the entire people of South Africa'". He elaborated on this:

> *I was fighting for a United South Africa in which there would be the greatest possible freedom, but from which the disturbing influence of Downing Street would have been finally eliminated. I was not fighting for 'Dutch' supremacy or predominance over English Afrikaners.... Let us try so to arrange our politics, our administration and our legislation that a compact South African nationality may be built up with the best elements of both parts of the colonial population, so that when eventually we become politically independent (as we necessarily must in course of time and who knows how soon) we shall no longer be at our old battle of the Kilkenny cats but shall be united within and present a united front to the outside world. Then this war which we have gone through will remain for all South Africa as a memory and heritage of glory and not as a nightmare.*[86]

Once Smuts had decided on his strategy to neutralise Milner and his *kindergarten* he attacked his opponents whenever he got the chance. In this *modus operandi* Botha and the other Boer leaders solidly backed him. Milner reacted to this by inviting Smuts, Botha, and De La Rey to serve on the legislative council of the Transvaal. Not surprisingly they declined.[87] "As usual," wrote Hancock, "it was Smuts who drafted the consequential documents for signature by his two friends and himself. The first was a most skilful letter to Lord Milner, arguing that the country's immediate need was not a nominated legislature but a rest from politics and a clear recognition of the government's unfettered responsibility...."[88] A Rand capitalist newspaper launched a vicious attack on Smuts: "Who is Mr Smuts? He is one of the five men chiefly responsible for the war; a man of intensely bitter feelings; a type of Afrikaner who ... used every effort to keep the races apart."[89] But Mansergh contradicts this accusation: "Anglo–Afrikaner cooperation remained ... his first priority."[90] Smuts ignored, as usual, these personal attacks without any visible emotion. Mrs Isie Smuts once wrote of her husband in this regard: "But the 'Ou Baas' didn't care much. He never cares what people do to him."[91] Smuts continued, with enthusiasm, on the road which he had decided upon. At one stage, people referred to the two prominent faces of Smuts as: Mr J. Smuts, known to Milner's young men as "the other Mr Smuts", and the vicious ex-state attorney, the "altogether inadmissible" Mr J.C. Smuts.[92]

The decline of the gold output was a serious blow to Milner's reconstruction initiatives. He relied on the gold-mining industry for his reconstruction of the former Boer republics in the post-war era. He had no choice but to import very cheap Chinese labour. This was gross miscalculation! It resulted in serious problems for Milner.[93] He was attacked from two different sources—the Liberals in England shouted vigorously against the "Chinese Slavery" while Afrikanerdom protested against "the wilful importation ... of another colour problem".[94]

Smuts became the ardent champion in the attack on the governor of the Transvaal. Milner, his *kindergarten* and his whole administration came under severe fire.[95] On the public platform, in private conversation, in letters and in the press, Smuts subjected Milner to extreme pillory. "He accused the governor," wrote Crafford, "of seeking to benefit his friends with an administration which was a 'carnival of extravagance' in a 'country, which seems to be verging on public bankruptcy', and charged him with plotting to extirpate the very soul of the Afrikaner race."[96] The Repatriation Department was written off as "a complete failure"; the credibility of Milner's despatches were questioned; the denationalisation policy was vicariously denounced; the Chinese labour question was once again intensively scrutinised and denounced without any reservation; and finally, the alleged alliance between the mine magnates and the governor was "fiercely taken to task".[97] Smuts called the mines "a sham industry ... a bogus industry, with its reputation kept going for the purpose of still further swindling the investing public of Europe." He made the allegation that "the Transvaal government is almost completely dictated to by the magnates. The whole policy of the government is inspired by fear and distrust."[98] And Smuts wrote further: "We are convinced of the utter selfishness of these magnates, as well as of their stupidity and want of foresight in all matters of politics."[99]

In spite of the fact that much of Smuts' criticism was based on "incontrovertible facts" and a great deal of it being "wanton misrepresentation", it had in the long run the desired effect. It brought Milner and his *kindergarten* in disrepute locally as well as in Britain. Signs of physical and mental strain and fatigue were, at this stage, evident in Milner.[100] His disrepute, especially amongst Afrikaners, also stimulated the awakening of a "Spirit of South African Nationalism". This nationalism resulted in an increasing demand for self-government. Milner's tenure as British high commissioner in South Africa and governor general for the Transvaal and the Orange River Colony came to an end in April 1905. The changing political conditions in Great Britain convinced Milner and the Colonial Office that his retention would only render less likely the achievement of the goals for which he had been striving.[101]

Smuts now looked upon Milner as a defeated man. He wrote an extraordinary and most peculiar farewell letter to the departing high commissioner and governor general. "In victory," wrote Hancock, "he (Smuts) had an unusual way with his enemies." Smuts wrote to Milner:

Will you allow me to wish you 'Bon Voyage' now that you are leaving South Africa for ever? I am afraid you have not liked us; but I cherish the hope that, as our memories grow mellower and the noble features of our respective ideals become clearer, we shall more and more appreciate the contribution of each to the formation of that happier South Africa which is surely coming, and judge more kindly of each other. At any rate it is a consolation to think what is noble in our work will grow to larger issues than we foresaw, and that even our mistakes will be covered up ultimately, not only in a merciful oblivion, but also in that unconscious forgiveness which seems to me to be an inherent feature of all historical life. History writes the word 'Reconciliation' over all quarrels....[102]

To Milner this must have been the most astonishing letter he had ever received. He must have had much to think about on leaving South Africa's shores. Did he achieve anything worthwhile during his period of high office in South Africa?

Milner and Smuts were to meet again face-to-face many years later in London. But this time it would be in altogether different circumstances. Both men would become members of Lloyd George's Imperial War Cabinet and later of the British War Cabinet during the First World War. Botha, realising that Smuts was the man for the job, suggested that Smuts represent South Africa in the Imperial War Cabinet. Smuts arrived in England on 12 March 1917. Shortly after his arrival he received an invitation from Milner to "a meeting of five or six men, mostly or all known to you, who are interested in the business of the Cabinet meeting which you have come over to attend."[103] Actually, Milner and his newly-formed *Round Table* reformers were trying to interest Smuts in their plans for constitutional reform in the Empire. They believed that the British Empire had no choice between federation and disintegration.[104] They realised that Smuts was "the principal architect of the South African Constitution and it was important for the *kindergarten* to build bridges to him."[105] But Smuts was not interested at all in meeting Milner and his *kindergarten*. Lloyd George invited him to address a joint meeting of both Houses of Parliament on the evening of 15 May at a banquet given in his honour.[106] Smuts began his speech by discussing the War. He continued by analysing the British Empire as an institution. He most effectively compared the advantages of a Commonwealth of Nations to that of a Federal State. He took a strong stance against Milner and his associates who wanted to transform the British Empire into a Federal State. Smuts received a letter the next day from L.S. Amery, secretary of state for the colonies: "I thought your speech tonight magnificent. So much of it was on lines akin to those on which my own mind has travelled ... "[107]

Smuts had always been a Commonwealth man. Once again he outwitted Milner who was the driving force for a federation. But, when they were colleagues in the British War Cabinet, the long tension between Milner and Smuts dramatically changed. Smuts struck a quick friendship with his former arch-enemy. Their joint contributions to the work of the War Cabinet proved to be of immense value.

1. Kenneth Ingham, *Jan Christian Smuts. The Conscience of a South African*, 18 – 19. Cecil Headlam, *The Milner Papers. South Africa, 1897 – 1899*. Volume I, 28.
2. Walter Nimocks, *Milner's Young Men. The "kindergarten" in Edwardian Imperial Affairs*, 8.
3. F.S. Crafford, *Jan Smuts. A Biography*, 34. Headlam, 7 – 11.
4. S.B. Spies, *et al, Jan Smuts. Memoirs of the Boer War*, 194.
5. Nimocks, 10. John Marlowe, *Apostle of Empire*, 16. Headlam, 24 – 27.
6. Spies, 194. Ingham, 19. Nimocks, 10. Headlam, 28.
7. Nimocks, 17.
8. Crafford, 35. D.W. Kruger, *Paul Kruger,* Volume II, 218 – 219.
9. Spies, 194.
10. Sarah Gertrude Millin, *General Smuts*, Volume II, 67. See Kruger, 153 – 4 for diplomatic ties between the Transvaal and Germany.
11. Nimocks, 11.
12. W.K. Hancock, *Smuts,* 1. *The Sanguine Years, 1870 – 1919*, 73. Kruger, 219.
13. Ingham, 19.
14. Millin, 89 – 90. Ingham, 19.
15. Ingham, 19.
16. Hancock, 1, 74.
17. Thomas Pakenham, *The Boer War,* 62. Crafford, 35.
18. Pakenham, 62.
19. Crafford, 35.
20. Pakenham, 61. Kruger, 229 – 233. Headlam, 409.
21. Spies, 24.
22. Crafford, 36. Kruger, 236.
23. *Ibid.*
24. *Ibid.* Kruger, 233 – 234.
25. Pakenham, 63.
26. Crafford, 36.
27. Millin, 1, 101.
28. Crafford, 37.
29. Millin, 1, 101 – 102. Spies, 24.
30. Marlowe, 85. Smuts Papers, Volume I, 14 September 1899, 283 – 293.

31. Pakenham, 63.
32. *Ibid.*, 102.
33. Spies, 24.
34. *Ibid.*, 24 – 25.
35. Crafford, 38.
36. Pakenham, 107. Spies, 24. Headlam, 525.
37. Headlam, 525.
38. Crafford, 38.
39. Smuts Papers, Volume I, 4 September, 1899, 329. Pakenham, 100.
40. Crafford, 44. Pakenham, 107. Headlam, 559 – 560.
41. Pakenham, 561. F.V. Engelenburg, *General Louis Botha,* 71.
42. Pakenham, 561.
43. *Ibid.*
44. *Ibid.*, 562.
45. *Ibid.*
46. Hancock, 1, 150 – 163.
47. Pakenham, 562. Ingham, 41 – 44.
48. Spies, 26.
49. Pakenham, 562.
50. Hancock, 1, 160.
51. Pakenham, 563.
52. Pakenham, 563 – 564. Hancock, 1, 152.
53. Pakenham, 564.
54. *Ibid.* See also 565.
55. *Ibid.*, 566.
56. *Ibid.*
57. *Ibid.*, 568.
58. *Ibid.*, 569.
59. Hancock, 1, 142.
60. Pakenham, 568.
61. Engelenburg, 91. Hancock, 1, 152.
62. Pakenham, 567. Hancock, 1, 152.
63. Smuts Papers, Volume II. 1 Junie 1902, 4. Hancock, 1, 164.
64. Spies, 30. Hancock, 1, 159.
65. Hancock, 1, 152.
66. Pakenham, 570.

67. *Ibid.* Hancock, 1, 171 – 4. Ingham, 45. Marlowe, 132 – 133.
68. Marlowe, 132.
69. Nimocks, 30.
70. Hancock, 1, 246.
71. Marlowe, 134.
72. Hancock, 1, 171.
73. Crafford, 64. Marlowe, 133.
74. Marlowe, 133.
75. Crafford, 65.
76. Millin, 1, 191.
77. *Ibid.,* 193 – 5. Hancock, 1, 179.
78. Millin, 1, 195. Crafford, 64.
79. *Ibid.,* 195 –196.
80. Hancock, 1, 179.
81. Crafford, 65.
82. Nicholas Mansergh, *The Commonwealth Experience,* 377.
83. *Ibid.,* 373.
84. Marlowe, 122. Crafford, 65.
85. Crafford, 61.
86. Hancock, 1, 199.
87. Ingham, 47.
88. Hancock, 1, 193.
89. Crafford, 66.
90. Mansergh, 375.
91. Millin, 1, 192.
92. Hancock, 1, 179.
93. Marlowe, 160 – 75. Hancock, 1, 173, 178, 195.
94. Crafford, 66. Millin, 1, 202.
95. Hancock, 1, 179.
96. Crafford, 66.
97. *Ibid.,* 66 – 67.
98. *Ibid.,* 67.
99. *Ibid.*
100. Nimocks, 54.
101. *Ibid.*
102. Headlam, Volume II, 541, 542.
103. Smuts Papers, Volume III, 12 March 1917, 461.
104. Hancock, 1, 427.
105. Marlowe, 208.

106. Smuts Papers, Volume III, 15 May 1917, 506 – 517. Ingham, 93.
107. Smuts Papers, Volume III, 15 May 1917, 517.

A cartoon of Sir Henry Campbell-Bannerman. The German Kaiser, William II, is in the background. (Central Archives Repository)

3

Henry Campbell-Bannerman

"But what a wise man, what statesmanship in insight
and faith, and what sure grip on the future."
J.C. Smuts (Hancock, *Smuts*, 1, 215)

"I have made up my mind that we must ... make
partners of the Boers."
Henry Campbell-Bannerman (Sarah Gertrude Millin,
General Smuts, 1, 213-214)

Lord Alfred Milner's tenure as high commissioner for
South Africa and governor general of the Transvaal and
the Orange River Colony ended in April 1905. Milner,
who was never in good health, suffered severely under the
physical and mental strain imposed on him by the heavy
responsibilities of his post. This was later partly responsible for
his departure and return to England.[1] On the other hand, it
became clear that the Unionist government in Great Britain
would most definitely be ousted by the Liberals in the upcoming
general election. "Mounting resentment," wrote Walter
Nimocks, "over internal affairs and the anti-imperialist
sentiment which had been growing since the Boer War seemed

to presage a Liberal victory in the next general election."[2]
Should the Unionists lose at the polls there would undoubtedly
be no place for Milner in the new governmental structure. He
therefore decided that his replacement should be chosen well in
advance of the election.

Convinced that it was necessary he retire, Milner
immediately brought the matter to the attention of Alfred
Lyttelton. Lyttelton succeeded Joseph Chamberlain in the
Colonial Office. Due to the conflicting qualifications that the
job demanded, it was surely not an easy task at all to select a
suitable successor for Milner. Milner became impatient when,
after several weeks, a successor was still not named. In January
1905 he cabled Lyttelton and asked if he might "begin quietly to

Lord Selborne. (Cape Archives Repository)

make preparation for leaving in the second or third week in March? Unless there is some grave reason to the contrary, I am most anxious not to defer my departure".[3] It was announced in London in late February that the Earl of Selborne was to succeed Milner in due course. The latter received this welcome news with great satisfaction and relief. Lord Selborne, who had served as Chamberlain's under-secretary from 1895 to 1900, before becoming first lord of the Admiralty, was "an exponent of vigorous imperialism". Geoffrey Robinson of *The Star* wrote to his father in England: "Lord M. quite overjoyed. He had long given up all hope of getting anyone so good."[4]

Article 7 of the Peace Treaty of Vereeniging, which concluded the Anglo-Boer War, had promised the Boers representative institutions leading up to self-government "as soon as circumstances allowed".[5] Four years had passed since that time. The Transvaal and the Orange River Colony had been well governed as Crown Colonies by Milner and his *kindergarten*. But in the Milner administration there was no place for self-government.[6] In March 1905 the Unionist government in Britain put forward, for the Transvaal, what came to be known as the Lyttelton Constitution.[7] Smuts was not enthusiastic about it at all. He told Emily Hobhouse exactly what he thought of the Lyttelton Constitution. "We are viewing with the gravest concern the grant of 'representation' to us," he wrote. "I have drafted a strong memorandum to Lord Milner which is now being circulated for approval among our leaders. So long as we are distrusted we don't want anything, and if we are not distrusted why retard self-government? God save us from our present friends and rulers—and He will."[8] At this stage, nothing had been proposed for the Orange River Colony.

On the fall of the Unionist government in Britain, the *Het Volk* Party sent the former attorney general of President Paul Kruger to London. He was the 35-year-old J.C. Smuts, whom they regarded in the Transvaal as "their most intelligent young man". Lord Selborne telegraphed on 28 December to London, warning the British government that Smuts " ... is a clever, well-educated man, agreeable to meet, and personally I much like him; but please remember that he is an absolutely unreconciled (sic) Afrikander Republican".[9] This was Smuts' first entry as a politician onto the international stage of politics. In December 1905, on the eve of his mission to the new British prime minister, Henry Campbell-Bannerman, he led ex-president M.T. Steyn to believe that he was going to England for the benefit of his health.[10] It might have been better, for good personal relations, if he had avoided "that small equivocation". But, on the other hand, Smuts might have felt that it would be better, for political reasons, to put a private colour to his visit. "Certainly," wrote Hancock, "that was not a time for slow committee work, cumbersome deputations and newspaper publicity."[11]

Smuts took with him to London a "very able and persuasive memorandum" on the Transvaal Constitution. Le May called it a memorandum "which read like an anthology of Liberal principles."[12] The memorandum was certainly meant to "strike a responsive chord" in a man like Campbell- Bannerman. It was most certainly Campbell-Bannerman's very own language which paved the way for granting self- government to the two former Boer republics: "I can conceive no nobler task for Liberal statesmanship," said Campbell- Bannerman, "than that it may inaugurate in South Africa such an era of trust and goodwill and reliance on the people of the land, and bring healing to the wounds which the errors of the past have inflicted."[13] It made less impact on colonial officials—one of whom minuted on it: "Mr Smuts is a Boer and a lawyer. His Memorandum ... exhibits all the cunning of his race and calling."[14] The memorandum was entitled *Memo of Points in reference to the Transvaal Constitution.*[15] It was distributed among members of the new government in London. "It was," wrote Hancock, "persuasive, forceful and short." In language closely attuned to the mood of British liberalism Smuts went straight to the point:

> *What South Africa needs above all things after the storms and upheavals of the past is tranquillity. But that can only be secured by the removal of all just grounds of discontent and the unreserved application of Liberal principles to the government of the new Colonies, by showing a statesmanlike trust in the people of the land, of whatever*

race, and granting them a fair and equitable Constitution under which they can work out their own salvation.

There may be some danger in trusting the people too soon, but there may be much greater danger in trusting them too late.[16]

On receiving a letter and several enclosures in respect of the above, Winston Churchill wrote to Smuts from the Colonial Office acknowledging receipt with gratitude:

I have no doubt that by this time you will have had some opportunity of laying your views before the Commission and I feel convinced that you have expressed yourself to them with your usual force and fluency.

I am not without hopes that the darkest days of South African history may have drawn to their close. The power of the Government has greatly strengthened as the Session has advanced, and our great majority is proving a much more stable foundation than many people had at first supposed.

If there should be any matter on which you wish to write to me, I shall always be very glad indeed to hear from you, though it will not always be possible for me to reply with unfettered freedom while I continue to occupy my present post.[17]

In his memorandum Smuts argued that the issue at stake was not one between the Dutch and the English, but between "the mine-owners and the permanent population of the land; English as well as Dutch". He strongly made the point that the time for self-government had come. It was, to Smuts, of the utmost importance that self-government be established on a fresh basis, and not on any adaptation of the Lyttelton Constitution.[18]

In London the devising of a political settlement in South Africa was the first major task that faced the new Liberal government of Campbell-Bannerman. The decisions Campbell-Bannerman and his colleagues took in the Cabinet, in the early months of their term of office, were of great political and historical significance. The evidence about how these decisions were reached, and especially the role Campbell-Bannerman personally played in them, is still, unfortunately, largely unknown and conflicting. Amongst many in parliamentary circles there was never any doubt about Campbell-Bannerman's own views on this matter. His was a lone voice when he said at Glasgow in June 1900: "Let us restore as early as possible and let us maintain those rights of self-government which give ... contentment and loyalty to every colony which enjoys them."[19] He never wavered in his belief that the only viable policy for South Africa was self-government and trust. He wanted, incidentally, the same policy for Ireland. He consequently made this point in speech after speech. Alfred Milner regarded this line of thought as totally insane. In his diary on 11 January 1906, he described the outlook "as very black owing to the ignorance and evil dispositions of this wretched *pro-Boer* Cabinet."[20] This was a policy that the Liberal Imperialists had throughout been doubtful and hesitant about. They believed in "continuity of policy" in South Africa. Viscount Haldane, in particular, urged the importance of that view. Massingham returned from a visit to South Africa. Campbell-Bannerman invited him to breakfast. Massingham later wrote of this meeting: "Long before I had finished my account of their (Boers) perfect ability ... to work self-government I divined that there was no call to persuade C.B. of/or to anything."[21]

The Liberal government now had to decide whether to implement or to amend the Lyttelton Constitution. There was also the option to scrap it and make an immediate grant of self-government. The Colonial Office was strongly in favour of preserving continuity of policy. This meant that if they built on Conservative foundations, to some extent, it would ultimately result in a continuation of Milner's work. Would this be advisable in the changing political circumstances? In 1904 the Boers' stance on this was revealed when Emily Hobhouse sent a private letter from Smuts (as discussed in the previous chapter), without consulting him, to *The Times*, in which Smuts took a strong stance against the British.[22] It was, for a long time, abundantly clear that Campbell-Bannerman wanted "a clean break with policy". This produced the same feelings in the Boer leaders as Smuts had portrayed in his letter.

To deal in depth with this thorny problem, the government set up a Cabinet committee. The committee had to deal with the problem and table suggestions for consideration. Lord Loreburn, the lord chancellor, was the chairman. The other members were Ripon, Elgin, Asquith and Bryce. Not much progress could be made during January, due to the preoccupation of ministers in the general election campaign. In spite of their hectic program, the committee circulated a draft for amending the Lyttelton Constitution. It was to be expected that a number of influential people would give their opinion on the issue of granting self-government to the Transvaal. They were all in favour of continuity. Milner's successor as high commissioner, Lord Selborne, "was of opinion that the grant of self-government would be a 'leap in the dark', and that the generation of Boers who had fought in the war were irreconcilable."[23] In November the governor of the Orange River Colony declared that immediate responsible government "would be a dire calamity to the people of the Colony". Colonial officials shared Selborne's doubts. Secretary Graham minuted: " ... for all the smooth words of General Botha and others we must lay our accounts with any Boer ministry containing a strong element of irreconcilables,"—among whom he numbered Beyers and Smuts.[24] The new British government was strongly in favour of a transitional government.

Lord Grey, surprisingly, was one of those who favoured a bolder course. He thought it best to have immediate self-government. The new under-secretary at the Colonial Office, Winston Churchill, had a more eloquent voice. It is significant to note that Churchill began his career in the House of Commons by criticising Campbell-Bannerman "for urging an early move to responsible government". But now he was at one with the prime minister of the day, believing that "the bold, generous course" was the correct one. Churchill wrote a memorandum on 2 January regarding this whole issue. He argued that the Transvaal should be given "forthwith a representative Assembly with an Executive responsible to it." He was of the opinion that unless this was done at the present appropriate time the whole issue could "be jerked and twisted from our hands ... without grace of any kind ... not perhaps without humiliation."[25] Although not a member of the Cabinet, Churchill was nevertheless allowed to take part in the work of the Cabinet committee. It was Churchill who would defend the government's policy in the House of Commons. On Elgin's request Churchill summarised, on 4 February, the conclusions of the committee for the Cabinet. These were *inter alia* "that the Lyttelton Constitution must be regarded as unworkable, that full responsible government should be granted and that elections should not be delayed".[26] It was emphasised that for all practical purposes an early decision was necessary.

Smuts arrived in London during the general election. He stayed the weekend with his Quaker friends, the Clarks, in Somerset. They were supporters of the Liberal Party. After the weekend Smuts left for London in order to persuade the new government to follow the course put forward in his memorandum. To another friend, Margaret Gillett, Smuts wrote on 1 February:

> *Most of the Ministers I have seen. Kindest of all were C.B. and John Morley ... I feel certain that the Government mean well, but whether we shall get justice is another matter. If God wills ... that we shall continue the victims of that Jewish-Jingo gang, and that our fate is to be a martyr people, so be it ...*[27]

Years later Smuts said that Churchill was the first man he saw regarding the issue of self-government for the Transvaal and Orange River Colony. Churchill undoubtedly played a political game with Smuts. What he exactly wanted to achieve with this, is not quite clear. After Smuts had stated his case, Churchill responded by saying that he had never heard anything so "preposterous".[28] He said to Smuts that England had conquered the Boer republics only three years earlier, and that it was unbelievable that he could come to London to ask for the former Boer republics back. "He declared," said Smuts, "that he would never stand for breaking up the British Empire.... I saw all the other ministers, too. I made no headway. Morley was sympathetic. He said he agreed with most of what I had said, but that British public opinion would never stand for it."[29] After the meeting between Smuts and Churchill the latter wrote to Smuts promising that he would read his memorandum with "attention and that he looked forward to a settlement 'fair to both parties in South Africa'".[30]

Smuts saw Campbell-Bannerman again on 7 February. He believed ever after that the conversation the two of them had had on that day had been decisive. During his lifetime Smuts gave many versions of the meeting. He truly overestimated the role he, himself, played in the discussions with Campbell-Bannerman.[31] In 1948 he wrote an article for the boys of Campbell-Bannerman's old school:

The man who wrought the miracle was Sir Henry Campbell-Bannerman, to all appearances an ordinary man, almost commonplace to the superficial view, but a real man, shrewd and wordly-wise, but rooted in a great faith which inspired a great action. I discussed my mission with many members of the Cabinet—perhaps the most brilliant Government Britain had had for a long time—and with men among them like Asquith, Edward Grey, Lloyd George, John Morley, and, last but not least, Winston Churchill. Campbell-Bannerman looked the least distinguished in that galaxy of talent. But what a wise man, what statesmanship in insight and faith, and what sure grip on the future! My mission failed with the rest, as it was humanly speaking bound to fail. What an audacious, what an unprecedented request mine was—practically for the restoration of the country to the Boers five years after they had been beaten to the ground in one of the hardest and most lengthy struggles in British warfare. But with Campbell-Bannerman my mission did not fail. I put a simple case before him that night in 10 Downing Street. It was in substance: Do you want friends or enemies? You can have the Boers for friends, and they have proved what quality their friendship may mean. I pledge the friendship of my colleagues and myself if you wish it. You can choose to make them enemies, and possibly have another Ireland on your hands. If you do believe in liberty, it is also their faith and their religion. I used no set arguments, but simply spoke to him as man to man, and appealed only to the human aspect, which I felt would weigh deeply with him. He was a cautious Scot, and said nothing to me, but yet I left that room that night a happy man. My intuition told me that the thing had been done.[32]

Smuts referred to his meeting with Campbell-Bannerman as "the creative encounter of his political life".[33] Hancock wrote of the meeting between Smuts and Campbell-Bannerman:

The older he (Smuts) grew, the more vivid grew his vision of it.... In his memory, Botha and Campbell-Bannerman became linked together with the greatest of political virtues, magnanimity.... In moments of doubt and depression he found reassurance in the portrait of Campbell-Bannerman, which hung on the wall behind his desk in the study at Doornkloof. Magnanimity had been achieved once, at any rate, in the dealings of man with man and nation with nation.[34]

Unfortunately there appears to be no account of Campbell-Bannerman's impressions of this meeting. It is, however, clear that his mind was already made up before he met Smuts that evening. So, to a certain extent, Smuts 'was preaching to the converted'. Wilson wrote: "C.B. always believed that the way to make your enemies friends was the way of forgiveness and trust."[35] Smuts went away that night with the impression that one talk convinced Campbell-Bannerman. This is certainly not justifiable. In this respect Wilson wrote:

Certainly C.B. impressed Smuts as a man who was unshakeable in his determination. Smuts referred to him at the time as 'the rock'. And it was true that it was he who had stood up for the principles of self-government and reconciliation all through the Boer War. In his person he represented, more than any one else, the faith and conviction that carried through the South African settlement.[36]

Perhaps the summary of this meeting by Professor Le May is the most acceptable assessment: "It is probable that the meeting of the two men had its largest consequence in its influence not upon Campbell-Bannerman, but upon Smuts ... his meeting with Campbell-Bannerman may have altered his opinion of British statesmen."[37] Le May argued that the meeting resulted in Smuts seeing "the England of John Bright, which he had learnt to revere, rather than the England of Joseph Chamberlain, whose dust he had cast off from his feet."[38]

The Cabinet met on 8 February. It is not clear what exactly happened at this very important and decisive meeting. Reports of the meeting are conflicting. Even Campbell-Bannerman's letter to the King throws no light on this very intriguing matter. The prime minister wrote to the King:

The desire of the Cabinet was to introduce responsible government into that Colony at the earliest possible time. Examination and discussion however disclosed the fact that much information is lacking ... and the Cabinet concluded that it would be necessary, by a Commission or otherwise, to ascertain these data before framing a plan of government.... The precise reference to the Commission could not well be settled today, and was deferred to an early Cabinet.[39]

The King was certainly not any wiser.

Campbell-Bannerman took the lead in the discussion in the Cabinet and directed it along the lines of his own thoughts. Lloyd George described the Cabinet meeting the next day to Smuts "as the most wonderful experience".

Sarah Gertrude Millin records Lloyd George's report in her discussion of Smuts' meeting with Campbell-Bannerman:

I have made up my mind that we must scrap the Lyttelton Constitution and start afresh and make partners of the Boers.

He spoke of the Boers' fight for freedom, and of how, for three years, the matter of the Chinese apart, they had given their conquerors a clear field. Such people, said Campbell-Bannerman, should be England's partners. He was full of emotion and he moved others too. They decided in a few minutes to give the Boers responsible government.[40]

The atmosphere in the Cabinet was initially unclear, but soon it became known that there was a difference of opinion. Elgin wrote to his wife: "Rather a disappointing Cabinet ... but one cannot always have one's own way." Days later he wrote to Ripon: "The result of Thursday's Cabinet was unexpected, and as it stands there is no very clear decision ... the prime minister rather took it out of my hands." What was ultimately decided was clearly not what Elgin was hoping for or what he had had in mind.

Lord Riddell gave a more detailed account when he recorded a conversation with Lloyd George in April 1913:

The South African constitution was the biggest thing established in our day. Who was responsible? Campbell-Bannerman or Asquith? Oh, C.B.! He deserves all the credit. It was all done in a ten minute speech at the Cabinet ... the most dramatic, the most important ten minutes' speech ever delivered in our time. In ten minutes he brushed aside all the checks and safeguards devised by Asquith, Winston and Loreburn. At the outset only two of us were with him, John Burns and myself. But his speech convinced the whole Cabinet. It was the utterance of a plain, kindly, simple man. The speech moved one at least of the Cabinet to tears. It was the most impressive thing I ever saw.[41]

Nevertheless, the controversy continued. The *Manchester Guardian* argued in a leading article that the settlement was due to Campbell-Bannerman alone and "that without him it could not have been done". In June 1912 Asquith wrote to J.A. Spender from 10 Downing Street: "(It) is ridiculous fiction. Between ourselves, he had little or nothing to do with the matter and never bothered his head about it.... There was never the faintest difference of opinion about it in the

Cabinet...."[42] But Lord Carrington, on the other hand, wrote to Campbell-Bannerman in a completely different tone:

You must allow me to congratulate you on having so magnificently saved the S. African situation today. The Party would have been in arms if we had capitulated to Lyttelton and the mine owners ... and you pulled us through entirely, and all alone.
Burns and I are very proud of our chief.[43]

On 13 February the Cabinet decided to send a committee of three to the Transvaal with the commission to investigate in depth the situation there and to prepare a scheme of responsible government. At this stage the King voiced his concern. "After all the blood and treasure we have expended," he wrote to the Prince of Wales on 2 March, "it would [be] terrible indeed if the country were handed over to the Boer."[44]

On 31 July Winston Churchill opened the debate in the House of Commons and announced the government's proposals. Within weeks of the announcement of the government's decision the atmosphere in South Africa changed considerably. The grant of self-government to the Transvaal, and directly thereafter to the Orange River Colony, cleared the way for the Union of South Africa in 1910.

As some of the detractors alleged, the Liberal government was definitely not seeking to "give the republics back to the Boers". Milner called it "the great betrayal". Liberal policy intended a continuance of imperial predominance in a new form. Churchill emphasised this in the debate in the House of Commons:

There is a profound difference ... between the schools of thought which exist upon South African politics in this House. We think that British authority in South Africa has got to stand on two legs. Hon. Gentleman opposite have laboured for ten years to make it stand on one. We on this side know that if British dominion is to endure in South Africa, it must endure with the assent of the Dutch. We think that the position of agents and ministers of the

> *Crown in South Africa should be just as much above and*
> *remote from racial feuds as the position is above our party*
> *politics.*[45]

It was now six years after Vereeniging and the two former Boer republics, granted self-government by the Campbell-Bannerman government, were to go to the polls to elect a government of their own choice. In the Transvaal the general election took place on 20 February 1907. Despite all their efforts, the Progressive Party and Milner's *kindergarten* suffered a resounding defeat. The results were: *Het Volk*—37; *National Party*—6; *Labour Party*—21; *Independent*—2.[46]

Smuts was jubilant—"We are in forever".[47] Louis Botha, the leader of *Het Volk*, had fought the election in alliance with the Nationalists. Richard Solomon, the leader of the Progressive Party, saw the premiership, which was initially promised to him, slip through his fingers. Lord Selborne had turned to General Botha and requested that he form a government. Botha invited four of *Het Volk* to his Cabinet. The other two members of the Cabinet came from the Nationalists—Botha "scrupulously honouring the pact!"[48] The *kindergarten* expected defeat, but still they experienced the defeat with extreme pain.[49] With the defeat came changes directly affecting the lives of Milner's young men. "Those who before the election held positions in the Crown Colony government," wrote Nimocks, "quickly resigned to make way for appointees of the new administration."[50]

It was widely expected that Smuts would become the first prime minister of the Transvaal. He had an excellent track record for public duty; he had served as a member of President Kruger's government; he had played a major and, to a certain extent, decisive role in acquiring self-rule for the Transvaal and the Orange River Colony; intellectually he was far superior to all his colleagues. Nevertheless, without the slightest doubt, he supported Botha for the premiership. Later he wrote to John X. Merriman: "I might have been premier, but considered that it would be a mistake to take precedence over Botha, who is really one of the finest men South Africa has ever produced. If he has culture as he has chivalry and common sense, there would not be his equal in South Africa. The varsity boys in the team will help him most loyally, and I hope that events will justify the arrangement of the Cabinet."[51] It was one of Smuts' wisest acts, throughout his long and eventful political career, to stand down in favour of Botha. Thus Botha became prime minister with Smuts as his colonial secretary and minister of education.[52]

The new regime in the Transvaal took over the Milner administration with great and impatient enthusiasm. "Eagerly, indeed, almost too eagerly," wrote Crafford, "the new regime took over the Milner administration and rapidly brought about changes in it. Smuts was the brain of the ministry."[53] Smuts was widely referred to as the "Power behind the throne".[54] Referring to the role Smuts played in this respect, Crafford wrote: "A cartoon by A.W. Lloyd, in an English paper, depicting a meeting of Botha's Cabinet gave to each of the ministers the face of Smuts. Underneath was this explanation of the picture: 'The controlling interest of General Smuts in the Cabinet is so apparent that the government may be said to be concentrated in him alone'."[55]

Smuts worked feverishly behind the scenes. Whenever it was possible he painstakingly tried to avoid the limelight. He was always pushing Botha into the foreground. In the House it was Smuts who acted as the mouthpiece of the government. He announced the government's policy on all-important questions; he submitted the various schemes for the approval of the members. He took all these schemes through all the different stages of legislation, reacting to all the questions. This *modus operandi* applied not only to his department but to departments of colleagues in the Cabinet as well. Very soon all those concerned realised that Smuts had an "invariably evincing encyclopaedic knowledge of all the affairs of the government".[56] He worked tremendously hard. As had been in the days of Kruger, Smuts worked much more than was really necessary. He was incapable of entrusting tasks to his subordinates in government administration. It was common knowledge that Smuts had absolute confidence only in his own powers. He was competent to take over, at the shortest notice, the department of a colleague who, through ill health or otherwise, might be absent on leave. "With the great prospect of a united South

Jan Smuts and his first motor car. (Central Archives Repository)

Africa," wrote Crafford, "always impinging on his thoughts, Smuts made tremendous efforts, particularly in the beginning, by effecting compromises and with every other means at his disposal, to smooth out those differences between the races which had been responsible for so much strife and misery."[57]

During the months to pass Smuts became restless and impatient. Constitutionally he wanted to move on. He became increasingly dictatorial in his manner. Gradually he became intolerant of all opposition. He had tasted the delight of having his own way and found it good. Those near to him gradually realised that he was a dictator at heart. His "masterful side" brought him into bitter conflict with Hertzog and Afrikanerdom, capitalists, organised labour and eventually with Mahatma Gandhi. Ghandi saw himself as the champion of Indian human rights and dignity in South Africa.

The greatest differences between Smuts and Botha lay in their transactions with other people. Botha, they said, regarded the world with the eye of a cattle farmer, while Smuts' outlook was

Jan Smuts, 1913. (Central Archives Repository)

described as that of a physicist. "Where Botha could charm," writes Le May, "Smuts could overawe."[58] Smuts sadly lacked in "the great gift of human sympathy and understanding." Botha was generously endowed with the gift that Smuts completely lacked.[59] Smuts placed Botha and Campbell-Bannerman, as far as personality and approach to political issues were concerned, in the same category. He regarded both as his mentors. In contrast to Botha, Smuts, in spite of his "sparkling intellect, energy, and general ability", could never successfully establish and maintain the confidence of people. He even frequently antagonised members of his own party. Botha, in complete contrast to Smuts, had the aptitude to manage all people in various situations with extreme and natural ease. People turned instinctively to Botha to discuss a problem or to ask for advice. True to his nature with people, Smuts alienated those who turned to Botha. Often Botha had to rescue Smuts and "with quiet, soothing words" calm furious men in whom Smuts aroused intense hostility. Smuts was well known, more than often, to act too hastily in coming to conclusions on matters of state.[60] He preferred making decisions without discussion or consultation. Botha would inquire into a matter at length with calm endurance. He would consider arguments, put forward by advisers and others, at considerable length before making a final decision. "Botha often perceived instinctively with an intuition transcending reason," wrote Crafford, "what his colleagues could achieve only by cold, logical reasoning."[61]

Smuts' ultimate goal of a united South Africa mainly inspired his discussions with Campbell-Bannerman and his colleagues in London. Smuts was now firmly entrenched in his new position. At last he had influence and power and he would use everything possible towards achieving his heart's desire. "Britain should trust the South African whites," Smuts wrote, "and if she did so they [she] would recognise the gravity of their [her] responsibilities."[62] It was at this stage that he recalled the wisdom of the man whose action he valued so much and who, according to him, made the developments to a closer unified South Africa possible—Henry Campbell-Bannerman. The latter's treatment of the Boers was, according to Smuts, "one of the wisest political settlements of the English nation".[63] John Wilson also emphasised this aspect of Campbell-Bannerman's premiership:

> *C.B.'s greatest achievement was the settlement with South Africa, under which the defeated Boer states ... the Transvaal and the Orange Free State ... were given full self-government and allowed to elect Boer governments. This was a wise, large-minded and imaginative solution, which turned Botha and Smuts into lifelong friends of Britain and resulted in South Africa coming to Britain's help in two world wars.*[64]

Smuts' conversion to British imperialism became complete when the Liberals granted responsible government to the Transvaal and later to the Orange River Colony. In the future he was to become, almost naturally, with further constitutional development, one of the leading figures in a changing British Empire.

1. Walter Nimocks, *Milner's Young Men. The "kindergarten" in Edwardian Imperial Affairs,* 54. Sarah Gertrude Millin, *General Smuts,* Volume I, 216.
2. Nimocks, 54.

3. *Ibid., 55.*
4. *Ibid.*
5. John Wilson, *A Life of Sir Henry Campbell-Bannerman,* 477.
6. Millin, 216.
7. W.K. Hancock, *Smuts,* I. *The Sanguine Years, 1870 – 1919,* 188. Wilson, 477. Kenneth Ingham, *Jan Christiaan Smuts. The Conscience of a South African,* 50.
8. Hancock, 1, 188.
9. Wilson, 478.
10. Hancock, 1, 240 – 241.
11. *Ibid.,* 241.
12. G.H.L. le May, *The Afrikaners. An Historical Interpretation,* 137.
13. Wilson, 479.
14. *Ibid.*
15. Smuts Papers, Volume II, 216 – 227.
16. *Ibid.,* 216. Hancock, 1, 207.
17. Smuts Papers, Volume II, 12 May 1906, 272 – 273.
18. Wilson, 479. Hancock, 1, 188.
19. Wilson, 476.
20. *Ibid.*
21. *Ibid.*
22. Smuts Papers, Volume II, 21 February 1904, 147 – 149.
23. Wilson, 478.
24. *Ibid.*
25. *Ibid.* Herbert van Thal, *The Prime Ministers,* 190. See chapter on Campbell-Bannermann by John Wilson.
26. Wilson, 478.
27. Smuts Papers, Volume II, 1 February 1906, 228.
28. Wilson, 479.
29. Wilson, 479 – 480.
30. Hancock, 1, 213 – 214.
31. Le May, 139. Hancock, 1, 215 – 216.
32. Hancock, 215. Wilson, 481.
33. Hancock, 215.
34. *Ibid.,* 215 – 216. Wilson, 480 – 481.
35. Wilson, 481.
36. *Ibid.*

37. Le May, 139. Wilson, 481.
38. Le May, 139.
39. Wilson, 481.
40. Millin, 1, 213.
41. Wilson, 483.
42. *Ibid.*
43. *Ibid.*, 483 – 484.
44. *Ibid.*, 485.
45. Le May, 140.
46. Hancock, 1, 228. Le May, 140 – 141.
47. Le May, 141.
48. *Ibid.* Nimocks, 68.
49. Nimocks, 68.
50. *Ibid.*
51. Smuts Papers, Volume II, 4 March 1907, 326. Crafford, 72. Hancock, 228.
52. Millin, 1, 228. Ingham, 54.
53. Crafford, 73.
54. *Ibid.*
55. *Ibid.* Millin, 228.
56. Crafford, 73.
57. *Ibid.*, 74.
58. Le May, 134. F.V. Engelenburg, *Generaal Loiuys Botha,* 115, 331.
59. Crafford, 80.
60. *Ibid.*, 81.
61. *Ibid.*
62. Ingham, 57.
63. Crafford, 72.
64. Herbert van Thal, 191 – 192.

Jan Smuts, 1910. (South African Library)

Smuts and Lloyd George seated in the back of the car, Peace Conference, Paris, 1919. (South African Museum of Military History)

Jan Smuts in Lloyd George's Imperial War Cabinet. Smuts is seated in the front row, far right. (Central Archives Repository)

4

David Lloyd George

"I am bitterly disappointed in both Wilson (United States president) and Lloyd George, who are smaller men than I should ever have thought."
J.C. Smuts (Smuts Papers, IV, 176)

"We insisted on keeping him here to help us at the centre with our war efforts."
Lloyd George (Hancock, *Smuts,* 1, 432)

Louis Botha decided that Smuts should represent South Africa at the Imperial Conference in London in March 1917.[1] Circumstances at home prevented Botha from going to London. On the other hand Botha realised that Smuts was the man who was actually best equipped to handle international affairs with competence. For Smuts this was a "heaven-sent opportunity" to relinquish his command in East Africa. For various reasons the campaign no longer interested him. Back in South Africa he spoke in glowing terms of the South Africans' achievements in German East Africa. "Through our own efforts and our own sacrifices," he said, "we have secured a voice in the ultimate disposal of this sub-continent.... And we have done our duty, and nobody will be able to say we have been petty or small.... We have followed in the steps of the *Voortrekkers* and Pioneers .... "[2] His words echoed throughout South Africa. Generally he received no positive response. Who was he, it was argued, to identify himself with the cause of the *Voortrekkers*? Smuts was looked upon as the reincarnation of Rhodes. "Let him go to England," he was snarled at, "his spiritual home, there to become a privy councillor like Botha. South Africa was obviously too small for him and his great ideas. Let him get out and stay out."[3]

Smuts was initially not at all excited by the accession to power of Lloyd George. He disliked the look of the new British government. "What do you say of the new government in England with Milner and Curzon in it?" he wrote to his wife. "I think very little of them. It is a 'damn the consequences government', and I expect little good of them. And then the half German Milner in it!"[4] And to John X. Merriman he wrote: "I go with some misgivings to this conference, and only hope I

Jan Smuts, 1917 (Central Archives Repository)

shall not be overborne by some of my colleagues to acquiesce in schemes which will be good neither for South Africa nor the Empire."[5] He was most probably referring to Milner and his *kindergarten's* attempts to federalise the British Empire. "Do, I implore you," Merriman replied, "make head against the gasbags! Do not give way to them.... Do not be *forced* to do anything; you can be dour enough when you choose.... I fancy I see you surrounded by the *kindergarten* revolving round those twin luminaries, Milner and Northcliffe...."[6] Smuts sailed for England in the midst of a hostile public opinion. He was severely criticised by the Afrikaners. They accused him of giving more attention to matters concerning the Empire than to those of South Africa. It seemed as if he wanted to leave all this behind him and indulge in the world of international politics, with London as the focal point.

Smuts arrived in Southampton on 12 March 1917. In complete contrast to his experience in South Africa, he was, on his arrival in England, hailed as a hero. "At this moment," Churchill wrote, "there arrives in England from the outer marches of the Empire a new and altogether extraordinary man."[7] From now on the focus was on the young former Boer general. Sir Arthur Steel Maitland invited him to *All Souls* and Lady Astor invited him to Clivedon. Other invitations came from the archbishop of Canterbury; Lady Brassey; the Duchess of Rutland and various other leading personalities. Mrs Asquith, wife of a former British prime minister in the period 1908–1915, wrote to Smuts: "I have made a new friend, and as one is able to stretch the power of love so much the more grateful we should be. You are sane, clever and kind (a rare combination). DON'T

Jan Smuts on his way to receive the Freedom of the City of Cardiff, Wales, 1917. (Central Archives Repository)

go away just yet...."[8] Honours poured in—London, Plymouth, Edinburgh, Cardiff, Manchester, Bristol and various other cities bestowed on him their freedom. *The Middle Temple* and *The Society of Law Teachers* made him an honorary fellow. King George V made him a privy councillor and a *Companion of Honour.* "People make rather much of me here," Smuts wrote to his wife in South Africa, "but I am keeping apart from everything to avoid too much attention."[9] On his arrival in London a letter from Emily Hobhouse awaited him:

> *So off this goes to welcome you.... Years ago I prophesised to you that the day would come when your name would be seen in big print in the Times, that mighty organ that emulates Divinity for 'it putteth down one and setteth up another'—and I further said that I should live to see you Earl of Irene and Lord of Doornkloof and lo! are not these words fulfilling themselves? In essence if not the letter? For I know from old that honours come showering down upon those who tread 'Imperialist' paths. Still, I hope that something of the old 'Oom Jannie' yet remains, enough to enjoy association with the Pacifist and Anti-Imperialist I am prouder than ever to be.[10]*

It was first and foremost war business that brought Smuts to London. But he had made up his mind that he had no intention of spending his leisure time with the "important new acquaintances who tried to take possession of him".[11]

The Imperial Conference in London, which Lloyd George had in mind, to be attended on invitation by representatives of the dominions, would be a war-and-peace conference of the whole Empire. He eventually wanted something more than that. Apart from exchanging information and ideas he also wanted the statesmen of the Empire to make decisions—to take joint responsibility in the process of war. At the first meeting of the Imperial War Conference, Lloyd George informed the representatives that the War Conference was bound to be far more. He also envisaged an Imperial War Cabinet.[12] In constitutional terms this was something extraordinary, because a Cabinet "was hardly conceivable except as a body of men collectively responsible to a parliament".[13] The prime minister of Canada, Sir Robert Borden, called it a "Cabinet of Governments". Smuts found the Cabinet meetings far more satisfactory than the conference meetings.

When Lloyd George introduced Smuts to the Imperial War Cabinet he referred to him as "one of the most brilliant generals in this war".[14] Smuts made a lasting impression on Lloyd George. "So deep was the impression that General Smuts made at this time upon his colleagues," he wrote later, "nay, upon the nation, that we would not let him leave us when the conference ended. We insisted on keeping him here to help us at the centre with our war efforts."[15] At the numerous meetings Smuts attended he constantly kept a low profile. But when he spoke everybody listened attentively to what he had to say. "At the

Smuts and Lord Milner, London, 1917 (Central Archves Repository)

Imperial War Conference, London, 1917. Smuts is seated in the front row, third from the left. (Central Archives Repository)

meetings of the Imperial War Cabinet," wrote Crafford, "Smuts gave ample evidence of wisdom and foresightedness. He spoke rarely, but whenever he rose to address the council he was listened to with attention and respect."[16]

Smuts thought it a waste of time to discuss small issues, which crowded the agenda of the conference. Simultaneously, he thought it more meaningful to postpone big issues until the War had been won. "When the former was raised," wrote Hancock, "he sat in silence, when the latter was raised he protested."[17] Smuts adopted different tactics when the constitutional question came up. He argued that the question was so important that it couldn't wait, but on the other hand so comprehensive that it could not be rushed into. The only way to handle it, would be to settle it in principle. At first these two affirmations appeared to be "contradictory but in reality so coherent". They were both contained in a resolution, which Smuts drafted and which later proved to be of immense historical importance. Smuts carried the resolution through the Imperial War Conference on 16 March 1917:

The Imperial War Conference is of opinion that the readjustment of the constitutional relations of the component parts of the Empire is too important and intricate a subject to be dealt with during the War, and that it should form the subject of a special Imperial Conference to be summoned as soon as possible after the cessation of hostilities.

They deem it their duty, however, to place on record their view that any such readjustment, while thoroughly preserving all existing powers of self-government and complete control of domestic affairs, should be based upon a full recognition of the Dominions as autonomous nations of an Imperial Commonwealth, and of India as an important portion of the same, should recognise the right of the Dominions and India to an adequate voice in foreign policy and in foreign relations, and should provide effective arrangements for continuous consultation, as the several Governments may determine.[18]

This was a constitutional development of extreme significance and importance for the future, not only for the British Empire but also for the developing dominions. Smuts found himself at the centre of it all! "Here in England," wrote Crafford, "far removed from the rancour and harassment of South African politics, he was happy. He loved to be busy all day with important work ... doing big things, playing a very important part in directing the destinies of a great Empire at the time of her greatest need.... "[19] Smuts was completely convinced that Imperial Federation was *not* the solution to the demands of growing nationalism in the dominions. It is clear that phrases such as "self-government", "consultation", "such necessary concerted action ... as the several governments may determine", were decisive. In a speech, which supported the resolution, Smuts pointed out that these phrases "embodied a principle completely incompatible with Imperial Federation".[20] By now Smuts had dealt the Federalists a severe blow. The resolution passed by the Imperial War Conference on 16 March would undoubtedly always remain a historical landmark. From here the constitutional road ran straight to the *Statute of Westminster* of 1931.

Smuts was working for a necessary transformation of the British Empire and not for a disruption of the Empire. He realised that it was necessary for the Empire to adapt to a changing world order. Reconstruction was high on the agenda. Smuts recognised that the Empire rested on the heroic principles of freedom and equality, but pointed out that those principles were still caught up in "the legal clutter of a past age". Imperial sovereignty and colonial subordination was still too much in the forefront. "People were talking," Smuts argued, "about a League of Nations, but the British Empire was already taking shape as 'the only successful experiment in international government' that the world had yet seen."[21] He analysed the new structure he envisaged for the British Empire in a historical speech to both Houses of Parliament on the evening of 15 May.[22] The speech made a great impact on his audience. It is not far-fetched to claim that this speech indicated the way for the transformation of the British Empire. He asserted that in the light of Britain not being an Empire in the true sense of the word, it had become necessary and appropriate to take a new name. He suggested the name: Commonwealth.[23] Later that night, Lord Amery wrote Smuts a letter and congratulated him on a "magnificent" speech.[24]

At this stage, the British realised that they had discovered a "handy-man of the Empire".[25] They felt that at present he could not be spared! The serviceableness of Smuts was in the mind of Lloyd George all the time. What kind of assistance could they get from him at a time like this? Could he perhaps help to settle the thorny Irish problem? As prime minister, between 1916 and 1921, Lloyd George was too preoccupied with the urgent demands of war and peace to give Ireland the necessary attention it needed.[26] As a first contribution to British politics, Smuts proposed a convention based on the South African model—the Irish should settle things for themselves. Lloyd George and John Redmond agreed.[27] Perhaps a convention, it was argued, could reconcile and pacify the alarming increase in Irish nationalism. Smuts was the obvious choice as chairman of such an important and crucial convention.[28] Up until then Smuts' record presented almost everything an Irishman might claim and hope to be: nationalist, rebel, reconciler, state-builder.[29] Smuts had, since his arrival in London, shown a keen interest and concern for the ongoing Irish hostilities.[30] His old friend from Cambridge, John Wolstenholme, also urged him to involve himself in the cause of Irish reconciliation.[31] John Gregg, who shared lodgings with Smuts at 13 Victoria Street, Cambridge, also encouraged him to get involved.[32] Gregg was at the time archbishop of Armagh. Smuts could also have been persuaded to become involved in the Palestine issue. He could likely be the man to beat the Turks in Palestine and drive them out of the War. It was Amery who first thought of Smuts for the Palestine command. He referred to Smuts as the only soldier who "has not got trenches dug deep into his mind".[33] Smuts was regarded as ideal to lead the offensive against the Turks. Sir William Robertson, chief of the Imperial General Staff, told Smuts that, in the War Office's view, Palestine was already an obsession of the prime minister. Not satisfied with General Murray's progress against the Turks in the Near East, Lloyd George asked Smuts formally to take over the Palestine command.[34] Smuts contacted Louis Botha for his advice. Botha responded almost immediately:

I regard the offer by the Imperial Government of the Palestine command as a great honour, not only to you but also to the people of South Africa. Please accept our congratulations. As regards the wisdom or advisability to accept this offer, this will depend upon the scale on which the operations there are to be carried on. If on a large scale it would be very difficult to refuse the offer. I have no doubt that South Africa will appreciate with thankfulness this personal sacrifice by you. It is true that your colleagues will miss you greatly, but we are anxious to give you all facilities.[35]

Botha further advised Smuts that, should he decide to accept the Palestine command, he must remain a member of the Union Cabinet as minister without portfolio, and by doing so remain on the payroll of the Union, rather than of the British government.[36] Smuts eventually declined the offer of the Palestine command.[37] Lloyd George's disappointment was to be expected. "Smuts made a great mistake in not accepting the command in Palestine," he said afterwards. "The conquest of Palestine would have been an historic feat of arms."[38]

The Imperial War Cabinet was dissolved by May 1917, and Smuts decided that it was time to go home. Back in South Africa he would be "on the reserve, to be called up in time of need".[39] A month earlier Lloyd George had hinted that he would most probably need Smuts in a more permanent British War Cabinet. Eventually Lloyd George invited Smuts to stay on in England and become a permanent member of the British War Cabinet. Smuts accepted the invitation, which was extended at Milner's suggestion. The two former enemies became colleagues under these extraordinary circumstances.[40] The other members of the War Cabinet were Lloyd George, Lord Curzon, Bonar Law, Lord Carson, George Nicoll Barnes, and Lord Milner.[41] Many people were totally amazed when this became known. Smuts' inclusion in the War Cabinet was called "one of the greatest paradoxes of imperial history". This was after all, the premier's "innermost Cabinet", which virtually ran the War for Britain. How could a South African politician join the British Cabinet without becoming a British politician? Fifteen years previously Smuts had been a Boer general and now he was a member of a British War Cabinet in which was vested more power than in any other similar body since the dawn of time! "It has been suggested," wrote Crafford, "that Kruger's former lieutenant was taken into the War Cabinet not only because of his indispensable qualities as counsellor and plenipotentiary and the confidence he inspired, but largely also because the man in the street regarded him 'as a counterpoise to elements it distrusted wholly'." There is no denying the fact that in the dark days of 1917 and 1918 the War Cabinet on several occasions took "shelter behind the prestige of his name".[42] Lloyd George later tried to persuade Smuts to take a seat in the House of Commons. After consulting Botha once again, Smuts declined.[43] He took this step lest his political position in South Africa be jeopardised.[44]

The Imperial War Cabinet was still in session and Smuts was merely a representative of it in the newly-formed British War Cabinet. It is nearer to the truth that Lloyd George and his colleagues, including the King, held Smuts in high regard. Lloyd George and his colleagues were convinced that Smuts could contribute amply to the British war effort.[45] Smuts solved, during his stay in London, several problems in the British political set-up, including the very thorny coal strike in Wales. People from different spheres sought Smuts' advice. Winston Churchill suggested to Lord Riddell that Lloyd George would certainly be wise to appoint Smuts as a member of the British War Cabinet. Winston Churchill *inter alia* referred to Smuts as "the only unwounded statesman of outstanding ability in the Empire".[46] In a letter to his brother, Frederick Scott Oliver, a former member of Milner's *kindergarten,* he wrote: "I regard the taking of Smuts to the War Cabinet as a most important step. So far as pure intellect goes he is superior of any member at the present on it.... "[47]

It seemed that, from the British point of view, the special circumstances of national emergency justified Smuts' appointment. Nobody found it necessary to fuss about the constitutional and political niceties at a time like that. Lloyd George wanted Smuts in the Cabinet and true to his custom, he made sure that he got his way. Without doubt this was an extremely difficult situation for Smuts. He was on the fringe of British politics and there was no means by which he could become directly involved without becoming a Member of Parliament. This could result in tearing his roots up in South Africa. He just had to come to terms with the situation. Hancock wrote that Smuts found a middle course in this respect:

> In effect, he joined the War Cabinet on long loan from his own country and government. The price he had to pay proved to be a heavy one, not only in the prolongation of his loneliness and homesickness but in being cut off from the sources of political strength both in South Africa and in England. It may well be that he did not discover until two years later how high and dry he would be left; but even if he had foreseen his agonies at the Paris Peace Conference he might still have decided that London—but not as an MP—was the place for him.[48]

A.J.P. Taylor emphasised the unique situation in which Smuts found himself.[49] In modern times he was the only full Cabinet

Lloyd George introducing Smuts to both Houses of the British Parliament. (Central Archives Repository)

minister without any connection whatsoever to either Houses of Parliament: "As a weapon against the generals, Smuts did not meet the expectations. Professional loyalty worked even with a former rebel, and Smuts became the champion of the British generals whom he had once beaten in the field."[50]

The South African prime minister, Louis Botha, and his colleagues in the Cabinet supported Smuts in accepting Lloyd George's offer to join the War Cabinet. Smuts eventually accepted. His status was equivalent to that of minister without portfolio. "But was it not odd," asks Hancock, " that the British Parliament and people should tolerate in the government of their country a person who stood quite apart from the rules and conventions of the United Kingdom?"[51]

From now on Smuts was to be directly involved in the War; firstly, with the War strategy, and secondly, with peace-making. In this respect Mansergh makes mention of Smuts' "contribution to the creation of the Royal Air Force, the transformation of Empire, and to planning for international order and thinking about war and peace, without enlarging his understanding of the history of those years, without sensing in

Smuts the quality, albeit fallible, of greatness and without recognising how much even one man of vision and political stature might do to give meaning to the new idea of Commonwealth".[52]

Smuts was to assist actively with the reorganisation of British air power and governmental control of industrial production. Lloyd George sent him on various missions to Europe. In his *War Memoirs* Lloyd George wrote: "Smuts more perhaps than any other man, has the right to be called the father of the Royal Air Force."[53] Lloyd George sent Smuts to Belgium and France on an important mission. He was to examine the situation on the Western Front, interview Painlevé, the French president, and visit King Albert of the Belgians whose dejection at the time was causing grave concern.[54] Smuts' talks with the French president were confined to a close examination of the Allies' ultimate war aims. On the Western Front he received decorations from Belgium and France. He held discussions with Sir Douglas Haig and afterwards undertook a thorough examination of the over-all military situation. He then hastened back to London to report to Lloyd George. His memorandum, dated 29 April 1917, was tabled at a meeting of the War Cabinet.

Everybody did not always agree with Smuts. On 3 July 1917, Sir Henry Wilson entered in his diary: "I explained the situation in France and finished by saying that although not desperate, it undoubtedly was serious. I was struck by the tone of the committee, except Smuts, who seemed rather to revel in the idea that the situation was desperate and impossible. Of course, this is nonsense."[55] Next Smuts was off to Switzerland under the name of Mr Ashworth. Apart from the members of the War Cabinet only a few knew of Smuts' mission. In spite of all the secrecy, the news leaked out quickly. Shortly after his arrival Smuts negotiated with Count Albert Mensdorff, who was the Austro-Hungarian ambassador to London before the War. After two days of negotiations, nothing constructive was accomplished. "Lloyd George is a fool," said Clemenceau to Henry Wilson, "and an extra fool for sending Smuts, who doesn't even know where Austria is."[56] Nevertheless, Smuts was as busy as ever before. "It was an immense burden of work that he was carrying," writes Hancock. "Still, it was not beyond his physical strength nor did it depress him."[57] Subsequently, Lord Northcliffe asked the British government earnestly to send Smuts on a special mission to America.[58] Somebody had to enlighten the Americans regarding the effectiveness of the British war effort. "All people heard about," wrote Gertrude Millin, "was the doings of the French and Italians, who were flooding the country with their propaganda."[59] At the time Lord Northcliffe argued that Smuts was "the only big military man who could help here".[60] Finally Sir F.E. Smith went to America because the War Cabinet felt that Smuts was indispensable in England. On 9 September he wrote to Isie at Doornkloof:

> *The King and I then had a long talk about the war and he advised me not to accept the invitation to America, but to remain helping here to the end. We shall see! I feel lonely and alone here in England and would much rather be with you in beloved South Africa ... there are some here who love me. But the old heart is where the hills and ridges look down to the beloved Hennops.*[61]

Smuts was also offered the leadership of a secret expedition to Russia, but he turned it down after due consideration believing "that Russia in the throes of a revolution could no longer be of any assistance to the cause of the Allies".[62] Smuts was undoubtedly of the opinion that he was "on active service for humanity".[63]

Although there were intellectual and temperamental differences between Smuts and Lloyd George, these two men nevertheless still had much in common. The differences though were bound, sooner or later, to surface. But throughout 1917 they remained intact. Smuts admired Lloyd George as a war leader. There was a similarity between Smuts' outlook on the Boer War, and that of Lloyd Georges' on the First World War. This can be seen in the paper Smuts wrote on the eve of the Boer War.[64] Hancock refers most effectively to the similarities between Smuts and Lloyd George:

> *Both men had the gift of envisaging the problems of war comprehensively, not just as a heap of bits and pieces. They*

both possessed a sense of urgency and fiery determination.
Before Lloyd George came to power, it had seemed so easy
to postpone urgent tasks or to declare them insoluble. The
land could not be ploughed up. The ships could not be
controlled or convoyed. Hesitations such as these were
finished with when Lloyd George took control. Difficult
things could be done, they must be done, they were done.
Lloyd George, like Smuts, was audacious, experimental,
resilient. Both men possessed the gift of coming fresh to
work of each successive day. But beyond that? Whereas
Smuts was never content unless he could see his day-to-day
task in deep perspective, Lloyd George was intent upon the
immediate foreground. Smuts, so Merriman had said, was
a 'ruthless philosopher'. Nobody had ever accused Lloyd
George of being philosophical.[65]

The Peace Conference in Paris after the War was chiefly
responsible for the rift that gradually developed between Smuts
and Lloyd George. It is difficult to believe that something of this
nature could have happened to these two men who held each
other in such high regard and who were fighting for a cause in
which they both believed. Both went to Paris with a different
view regarding the peace they wanted for Europe and the
world. Smuts' point of view was entirely objective and,
therefore, in sharp contrast with that of Clemenceau, Lloyd
George, Orlando, and the other war leaders. " ... the war,"
wrote Crafford, "had bitten too deeply, and [their] outlook, in
consequence, was dominated by a chauvinistic subjectivity."[66]
In March 1919 Smuts wrote to his friends in Oxford: "I find the
prime minister still leans on me more than I thought he was
doing as we had tended to drift apart since the General Election
and its orgies of wild statements and doings. However, the still,
small voice is always there."[67]

The Allies won the War. Smuts was now determined to win
peace as well. It is understandable, in the light of this attitude
towards the peace talks in Paris, why Smuts went to Paris in a
most pessimistic mood. He resigned from the War Cabinet and
several committees. He was not a representative of the British
government at the Peace Conference but a representative of the

South African government. And this made quite a difference! Louis Botha also attended and Smuts was therefore second in command. Smuts was tremendously frustrated after being at the centre of events as a member of the British War Cabinet during the War. He was not a member of the Council of Four: Lloyd George, Clemenceau, Wilson, Orlando, and he could thus not directly influence the decisions taken. "Smuts was not an important person in the official hierarchy," wrote Hancock, "as he put it himself, he was 'only the second representative of South Africa'."[68] Situations like these were naturally frustrating to Smuts. He always wanted to be amongst those who determined destiny.

Smuts' approach to the Peace Conference in Paris differed totally from that of the other representatives. He was always concerned with a situation that could develop after the War. During the Second World War he once said: "I am not worried about the war, it will be difficult but we shall win it; it is after the war that worries me. It will take years of patience, courage and faith."[69] At the time he was distressed, and immensely concerned, about what the Allies intended to do to the defeated Germans. He urged the Great Powers to think "beyond the emotions of the moment". Smuts argued that there were greater issues at stake than mere retribution. "It is not merely that thrones and empires are falling, and ancient institutions suddenly collapsing," Smuts said. "A world order is visibly passing before our eyes, and the danger is that things may go too far and a setback be given to Europe from which she does not recover for generations."[70] But it was about Germany in particular that Smuts was most concerned:

> *What a doom has come over Germany! What a price she has paid for her ambitions and her crimes.*
>
> *Now as we organized the world for victory let us organize it against hunger and unemployment. Not only the liberated territories of our Allies, not only our small neutral neighbours, but the enemy countries themselves, require our helping hand. Let us extend it in all generosity and magnanimity.*[71]

Smuts was in constant contact with Lloyd George, conveying to him his observations and experiences. On 26 March he wrote that he was "seriously afraid" that the peace to which they are working "is an impossible peace".[72] He was afraid that it could result in promoting "the anarchy which is rapidly overtaking Europe". He stressed that certain vital points must be taken into consideration. He pointed them out:

* *We cannot destroy Germany without destroying Europe.*
* *We cannot save Europe without the cooperation of Germany.*
    Yet we are now preparing a peace, which must destroy Germany, and yet we think we shall save Europe by so doing! The fact is, the Germans are, have been, and will continue to be, the dominant factor on the continent of Europe, and no permanent peace is possible which is not based on that fact.[73]

Lloyd George and his European colleagues did not agree. But Smuts would not be intimidated by any of the senior representatives at the Peace Conference. He had his views on the type of peace that would, according to him, be to the best interest of Europe, its peoples and the world, and he would stick to that:

Even at this later hour, I would urge that we revise our attitude towards Germany, and, while making her pay heavily, and also making her undertake burdens for the defence and assistance of Central Europe which we have neither the men nor the means to undertake ourselves, treat her in a different spirit from that in which our proposals have so far been framed; avoid all appearance of dismembering her or subjecting her to indefinite economic servitude and pauperism, and make her join the League of Nations from the beginning.[74]

In spite of all his efforts, Smuts could not penetrate the minds of the Big Four. "From the outset," wrote Crafford, "Clemenceau was determined to dictate a peace of his own making or precipitate a bloody anabasis. What Germany had done since 1870 must be undone. The destruction of this country was a fitting end to what had been a veritable jehad ... he was determined to break Germany."[75] In complete contrast to this Smuts wrote to Lloyd George on 14 May: "Democracy is looking to you who have killed Prussianism ... the silent masses who have suffered mutely appeal to you to save them from the fate to which Europe seems to be lapsing."[76]

The growing tension between Smuts and Lloyd George was by now close to breaking point. In May, Lloyd George invited Smuts to serve on the *Commission on Austrian Reparation*. Smuts replied to Lloyd George in a letter dated 26 May:

> *[The] imposition of reparation on a broken, bankrupt, economically impossible State like Austria, or a new friendly allied State like Czechoslovakia ... seems to me a hopeless policy, which could only lead to the most mischievous results. I am against payment of all reparation by those countries for damage done by the dead and dismembered Austro-Hungarian Empire. And if it is (as it appears) your policy to exact reparation in these cases, I hope you will excuse me from serving on the Commission.*[77]

Lloyd George replied the same day and asked Smuts whether he was proposing "that Great Britain or South Africa are to bear a crushing loan of debt for the next 30 or 40 years, while Czecho-Slovakia, Jugo-Slavia, and the States which have been liberated by our arms, to say nothing of Austria and Hungary, are to carry no war debt at all. I must say that I cannot see how I am to justify to my own Parliament ... ."[78] Smuts was not impressed with Lloyd George's point of view. He was now in open conflict with the British prime minister with whom he had worked for many months in a close relationship. Smuts now knew that he was completely isolated. Whatever strategy he might have planned, he was totally without support.[79]

"I now began to think," Smuts wrote on 19 May, "I made a mistake in 1917 when I did not plunge right into British politics so as now to occupy a position at the centre instead of on the periphery."[80] Hancock is of the opinion that the Treaty of Versailles was "only one of a series but it was the one above all to whose making Smuts had committed himself, intellectually and emotionally."[81] In spite of all his efforts, Smuts was in the end a disillusioned and disappointed man. Years later he wrote, referring to the Peace Conference of 1919 in Paris: "I was as bad as the rest, as I was also partly responsible for some of the mistakes made in that awful time of confused thinking and counselling."[82]

Smuts returned to South Africa from England and Paris to take up his responsibilities in the government as a minister. Very soon he would lead the government. Lloyd George's Coalition government fell from office over the Chanak Crisis in 1922 and he remained an isolated figure, never again in office. The former good relations between Smuts and Lloyd George were never completely restored.

1. W.K. Hancock, *Smuts,* I. *The Sanguine Years, 1870 – 1919,* 432 – 434.
2. F.S. Crafford, *Jan Smuts. A Biography,* 133.
3. *Ibid.,* 133 – 134.
4. Smuts Papers, Volume III, 27 December 1916, 436 – 437.
5. Smuts Papers, Volume III, 15 February 1917, 444.
6. Smuts Papers, Volume III, 22 February 1917, 452.
7. Crafford, 134.
8. Hancock, 1, 425 .
9. Smuts Papers, Volume III, 31 March 1917, 471.
10. Smuts Papers, Volume III, 7 March 1917, 459 – 460.
11. Hancock, 1, 426.
12. *Ibid.,* 427.
13. *Ibid.*
14. Sarah Gertrude Millin, *General Smuts,* Volume I, 354 . Crafford, 134. David Lloyd George, *War Memoirs.* Volume IV, 1831.

15. Hancock, 1, 432.
16. Crafford, 137.
17. Hancock, 1, 429.
18. *Ibid.*
19. Crafford, 142.
20. Hancock, 1, 429.
21. *Ibid.,* 430.
22. Smuts Papers, Volume III, 506 – 517.
23. Crafford, 136.
24. Smuts Papers, Volume III, 15. May 1917, 517.
25. Nicholas Mansergh, *The Commonwealth Experience,* 373. Crafford, 149.
26. Herbert van Thal, *The Prime Ministers. From John Russell to Edward Heath,* Volume II, 226.
27. A.J.P. Taylor, *English History*, 1914 – 1945, 121.
28. Denis Gwynn, *The Life of John Redmond,* 532.
29. Taylor, 120. Franciscan Library (FLK): Colonel Maurice Moore Papers: Moore to Smuts, 20th August, 1921.
30. James Lawrence, *The Rise and Fall of the British Empire,* 382.
31. Smuts Papers, Volume III, 23 May 1917, 521.
32. Smuts Papers, Volume III, 19 May 1917, 521.
33. Hancock, 1, 435.
34. Crafford, 139.
35. Smuts Papers, Volume III, 26 April 1917, 494 – 495.
36. Hancock, 1, 434.
37. Smuts Papers, Volume III, 31 May 1917, 528. Lloyd George, 1831 and 1833.
38. Crafford, 140. Millin, Volume II, 39.
39. Hancock, 1, 435.
40. John Marlowe, *Milner. Apostle of Empire,* 268 . Millin, Volume I, 355.
41. Crafford, 140. Lloyd George, 1833.
42. *Ibid.,* 141.
43. Hancock, 1, 436.
44. Mansergh, 373. Millin, Volume II, 56 . Crafford, 140.
45. Hancock, 1, 432.
46. Crafford, 137.
47. *Ibid.,* 141.

48. Hancock, 1, 436 – 437.
49. A.J.P. Taylor, *English History, 1914 – 1965,* 120.
50. *Ibid.*
51. Hancock, 1, 436.
52. Mansergh, 373. Philip Ziegler, Mountbatten, 97. Stephen Roskill, *Churchill and the Admirals,* 70. Lloyd George, 1863.
53. Hancock, 438. Millin, Volume II, 80.
54. Crafford, 138. Hancock, 1, 448 – 449.
55. Crafford, 151.
56. *Ibid.,* 153.
57. Hancock, 1, 442.
58. Millin, Volume II, 129.
59. *Ibid.,*
60. *Ibid.,* 129.
61. Smuts Papers, Volume III, 9 September 1917, 550 – 551.
62. Crafford, 144.
63. Hancock, 1, 438.
64. Hancock, 1, 444. Spies, 24.
65. Hancock, 1, 444.
66. Crafford, 156.
67. Smuts Papers, Volume IV, 27 March 1919, 87.
68. Hancock, 1, 508.
69. Brian Gardener, *Churchill in his time. A Study in Reputation,* 36.
70. Crafford, 156.
71. *Ibid.*
72. Smuts Papers, Voume IV, 26 March 1919, 83.
73. Smuts Papers, Volume IV, 26 March 1919, 83 – 84.
74. *Ibid.,* 87.
75. Crafford, 162 – 163.
76. Smuts Papers, Volume IV, 14 May 1919, 158.
77. Smuts Papers, Volume IV, 26 May 1919, 197.
78. Smuts Papers, Volume IV, 26 May 1919, 198.
79. Hancock, 1, 532.
80. *Ibid.,* 531.
81. *Ibid.,* 536.
82. *Ibid.,* 545.

Smuts and Churchill in Cairo. (Central Archives Repository)

Churchill (far right) after his capture by the Boers. (Transvaal Archives Repository)

5

Winston Churchill

" ... the one in all the world to whom so many owe so
much."
Jan Smuts (Martin Gilbert, *Road to Victory*, 1079)

"My faith in Smuts is unbreakable. He is a great man."
Winston Churchill (Lord Moran, *Diaries*, 317)

It is extremely difficult, almost impossible, to find a
friendship comparable to that of Smuts and Churchill. It
was a friendship that lasted for almost 50 years. Anthony
Eden, who succeeded Churchill as prime minister, once said of
the friendship between Smuts and Churchill: "The friendship
of Churchill and Smuts always fascinated me. They were such
contrasting personalities; the one with his neat philosophic
mind, the other a man 'rammed with life'."[1] Smuts never
smoked and rarely used alcohol—perhaps a beer and sometimes
a whiskey after a day mountain climbing.[2] Churchill on the
other hand smoked and drank heavily. He once told King Ibn
Saud of Saudi Arabia: " ... my religion prescribed as an absolute
sacred rite smoking cigars and drinking alcohol before, after,
and if need be during all meals and the intervals between

them."[3] Kenneth Ingham wrote of Smuts' and Churchill's friendship: "Theirs was a strange but none the less deep friendship. They were men of utterly different characters yet they seemed to be drawn together by a powerful attraction."[4] Lord Moran, Churchill's personal physician, knew these two men intimately and he wrote: "Smuts had few heroes, but to him Winston was the one indispensable man; the only man with ideas. Smuts' cool, scientific habit of mind turned to measurements. He was concerned that history should be informed about the size of the man, the measure of his achievements."[5]

Smuts mentioned Churchill's name for the first time during the Anglo-Boer War. On 13 November 1899, still in his capacity as *staats procureur*, he wrote to one of the Boer generals: "What truth is there in the rumour that Churchill has escaped but has been caught again?"[6] This escape of course made Churchill a national hero in England. The British newspapers reported this "heroic escape" to its fullest extent to their readers. After the War Louis Botha came to London as leader of a delegation of Boer generals. He met Churchill at a private luncheon where the latter recalled his capture and escape as a war journalist during the Anglo-Boer War.[7] Smuts, as attorney general, interrogated the "defiant young man" who claimed immunity from him as a non-combatant.[8]

The next encounter with Churchill was during Smuts' visit to London in January to February 1906. Smuts arrived in London, as a delegate of the Transvaal government, in order to meet Prime Minister Campbell-Bannerman. He was to request that the prime minister consider sovereign independence for the defeated Boer republics. This would be Smuts' second encounter with Churchill who was at the time a member of Campbell-Bannerman's Liberal government as under-secretary of state for colonies. Churchill was initially unenthusiastic about Smuts' visit to Campbell-Bannerman, but eventually he changed his point of view. It was left to him to write a letter to Smuts after the Cabinet's decision to grant self-government to the two former Boer republics. This private 'dictated' letter to Smuts clearly portrays a growing relationship between Smuts and Churchill:

*You will, I dare say, also have followed the course of affairs
in the House of Commons.... From all this, I trust you will
have concluded that it is the desire and intention of those
who now advise the Sovereign to do their best to strike a
fair and just balance between the Dutch and British races
in South Africa, to secure either race from danger of
oppression by the other, and then, while preserving at all
risks and at all costs the authority of the British Crown, to
leave South Africa as much master of its own fortunes as
the Australian Commonwealth or the Dominion of
Canada. If we are enabled to carry this policy to its
conclusion, I am not without hopes that the darkest days of
South African history may have drawn to their close.*[9]

Smuts' involvement in British war strategy placed him in close
contact with Churchill. Churchill was at that time in Lloyd
George's Cabinet—first as secretary of state for War and for the
air, and then as minister of colonies.[10] Smuts and Churchill
were thus constantly in close contact during this period of war.
Churchill frequently mentioned Smuts' abilities to the prime
minister.

In mid-1915 Churchill and the British War Cabinet were
plunged into a political crisis. Churchill was fighting for his
political survival. The naval operation, authorised by the War
Council to occupy the Gallipoli Peninsula and then to sail on up
to Constantinople, eventually proved to be a catastrophe.
Churchill was not the mastermind behind the operation, but he
made it his own.[11] Lord Fischer, admiral of the fleet, whom
Churchill looked upon as a personal friend, obstructed the
whole operation in the Dardanelles in every way possible. "That
Churchill still referred to Fischer as a friend on 14 May 1915,"
wrote Grant, "shows how naive he could be about people."[12]
Churchill became "the favourite whipping boy of the Tory
press."[13] The Tories blamed Churchill for Gallipoli and every
misfortune suffered by the navy since the beginning of the
War.[14] The Tories actually enjoyed battering Churchill in this
way because they had never forgiven him for his treacherous
deed in forsaking the Tories for the Liberals. Eventually
Churchill had to pay the highest toll a man could pay in active

politics. He left the Cabinet and Lloyd George was in no hurry to bring him back into the government, despite the claims of friendship from the past![15] Grant wrote that in retrospect there was actually nothing surprising about Churchill's downfall.[16] "He will never get to the top in British politics," wrote Lord Asquith, "with all his wonderful gifts; to speak with the tongues of men and angels, and to spend laborious days and nights in administration, is no good if a man does not inspire trust."[17]

While Churchill was battling for political survival, Smuts was honoured once again by Cambridge University. On October 1915 A.E. Shipley informed him that Christ's College had enrolled his name on the List of Honorary Fellows. It is interesting that Shipley refers, *inter alia,* to the crisis in the Dardenelles. "Things are not going too well in Europe," he wrote to Smuts. "Bulgaria's decision will certainly prove a big factor; as we are almost held up in Gallipoli (and) it looks as if the Germans might get to Constantinople first."[18] In the meanwhile Smuts made his mark in international and British politics as a member of Lloyd George's British War Cabinet. The British prime minister relied heavily on Smuts' insight and consequent advice. Churchill's admiration for Smuts grew by the day.

After the War Churchill wrote Smuts a most interesting personal letter. This was actually the first time he had mentioned their friendship so prominently:

> *I have been keeping your letter by me in my boxes for an opportunity to tell you how deeply I value it. All the many kindnesses and services you rendered to me in the stormy ups and downs of the great struggle have made a lasting impression on my mind. I can never forget your sympathy and comradeship. We shall always look back upon those fierce crowded days and in them I shall always see your friendship and courage and wise counsel.*[19]

This was really an effusion on which to build for the future. And this was exactly what the two men did over a very long period.

In 1922 there was a miner's strike in Johannesburg, which caused the Smuts government and the country anxiety. After mobilizing the Active Citizen Force and thereupon declaring Martial Law on 10 March, Smuts left Cape Town for Johannesburg to command the government troops against the armed strikers. While travelling by car from Randfontein to his headquarters in Johannesburg, Louis Esselen, and Smuts' chauffeur, Hodgson, came repeatedly under rifle fire. When the news of this scary incident reached Churchill he was alarmed. He anxiously sent Smuts a telegram: "Warmest congratulations your escape. Urge you to take greatest care of yourself. Your life is invaluable South Africa and the British Empire."[20]

October 1922 witnessed the fall of Lloyd George's Coalition government. Bonar Law formed a Conservative government, and in November 1922 a general election was called.[21] Meanwhile Churchill took ill, and he was operated on for appendicitis—at the time it was a serious operation. This illness prevented Churchill from going to his Dundee constituency until the final days of the election campaign. He was still frail when he eventually arrived in Dundee. Most of his speeches had to be delivered while sitting down. Although Lady Churchill took a leading part in the campaign, "canvassing and speaking at rowdy meetings", Churchill's large majority at the former general election was simply swept away.[22] Smuts responded to all this with a letter of consolation:

My dear Churchill, First the news of your serious illness and then the news of your defeat at Dundee have come as great shocks to your friends in South Africa. I am really sorry, whatever view you may take of the defeat. But perhaps it is as well that you get a short spell of rest after the very heavy labours you have had to bear recently. I trust you will soon be all right and all the better to do the great work which is still before you.[23]

The outcome of the British general election was a clear indication of the changing political tide in the country. The Conservatives, however, eventually won by a substantial majority.[24] Now, freed from office, Churchill could take a long convalescence. The whole family moved to Cannes in the south of France where they stayed in a villa for several months. Churchill now found himself in the political wilderness. In this time he fell ill and his appendix had to be removed. With his customary subtlety he wryly commented that he was now "without an office, without a seat, without a party, and without an appendix".[25] Apart from his political setbacks Churchill lost, what was for him, a small fortune. Mary Soames wrote about this period in her father's life: "Despite the severe setback to his fortunes Winston was, by his brilliance and industry, able to keep his family, and live in style and comfort at his beloved Chartwell through his writings. At times it was a never-run thing between bills and books, and the fragility of the economic raft on which they lived was a cause of great anxiety to Clementine, and was certainly the main reason why her enjoyment of Chartwell was dimmed."[26] Churchill then, once again, moved by degrees and through several elections, from the Liberal Party to the Conservative Party. In the general election of February 1924, following the fall of the Labour government, he stood as a "constitutional" candidate with the support of many prominent Conservatives. He won the West Essex (Epping) constituency. He was to remain the Conservative member for this constituency (later renamed the Wanstead and Woodford Division of Essex) for the remaining 40 years of his political life.[27]

A year later it was Smuts' turn to enter the political wilderness in South Africa when he lost the general election of 1924. General J.B.M. Hertzog succeeded him as prime minister.

Churchill highly appreciated Smuts' kind words of compassion. He recalled with fondness their mutual experience during the First World War:

> *My dear Smuts, I never answered your very kind letter to me when I left office. But I have been looking forward ever since to sending you a copy of my new book about the opening phase of the war. I dwell a good deal in those dazzling terrible times, and I like to think of how we were together in so many important things ...*
>
> *Your friendship is always very much cherished by me.*[28]

Smuts received Churchill's gift with enthusiasm and gratitude. He undoubtedly admired Churchill's special gifts and interesting spirit of enterprise:

> *My dear Churchill, Thank you very much for your last letter and the most acceptable gift of your Book. I have read the Book with the deepest interest. It is indeed a very brilliant affair and its subject will remain one of the greatest of all time. I envy you the great gift of being a man of action and a great writer at the same time. Julius Caesar was that rare combination. And although you are not as Francophobe as he was, your book will stand comparison with the Gallic War!*[29]

Churchill and Smuts had a special way of communicating with each other. They both felt at ease knowing that there was an invisible bond between them from which they could draw spiritual inspiration for the difficult and sometimes intriguing problems and issues that lay ahead. It seems that both of them had a constant desire to keep in touch with each other. Smuts sent Churchill a "deeply interesting book" on philosophy in which he "peered with awe". Churchill then sent Smuts the third part of his book, *The World Crisis*, dealing with the period 1916 – 1918. He wrote to Smuts:

> *I follow always the course of your affairs with that enduring sympathy which springs from wartime comradeship. I hope it will not be long before you pay us a visit. You will find a warm welcome awaiting you from your many friends, and from none more than those who with you have faced the battle and the breeze of the twentieth century of the Christian era.*[30]

It was during the Second World War that Smuts and Churchill grew even closer to each other. In her *A Churchill Family Album* Mary Soames has a photo of Smuts and Churchill relaxing together. The caption to the photo runs: "Here Winston is seen talking to a man whose counsel and friendship were equally precious to him—Field Marshal Jan Smuts, prime minister of South Africa. Throughout the War, Winston kept in close and constant touch with him."[31]

Germany invaded Poland on 2 September 1939. Honouring their pledge to Poland, France and Great Britain declared war on Germany. The British prime minister, Neville Chamberlain, invited Churchill on the evening of 3 September to become first lord of the Admiralty. He arrived on 4 September at the Admiralty to take up his duties. "Nearly a quarter of a century earlier," wrote Mary Soames, "he had left this building on relinquishing office in the bitter aftermath of the failure of the Dardenelles. Now the Admiralty signalled the fleet: 'Winston is back'.[32]"

In the South African Parliament the differences between Smuts and Hertzog on the war issue automatically meant a split in the United Party. When Britain declared war on Germany the South African Cabinet was forced to come to an immediate decision.[33] Hertzog announced in Parliament that the Cabinet was divided on the war issue. Dr D.F. Malan, leader of the Purified National Party, assured Hertzog privately that his party would support a policy of neutrality. Hertzog consequently moved the adoption of his neutrality motion.[34] In his speech following on the motion, Smuts made the point that Nazi Germany was undoubtedly aiming at world domination.

Members of Parliament who supported Smuts in his motion on the war issue, 4 September 1939. (Central Archives Repository)

Members of the new Union Cabinet, 1939. Standing, left to right: Dr C.F. Steyn, minister of justice; H.F. Lawrence, of the interior and public health; Senator A.M. Conroy, minister of lands; Major P.V.G. van der Byl, minister without portfolio; F.C. Sturrock, minister of railways and harbours; C.F. Clarkson, minister posts and telegraphs and public works; Col. C.F. Stallard, minister of mines; W.B. Madeley, minister of labour and social welfare. Sitting, left to right: J.H. Hofmeyr, minister of finance and education; General Smuts, minister of external affairs and defence; the governor general, Sir Patrick Duncan; Col D. Reitz, minister of native affairs; R. Stuttaford, minister of commerce and industries; Col W.R. Collins, minister of agriculture and forestry. (Central Archives Repository)

According to Smuts there could be no question of the Union standing aside at such a moment. He then proposed the following amendment to Hertzog's motion: "It is in the interest of the Union that its relations with the German Reich should be severed, and that the Union should refuse to adopt an attitude of neutrality in this conflict."[35]

The debate on the war issue lasted a whole day. The count was taken at nine o'clock that evening. Smuts' amendment was carried by a majority of 80 to 67.[36] The prime minister's original motion lost, and this amounted to a motion of non-confidence in the prime minister and his government. Hertzog then advised the governor general to dissolve the House and to call a general election. Sir Patrick Duncan, the governor general, stated that the voting in Parliament already showed that Smuts had enough support to form a new government. At such a critical hour there was no need to consult the electorate. Duncan accepted Hertzog's resignation and he requested Smuts to form a new Cabinet. Smuts' first task was to hand the German minister, Plenipotentiary, his passport.

Major Piet van der Byl, minister without portfolio, recalls the first meeting of Smuts' War Cabinet on 6 September 1939. "He (Smuts) was cheerful," wrote van der Byl, "and started off by saying, 'Well, gentleman, we must now declare war on Germany'."[37] Smuts received the following telegram:

> To: General Smuts
> From: First Lord of the Admiralty
> Dated: [7 September 1939]
> I rejoice to feel that we are once again on commando together.[38]

For the first four months Smuts governed without Parliament. He followed this *modus operandi* because "he wanted time to build-up strength both on the military and on the home front."[39] Smuts now "embodied the tradition of personal leadership which the Union had taken over from the Republics."[40] It is true that South Africa never completely absorbed British conventions of Cabinet government. Furthermore, it was also true that each government since Union in 1910 had the personal stamp of the prime minister of the day. Therefore it was never asked ... "What is the Cabinet doing? They always asked ... What is Smuts doing?"[41]

To Churchill it must have been a great comfort to know that Smuts was once again in charge in South Africa and that the British War Cabinet would once again, as was the case during the First World War, have the opportunity of consulting Smuts directly on war issues and other international developments. At this stage it was already commonly known that Churchill held Smuts in high esteem as a friend as well as an advisor. John Colville wrote:

> *When Smuts came to England Churchill would drop all else and listen attentively to the accented words of wisdom,*

Smuts at the British Embassy, Cairo. Front row, left to right: Smuts, Churchill, General Auchinleck and General Wavell (Central Archives Repository)

spoken in high staccato tones, which poured from the South African patriarch on all the issues of present and future policy. In Pretoria they called him 'Slim Jan'; at Downing Street he was the Prince Charming.... There were few of Churchill's colleagues in the British Government whose opinions carried the same weight.[42]

Germany attacked Denmark and Norway simultaneously on 9 April 1940. Denmark was quickly overrun but Norway put up a heroic fight against the invaders. They called on Britain for help. Britain responded immediately by sending, with speed, naval and military forces.[43] "After all," wrote Taylor, "unlike Czechoslovakia or Poland, (they) seemed within range."[44] The campaign in Norway was a total disaster.[45] A great number of

105

Smuts and Churchill inspecting the south-eastern defences in 1942.
(Central Archives Repository)

British troops had been evacuated in less than three weeks.[46] All this resulted in a heated debate on the Norwegian operations, lasting two days, in the House of Commons.[47] The government's support diminished from 240 to 81. Many members, who later supported the government, turned angrily against the prime minister, Neville Chamberlain, and his colleagues.[48] Chamberlain now faced open revolt in his own party. The entire country showed clear signs of mounting indignation. The prime minister's attempt to form a national administration failed. During the negotiations it became abundantly clear that the Labour and Liberal parties would only serve a government under a new prime minister. The only man, at that moment of crisis, who could command confidence was Winston Churchill.[49] On the night of 9 – 10 May, Germany invaded Holland and Belgium. Chamberlain resigned on the evening of 10 May. The King then sent for Churchill.[50]

Churchill commenced his responsibilities as prime minister by forming his War Cabinet of Conservative, Labour, and Liberal members. The *Daily Mail* of 11 May 1940 wrote that the new prime minister "set about the task, with his customary

Smuts and the War Cabinet, during Second World War. Churchill in the centre and Smuts second from right, next to Anthony Eden.
(Central Archives Repository)

vigour, immediately".[51] When the House met on 13 May, members rose and cheered Chamberlain. Cheers for Churchill came only from the Labour benches![52] The new prime minister then addressed the House in his customary oratorical style:

> *I have nothing to offer but blood, toil, tears and sweat. You ask, What is our policy? I will say: It is to wage war, by sea, land, and air, with all our might and with all the strength that God can give us.... You ask, What is our aim? I can answer in one word: Victory— victory at all costs, victory in spite of all terror; victory, however long and hard the road may be.[53]*

It was common knowledge amongst Churchill's colleagues, his personal staff and his generals that Smuts had a great influence on the British War prime minister. It is true that no active statesman at the time, apart from Churchill, had longer political experience. According to Moran:

> *He (Smuts) is the only man who has any influence with the P.M., indeed, he is the only ally I have in pressing counsels*

of common sense on the P.M. Smuts sees so clearly that Winston is irreplaceable that he may make an effort to persuade him to be sensible.[54]

The other Commonwealth prime ministers did not always appreciate the special attention Churchill bestowed on Smuts. Colville refers to the "jealousy of the other dominions".[55] They often envied Smuts' constant presence in government circles in London. Nevertheless, it was in London that Smuts remained a key figure. On 3 October 1943 Harold Macmillan, a future British prime minister, entered in his war diary:

He (Smuts) is going to stay there (England) more or less permanently, as a member of the War Cabinet. This is most fortunate for us all. He has all the qualities which will make him an admirable addition to the P.M. And it will be very good for Winston to have a colleague older than himself whom he cannot browbeat.[56]

Churchill consulted Smuts on a regular basis regarding difficult and sensitive decisions he had to make on the war situation. Sometimes it was necessary to replace key, and at the same time senior, military personal in order to keep military operations effective and intact. Lord Moran noted in his diary on 4 August 1942: "I am glad he (Smuts) is here. The P.M. hates the thought of

Smuts and the Air Council, 1943. During the First World War Smuts was instrumental in establishing the Royal Air Force.
(Central Archives Repository)

removing one of his commanders. Smuts is more ruthless, and if the P.M. has to make changes in the higher command, even, it may be, to get rid of General Auchinleck, Smuts' presence and counsel will fortify and comfort him."[57] But this was actually not a true reflection of Smuts' character. He could sometimes be sentimental about people without showing it openly. "Smuts' own weakness," wrote Lord Harlech, British high commissioner in South Africa, in one of his reports to the British prime minister, "is extreme tenderness for old friends and colleagues in past struggles and a reluctance to try out new men."[58] John Colville entered into his diary that Smuts was the one who was responsible for Sir Stafford Cripps' transfer from the War Cabinet to the Ministry of Aircraft Production (MAP).[59] There was also the appointment of Field Marshal Montgomery as commander of the Eighth Army. It all had to do with replacing General Gott after he was killed. The transport aircraft he was flying was shot down along a desert route by two German fighters. Smuts was directly involved in the new appointment. Alan Chalfont recorded the events leading to the replacement:

Field Marshal Smuts.
(Central Archives Repository)
"One of the greatest living men" - (Winston Churchill)

After a brief discussion between Churchill, Brooke and Field Marshal Smuts (whose opinion meant a great deal to the Prime Minister), a telegram was despatched to Attlee in London: 'Prime Minister to Deputy Prime Minister 7 August 1942 CIGS decisively recommends Montgomery for Eighth Army. Smuts and I feel this post must be filled at once. Pray send him by special plane at earliest moment. Advise me when he will arrive.[60]

In Smuts' words Churchill was "the one indispensable man" and to Churchill Smuts was "one of the greatest living men".

---

1. Anthony Eden, *The Eden Memoirs. The Reckoning,* 350.
2. André P. Brink, *Heildronk,* 35.
3. Martin Gilbert, *Road to Victory. Winston Churchill,*1941 – 1945, 1225.
4. Kenneth Ingham, *Jan Christian Smuts. The Conscience of a South African,* 210.
5. Lord Moran, *Winston Churchill. The Struggle for Survival,* 1940 – 1965. Taken from the diaries of Lord Moran, XVI.
6. W.K. Hancock, *Smuts,* 1. *The Sanguine Years,* 1870 – 1919, 113.
7. V.N. Carter, *Winston Churchill. As I knew him.*
8. *Ibid.*
9. Smuts Papers, Volume II, 12 May 1906, 272 – 273.
10. Alan Moorhead, *Churchill. A Pictorial Biography,* 50.
11. R.G. Grant, *Winston Churchill, An Illustrated Biography,* 92.
12. *Ibid.*
13. *Ibid.,* 90.
14. Suanne Everett, *World War I,* 48, 54 – 59.
15. Grant, 99.
16. *Ibid.,* 93.
17. *Ibid.*
18. Smuts Papers, Volume III, 8 October 1915, 318.
19. Smuts Papers, Volume V, 30 October 1919, 16 – 17.
20. Smuts Papers, Volume V, 13 March 1922, 114.
21. Mary Soames, *A Curchill Family Album. A personal Anthology,* 146.
22. *Ibid.*
23. Smuts Papers, Volume V, 22 November 1922, 153.
24. A.J.P. Taylor, *English History,* 1914 – 1945, 251, 253 – 254.

25. Soames, 146.
26. *Ibid.*
27. *Ibid.*
28. Smuts Papers, Volume V, 7 April 1923, 172.
29. Smuts Papers, Volume V, 13 August 1923, 180.
30. Smuts Papers, Volume V, 21 February 1927, 343.
31. Soames, 303.
32. *Ibid.,* 239.
33. D.W. Kruger, *The Making of a Nation. A History of the Union of South Africa,* 1910 – 1961, 196. Hancock, 11, 318 – 319.
34. Hancock, 11, 320 – 321.
35. Kruger, 197.
36. Ingham, 206. Kruger, 198.
37. Piet van der Byl, *Top Hat to Velskoen,* 163.
38. Smuts Papers, Volume VI, 7 September 1939, 191.
39. Hancock, 11, 334.
40. *Ibid.,* 333.
41. *Ibid.*
42. John Colville, *Footprints in Time,* 127 – 128.
43. E. Bauer, *The History of World War II,* 47. Taylor, 573.
44. Taylor, 573.
45. Bauer, 45. Taylor, 574.
46. Reader's Digest *Illustrated History of World War II,* 38. Taylor, 574.
47. Taylor, 575.
48. Soames, 246.
49. *Ibid.* Taylor, 577 – 579.
50. Taylor, 578 – 579.
51. Grant, 151.
52. Taylor, 579.
53. *Ibid.* Martin Gilbert, *The Road to Victory. Winston S. Churchill,* 1941 – 1945, 139.
54. Moran, 146 – 147.
55. John Colville, *The Fringes of Power. Downing Street Diaries.* Volume One: *September 1939 – October 1941,* 319.
56. Harold Macmillan, *War Diaries. The Mediterranean,* 1943 – 1945, 247.
57. Moran, 50.

58. PREM: 4/44/1. *Harlech to British Prime Minister,* 2 October 1941.
59. John Colville, *The Fringes of Power,* Volume Two, 61.
60. Alan Chalfont, Montgomery of Alamein, 157. Montgomery, *The Memoirs of Field-Marshal the Viscount Montgomery of Alamein, K.G.,* 93.

Smuts and Churchill with Lady Clementine. (Central Archives Repository)

Smuts pointing out to Churchill a particular type of grass in the Middle East. (Smuts House Museum)

Mohandas Karamchand Gandhi as a young man. (Central Archives Repository)

Gandhi in later years. (Central Archives Repository)

6

Mahatma Gandhi

"It was my fate to be the antagonist of a man for
whom even then I had the highest respect.... "
J.C. Smuts (Hancock, *Smuts,* 1, 346)

"You have a great strength (he told Smuts), and I am
sure you will use it wisely with every regard for the
feelings of these unfortunate Asiatics...."
Mahatma Gandhi (Hancock, *Smuts,* 1, 332)

Smuts and Gandhi met for the first time in South Africa late
in the 19th century. The encounter between these two
remarkable men would eventually prove to be an
exceptional experience, which was ultimately of deep
significance to both of their lives. It was also to be of world
historical significance. It not only developed into a 12-year
conflict between them, but also led to the eventual reconciliation
between Britain and India. To a certain extent the clash between
Smuts and Gandhi was a clash of personalities.

Smuts and Gandhi were born within a year of each other
and, significantly, under the same flag. Gandhi was born in
Porbandar on 2 October 1869.[1] At first sight it would seem that

there was little else they could have had in common by inheritance or upbringing.[2] Smuts was raised in a Calvinist family on their spacious farm in the district of Riebeeck West. Gandhi was raised in a Hindu family in the tiny principality of Porbandar, on the north-western coast of India. While Smuts grew up on an African farm and attended his uncle's church at Riebeeck West, Gandhi was "experimenting with some transitory divagations, such as smoking and meat-eating, from the strict rule of middle-caste Hinduism".[3] When Smuts discovered, at the age of 12, the "delights of study" at the school of Mr Stoffberg at Riebeeck West, Gandhi lost a year of schooling when he "indulged in the excitement" of a Hindu child-marriage. He was then only 13 years old. Much later, the paths of these two young boys seemed to converge a little. Smuts concluded his matriculation at Stellenbosch while Gandhi bid his young wife and children farewell and boarded ship for England in order to qualify as a barrister. As young strangers, Smuts in Cambridge and Gandhi in London, both experienced more or less the same trauma throughout their stay—"a similar loneliness, a similar reliance upon his own resources, mitigated by a similar good fortune in finding a few friends".[4] But Gandhi's friends were entirely different from those of Smuts. Professor Keith Hancock wrote:

> *Between the young Indian and the young Boer the gap might have seemed to be as wide as the distance between the civilisations of East and West. But might not the orthodox of both civilisations be prone to exaggerate that distance? From their separate bases of ancestral belief Gandhi and Smuts were both exploring the simplicities of divinity and of morality, and if they sometimes discovered opposite norms of conduct—opposite convictions, for example, about the place of chastity in marriage or of force in politics—they could at least mutually understand the purpose of each other's quest. Moreover, they both knew themselves to be deeply in debt to their English teachers ...[5]*

Hancock points out that Gandhi had a higher regard for the British constitution than Smuts, as well as for the British habit of compromise. Gandhi believed that it was harmonious with the basic values of his own civilisation. "Hardly ever have I known anybody," he wrote in 1927, "to cherish such loyalty as I did to the British constitution. I can see now that my love of truth was at the root of this loyalty."[6] He continued: "But all my life through, the very insistence on truth has taught me to appreciate the beauty of compromise. I saw in later life this spirit was an essential part of Satyagraha. It has often meant endangering my life and incurring the displeasure of friends. But truth is hard as adamant and tender as a blossom."[7] Looking at these two men objectively, one can conclude that they could have worked amicably together for a common cause. They could have "work(ed) with each other rather than against each other". But circumstances beyond their reach decided otherwise. They were to meet in conflict!

Gandhi came to South Africa to "try his luck" and not, as some of his biographers allege, "incidentally". According to T.K. Mahadevan he even made provision, if it should come to that, to stay on longer than the 12 months of his contract. He wrote: " ... he had come to this faraway land of opportunity not simply to do a year's job and return to the frustrations of his Rajkot life, but with a mind fully made up to recompense for his abject failure in India."[8] In South Africa Gandhi and Smuts were to meet. It was clear that they came from two different worlds. While Smuts cherished youthful visions of public fame, Gandhi had no such obvious desires. He never in his wildest dreams envisaged a career in politics. How could he? He was so shy that he would never get onto a platform in public. He would not have been able to utter a word! When he returned to India from England in 1891, his only ambition was to earn money as an attorney in order to support his family and pay his brother back for supporting him in London and his family in India. Even in this he was not successful. He failed to establish himself in the legal profession. Luck struck when, through his brother's interference, he received an invitation to go to South Africa as a member of a team of lawyers. This team would handle a case of two "rich and litigious" Indians in the Transvaal. Surendra Bhana in any case refers to Gandhi's involvement in South Africa as "an important formative period for his role in India".[9]

On his arrival in Durban, Gandhi experienced for the first time the social inequality in South Africa. "White attitudes to Indians were traditionally equivocal," wrote Brian Pottinger. "They seemed such a thoroughly non-indigenous community, and the fact that they were largely Muslim or Hindu further estranged them in a way that was not true for coloured fellow-Christians or even black Christians."[10] Gandhi was to endure numerous insults in the weeks to come. This frustrated him immensely. On his journey by train from Durban to Pretoria he was violently removed from the first-class coach, in spite of the fact that he had a first-class ticket as a barrister. A white passenger protested to his presence in first class. "He had not understood what it meant to be a British Indian gentleman in South Africa," wrote Sarah Gertrude Millin. "Nor were South Africans accustomed to Indian gentlemen. They knew only the coolie kind of Indians. They spoke of Indians as coolies—all Indians."[11] In Pretoria he was pushed from the pavement into the gutter. "His white tormentors, if only they had known it," wrote Hancock, "were pushing him into politics, with consequences incalculable for the history of South Africa, of India and the world."[12]

Gandhi was not sure if his experience in this regard was the general pattern or perhaps only isolated occurrences. Gradually his shyness slipped away and he started to hold meetings in order to discuss the situation of the Indian communities in South Africa. This was not preparation for action at all. Gandhi had no clear intention of staying on in South Africa at this stage in order to fight specifically for the rights of Indians. It is most significant that he should learn incidentally on the eve of his return to India that the national legislature of Natal was to debate a franchise bill, which would exclude Indians from voting on grounds of race and colour. He decided to cancel his passage and indulge in a series of protest actions against this. When this failed, he focused on the secretary of state for colonies in London. He consequently founded the Natal Indian Congress in May 1894.[13] The NIC became instrumental in defending the rights of Indians in Natal and it simultaneously arose public opinion in India and Britain.

Gandhi thus entered the political arena in South Africa. For many years hence, Gandhi was to fight for the Indians' cause in

South Africa directly and indirectly. In so doing, it also became a struggle for Indians in the rest of the British Empire. It was during this time that the paths of Gandhi and Smuts crossed. In his encounters with Gandhi it was only natural that Smuts' background, upbringing and academic training at Stellenbosch and Cambridge would be a decisive factor. Could these two men penetrate each other's minds in order to understand each other fully? Smuts' political vision was obstructed by the "petty and embittered politics" of the Transvaal. In Cambridge his old friend and constant adviser, H.J. Wolstenholme, was following Smuts' dawning political career with great interest. He had something to say to his young friend regarding his attitude and consequent conduct towards Gandhi:

> *You look at home and are content to hope that the agitation with you is 'dying out', but its reverberations in India and its embarrassing effect on the English Government of India, its effect on the relations of East and West, will not readily die out.... A perfectly 'epoch-making' change is taking place in the relations between East and West. Less than half a generation ago the European peoples were calmly discussing the possibility of an agreement among themselves for the 'partition of China', and the policing and commercial exploitation of the Oriental peoples generally. That has all been quietly dropped now, as a grotesque mistake.... Many of these 'inferior peoples' are showing themselves by no means inferior in capacity, and only need the teaching and training which the Japanese have already in a great measure secured, and which even the Negroes of the USA are striving after, to enable them to take up competition on equal terms with the older nations, which are coming to see that they will have to bestir themselves in order to keep their place in modern progress. And it would surely be wise statesmanship, as well as good human fellowship, to concede in time and with a good grace what is sure eventually to be won by struggle.*[14]

Truly a remarkable letter. This was an exceptional appraisal of the shape of things by a man like Wolstenholme. But nevertheless Wolstenholme did not know anything about the "spiritual and political force" of Gandhi and the power of his new strategy, *Satyagraha* or 'non-violence', which was gradually taking shape in Gandhi's life.

Indians were gradually spreading throughout the British Empire. For the next three generations the colonies were assured of a steady flow from India's vast reservoir of labour. Between 1842 and 1870 Mauritius received 351 401 Indian labourers; British Guiana a total of 76 691; Trinidad 42 519 and Jamaica 15 169. Natal only entered the market for Indian labourers in 1860.[15] During the next ten years Natal received only 6 448 labourers. By 1891 Natal's Indian population was estimated at 35 000. And by the end of the century it passed the total of the white population.[16]

Gandhi was not convinced that he should immediately enter upon a crusade for complete and immediate equality in South Africa. He was able to understand and even sympathise with the white population's viewpoint. "Our different ways of living," he wrote in 1927, "our simplicity, our contentment with small gains, our indifference to the laws of hygiene and sanitation, our slowness in keeping our surroundings clean and tidy, and our stinginess in keeping our houses in good repair—all these, combined with the difference in religion, contributed to fan the flame of antagonism."[17] Gandhi admitted that the Indians had rights but that they also had a duty. He was furthermore convinced that Indians' backwardness "in hygiene, in civic seemliness and similar matters" was of their own doing. Gandhi, however, made the point that the Indians nevertheless had the desire to uplift themselves and that the state should not obstruct their attempts to improve their standard of living.[18] Indians were debarred by law in the Orange Free State from farming and trading; in fact, any kind of work. But this was really not of any importance as Indians had been debarred completely from entering the Republic. Their numbers were thus absolutely negligible. In the Transvaal, Indians were debarred by law from obtaining citizenship and land ownership. Furthermore, they had to pay a registration fee of £3. Before they were allowed to trade they had to supply their fingerprints. "The Indian community, thus," wrote Pottinger, "was condemned in white eyes to be a dubious import; culturally esoteric and religiously suspect. Worse still, they proved to be highly industrious and thus an economic threat—in the 13 years between 1895 and 1908 the number of Indian trading licence holders in Natal trebled and there were soon over 1000 compared to the 2000 held by white colonists."[19]

Gandhi regularly opposed all the offensive laws on grounds of economic and moral indefensibility. He argued that these laws were economically damaging and that they contained principles of racial discrimination. The British government was of the same opinion. They could, however, do nothing to alter the situation. Britain had moral and legal power and they could reject the doctrine of racial discrimination in principle when it occurred in the legislatures of the British colonies.[20] The grant of responsible government to Natal in 1893 was undoubtedly due to this issue. The Franchise Bill, which Gandhi opposed, was classified as discriminatory. "Natal's legislation," wrote David Welsh, "were [was] far more concerned with economic development, with relations between the different South African states, and with the Indian menace."[21] The British government "rejected the bill in form but accepted it in fact." The reason for doing this was clear—the Queen could be advised to disallow the original bill. The colonial legislature would be permitted to work in the direction of their original purpose but in a new formulation of words. The principle was thus saved, and Gandhi consequently decided not to react against the bill. On the other hand he was not satisfied so easily with the Taxation Bill, which was debated by the Natal legislature in 1894. In essence the purpose of this bill was to force the contracted labourers back to India after the expiry of their contracts. The bill imposed on each Indian a discriminatory tax of £25. Most Indians could not pay this tax seeing that it was, in many cases, more than their annual earnings. The Natal Indian Congress organised a vigorous protest against the passing of the bill. Unfortunately the viceroy of India was eventually also dragged into the conflict.[22] Gandhi's opinion was that the viceroy's intervention had failed. He explained the situation from an Indian point of view as well as from the European perspective. He argued that it was in principle wrong to impose a tax based on racial discrimination. In 1896 Gandhi returned to India for six months. In India he published a pamphlet on the condition and situation of Indians in South Africa. He decided to put this matter on the agenda of the next annual meeting of the Natal Indian Congress. He took great effort and time to explain in depth the matter and the difficulties. "My experience has shown me," he said, "that we win justice quickest by rendering justice to the other party."[23] This *modus operandi* naturally surprised and baffled Gandhi's opponents.

Gandhi was in the process of discovering the principle of "self-suffering", which lay at the root of his technique of non-violence.[24] But it would still take ten years before he really discovered and employed the technique itself. In this time he found himself more in conflict with his fellow Indians than with the Europeans. He was in an active process of converting the Indian community in South Africa to the basic habits of cleanliness and good sanitation. These were the years during which he was arranging his life into a pattern of chastity, poverty and menial service. His political philosophy remained extremely simple. He believed that as a British subject he had certain rights as well as responsibilities. For Gandhi rights and responsibility always went hand in hand. In 1899, during the Anglo-Boer War, he organised an Indian ambulance corps and personally joined the corps at Spioenkop. He then spent a year or two in India. S.K. Gokhale, a professor in English literature, history, economics and mathematics, at the time a respected leader of moderate Indian nationalism, became his mentor in the struggle for national freedom. The most important years of his involvement in Indian affairs still lay ahead of him. Gandhi was asked to prepare a memorandum on the Indian claims and to present it to the British colonial secretary, Joseph Chamberlain. This led him to various other briefings and ultimately to his conflict with Jan Smuts.

It was the Indians in the Transvaal, rather than those in Natal, who felt in the years to come that their material interest and their self-respect was disregarded.[25] President Paul Kruger of the Transvaal ignored the British government's dismay regarding their treatment of the "Queen's Indian subjects" residing in the Transvaal.[26] After they had won the Anglo-Boer War, Alfred Milner, British high commissioner in South Africa, treated the Indians in the Transvaal in no different manner.[27] Gandhi inspired the Indians to protest against this breach of faith. "What the Indians pray for is very little," Gandhi said. "They agreed the British race should be the dominant race in South Africa. They ask for no political power. They agree to the principle of restricting the influx of cheap labour, no matter from what source it may come. All they ask for is freedom for those that are now settled and those that may be allowed to come in future to trade, to move about, and to hold landed property without any hindrance save the ordinary legal requirements. And they ask for abrogation of legislation that imposes disabilities on them because they wear a brown skin."[28] It was now time for the Milner administration to fulfil the promises made to the Indians by the British government. Lord Milner, Lord Selborne and several other high officials admitted that promises were made. They nevertheless held the viewpoint that for the future of the Transvaal it would be disastrous if it were to be handed over to "a 'horde' of Asiatics".[29]

It is interesting to note that the laws of the old Republic under Kruger stayed virtually unaltered on the statute book. The laws were even enforced against the Indians with an "efficiency which had never been known in republican times". An Asian department was specially created to enforce the laws. In 1906 the department drew up a new code of extreme stringency. The code was embodied in the Asiatic Law Amendment Ordinance—referred to by the Indians as the "Black Ordinance". Basically these measures aimed at closing the Transvaal to future Indian immigrants and removing all illegal Indian residents in the Transvaal. All Indians were to apply for new certificates of registration. These certificates were to be carried on their person and produced on the demand of any official or policeman. But the whites were unprepared to accept the Indians as equals. In the true sense of the word, they used their monopoly of political power to handicap the brown men from another part of the Empire. In October 1906 Smuts asserted: "The Asiatic cancer, which has already eaten so deeply into the vitals of South Africa, ought to be resolutely eradicated."[30] And in an election speech at Standerton in January 1907, Louis Botha put it bluntly: "If my party is returned to office, we will undertake to drive the coolies out of the country within four years."[31]

Gandhi felt that these regulations were far more stringent than the pass laws imposed upon the African population. "I have never known legislation of this nature," he said, "being directed against free men in any part of the world."[32] The Black Ordinance became the Black Act, with effect as from 1 July 1907. Only a minority of the Indian population in the Transvaal registered. This, *inter alia,* was an indication that there was a vast number of Indians illegally in the Transvaal. It was further estimated that there were approximately 9 000 Indians who had set themselves against the law. How would the Transvaal government handle this extremely thorny problem? The fact that the coloured and native section of the population was watching developments closely complicated the whole affair even more. The possibility that a perception could develop amongst these people that passive resistance, which was something uncommon in the South African political context, could be an instrument in achieving their own political goals, had to be prevented by the Transvaal government at all times and at all cost. This was of special concern to Lord Selborne, British high commissioner in South Africa. "It filled him with foreboding," wrote Hancock, "because the coloured people and the educated natives were watching the struggle, realising 'that they have an instrument in their hands—that is, combination and passive resistance—of which they had not previously thought'."[33] It was Smuts' ultimate responsibility to handle the extremely difficult Indian problem.

The responsibilities of the members of the government, Botha as prime minister, and Jacob de Villiers as attorney general, were equal to that of Smuts. But Smuts took the main burden upon himself. He was of the opinion that it would be more effective "to strike at the head, not at the tail" of the problem. This implied legal action against the leaders. But, true to his nature, Smuts first wanted to explore the possibility of a compromise, before committing to a specific policy. First and foremost he sought the advice of Lord Selborne, who held the same responsibility as Smuts for the developing situation. The Black Act was merely a repetition of Lord Selborne's own ordinance of the previous year.[34] Lord Selborne never expected such a passionate resistance from the Indians. Smuts feared the possible reaction of the other population groups. He argued that the restriction of future Indian immigration was an absolute necessity—it was actually "the whole object of the legislation". In this respect Lord Selborne argued:

> *But the Asiatics, through the mouth of Mr Gandhi, demand the total repeal of the existing Act. This, in my opinion, would never be permitted by Parliament, and ought never to be permitted by Parliament. The Asiatic is a very bad person from whom to run away, and I do not think that any such repeal would be consistent with the self-respect of the Government or of Parliament. But if the Asiatics are at last prepared to be reasonable, then I would make the way easy for them. The one simple object of the Government is to get them registered so that the Government may control future immigration.[35]*

In the meantime Gandhi was preparing himself and his fellow Indians for reaction. He was promoting a complete new revolutionary technique; a technique, which Europeans would find difficult to understand. Only after proving its efficiency in action would they understand the technique in full. Gandhi contradicted those who argued that he had decided on "passive resistance". They said that he had no other option because the Indians in South Africa had no arms, no votes and they were few in number and consequently weak. Gandhi denied all this emphatically.[36] The Indians were, according to Gandhi, not weak, and definitely not passive. As a matter of fact, he said, they were strong and active. He was convinced that they were in the position of the strongest force imaginable—"soul force", in contrast with the so-called inferior instrument of conflict, "brute force". Gandhi realised that the phrase "passive resistance" was open for misconception. He therefore started looking for a more appropriate word. Through a competition in a newspaper, *Sadagraha* was suggested. Gandhi changed it to *Satyagraha,* which meant for him the following: "Truth *(satya)* implies love, and firmness *(agraha)* engenders and therefore serves as a synonym for force. I thus began to call the Indian movement 'Satyagraha', that is to say, the Force which is born of Truth and Love or non-violence."[37] It must be kept in mind that Smuts himself believed in "soul force".

Dealing with violence came naturally to Smuts. Passive resistance was something completely different. He just did not know how to deal with it and he said regarding Gandhi's political *modus operandi*:

> *I must frankly admit that his (Gandhi's) activities at that time were very trying to me—Gandhi—showed a new technique—his method was deliberately to break the law and to organise his followers into a mass movement—for him everything went according to plan. For me—the defender of law and order—there was the usual trying situation, the odium of carrying out a law which had not strong public support, and finally the discomfiture when the law was repealed.*[38]

Gandhi's passive behaviour really puzzled Smuts. It was extremely unpredictable. He threatened Gandhi, but this made no impression on him. As a matter of fact, he kept calm and collected. When Smuts imprisoned a number of Indians, Gandhi accompanied them. Gandhi was fully committed to his people.

Many other players in politics realised the difficult situation Smuts was in. They gave him moral support and sound advice. He appreciated all this, but did not always, true to his nature, react positively. Lord Selborne came straight to the point: "At the same time Mr Gandhi ardently desires martyrdom, and when a man ardently desires such a thing under such circumstances one's natural instinct is not to give it to him. Still, that consideration must be balanced against others."[39] And from London Sir Richard Solomon conveyed the ideas of Winston Churchill, under-secretary of state, on this matter:

Churchill returned from East Africa last week and I lunched with him two days after his return when he had a long talk with me on this vexed question. He will strongly support your Government on its policy of preventing further immigration of Asiatics into the Transvaal and on the policy of compelling those lawfully in the country to register as the only method of properly carrying out the Immigration Act.[40]

John X. Merriman shared Churchill's opinion. He had no love for the Indians, but he could nevertheless not sanction mere "petty persecution". Merriman wrote:

I agree with you in looking on this India business as a very serious and unpleasant one.... Rightly or wrongly a certain number of these people have been allowed to settle down, acquire property, and carry on their avocations. Is it worthwhile to harry them by imposing what may be considered vexatious regulations, provided that you can obtain a registration that will secure you against any further influx by other means?... If you persist as you are entitled to do, you will succeed but I much fear that you will alienate the bulk of liberal opinion in England, you will give the Imperial Government a most serious blow in her most vital part ... India, and you will above all furnish a pretext for a great deal of mischievous interference in Native matters....[41]

For the time being Smuts decided to uphold the law as it stood.[42] By the end of January 1907 approximately 150 *Satyagrahis* were in prison. Mr Albert Cartwright, the editor of the *Transvaal Leader,* was constantly in touch with Smuts and Gandhi in an attempt to bring them to a compromise.[43] Smuts made a speech in Pretoria on 28 January in which he foretold an amicable settlement. Gandhi and two of his associates reacted to Smuts' speech in a letter the next day—also dated 28 January:

Our opposition has never been directed so much against the fingerprint requirements Regulations under the Act, in so far as such fingerprints were deemed necessary for the identification of Asiatics who could not very well be otherwise identified, as against the element of compulsion in the Act itself. On that ground we have repeatedly offered to undergo voluntary registration if the Act were repealed.[44]

The exchange of letters between Smuts and Gandhi ultimately led to a personal meeting. In spite of their differences there was much that these two had in common, which could form a firm basis for constructive negotiation. On 30 January 1908 the Johannesburg chief of police personally guided Gandhi from his prison cell to Pretoria.[45] Smuts received Gandhi with notable respect and courtesy. "I could never entertain a dislike for your people," Smuts said to Gandhi. "But I must do my duty ... I have consulted General Botha also, and I assure you that I will repeal the Asiatic Act as soon as most of you have undergone voluntary registration."[46] Their meeting lasted for about two hours. There is no written record of this meeting. It is nevertheless clear from Gandhi's reaction to their discussion that there must have been a positive atmosphere throughout. There was a Cabinet meeting in the afternoon and Gandhi waited in the anteroom. After a long wait he was once again summoned to Smuts' office at about seven o'clock. Smuts told Gandhi that the Cabinet had approved their agreement. On Smuts' indication that the meeting was over, Gandhi asked: "Where am I to go?" Smuts laughed and assured him: "You are free this very moment. I am telephoning the prison officials to release the other prisoners. But I must advise you not to go in for many meetings or demonstrations."[47]

Gandhi was a happy man. He explained the nature of his agreement with Smuts to the Indians at late-night meetings. He argued that this was in essence a victory for the community. In future all registration would be on a voluntary basis. He explained further that the Black Act would be repealed as soon as Parliament resumed its work.[48] But as was usually the case with Gandhi, he pointed out that now the community also had a responsibility. "We must register voluntarily in order to show that we do not intend to bring a single Indian into the

Transvaal surreptitiously or by fraud. And it is only when we have thus worthily fulfilled our part that we shall reap the real fruit of our victory."[49]

Smuts introduced a bill validating the voluntary certificates, but he did not repeal the Black Act. Gandhi was extremely upset with this and accused Smuts not only of a breach of promise but also of ungentlemanly behaviour.[50] He then met with the mediator, Albert Cartwright. "Really, I cannot understand this man (Smuts) at all," Cartwright said. "I perfectly remember that he promised to repeal the Asiatic Act. I will do my best, but you know nothing can move General Smuts when he has once taken up a stand."[51] Smuts was not moved. The situation was extremely tense. Gandhi wrote articles in the *Indian Opinion* under the caption *Foul Play*. He called Smuts a "heartless man".[52] Smuts most probably hoped and even intended to repeal the Black Act and, without making any firm promise, had mentioned it to Gandhi. But later he found himself unable to carry through his intentions. Gandhi now firmly believed that Smuts had deceived him. He accused Smuts of a "breach of faith". This alone was ample justification for Gandhi to resume the struggle. "I am very sorry at the revival of the Asiatic agitation," wrote Richard Solomon to Smuts. "I think Gandhi is a dangerous fellow."[53]

Many years later Gandhi changed his attitude towards Smuts on this issue. He definitely had second thoughts about Smuts. Gandhi wrote of Smuts:

Even today, I look upon the incident as a breach of faith from the Indian community's standpoint. However, I have placed a mark of interrogation after the phrase, as in point of fact the General's action did not perhaps amount to an intentional breach of faith. It could not be described as a breach of faith if the intention was absent. My experience of General Smuts in 1913 – 14 did not then seem bitter and does not seem so to me today when I can think of the past events with greater detachment. It is quite possible that in behaving to the Indians as he did in 1908 General Smuts was not guilty of a deliberate breach of faith.[54]

Gandhi was again arrested because he could not, on request, submit his registration certificate on 25 February 1909. He was fined £50 or three months imprisonment with hard labour. He managed to do much reading in his spare time. From Smuts he received a gift of two religious books. After the completion of his three-month sentence, Gandhi was released from prison. To prevent a demonstration he was released early in the morning. On his arrival in Parktown, *en route* to Johannesburg, Gandhi was enthusiastically greeted at a meeting by a number of excited supporters.

The majority of Gandhi's biographers seized incidents like these to boost his image. This resulted in a "Gandhi-centredness" which did not allow "a proper assessment of the role of numerous other individuals and groups"— "which made Gandhi appear the popular leader overcoming all obstacles".[55] In contrast to the majority of Gandhi's biographers T.K. Mahaderan and Maureen Swan portray a more objective and critical approach to Gandhi. Mahadevan states that Gandhi "was not quite as modest as biographers have made him out to be" and that the *chapeau* incident, when he attended a court case in Durban as a mere interloper, was part of Gandhi's "carefully premeditated plan" to win publicity—"he was craving publicity".[56] Mahaderan wrote further "that the magic spell of Gandhi lulled their critical faculties to sleep and they did not think it needful to subject his account".[57] Swan thought that Gandhi was merely "an efficient organiser", and that he could hardly be called a "leader", at least not before 1906—his leadership role in South Africa "has been consistently over-rated".[58]

Gandhi found it increasingly difficult to keep the ongoing interest of his followers. The rich trading class lost their trust and interest in Ghandi and his cause. It was difficult for them to submit themselves without active protest to the harsh measures that the government was imposing on them. These measures were a real threat to the *Satyagraha* movement. But there was even a bigger and more dangerous threat emerging for the Indians in South Africa. A Union of South Africa was in sight, which meant that the anti-Indian tendencies of the colonies would be incorporated nationally. This would place the Indians in South Africa in a far worse situation.

On the eve of the creation of the Union Smuts and Louis Botha were in London. At the same time Gandhi and Sheth Haji Habib, a Muslim—the latter sent to London to voice the interests of South African Indians—arrived in Southampton on 10 July. In a meeting Smuts told Arthur Oliver Russell (the second Baron of Ampthill, a former acting viceroy of India, and a member of the House of Lords), that he could grant some minor concessions, which included the entry of six "approved Asiatics" per year on temporary permits only. Smuts was unwilling to repeal the Asiatic Act or the Immigration Act. He bluntly refused to remove the racial bar from the law. "We cannot recognise in our legislation," Smuts told Lord Crew on 26 August, "the equal rights of all alike to emigrate to South Africa. Under our special circumstances we leave the door open as wide as possible to white immigrants, but we could never do the same to Asiatic immigrants."[59] The Baron of Ampthill advised Gandhi to accept what Smuts had to offer them, although they were merely minor concessions. The baron acted as their intermediary with influential men in the Foreign and Colonial Office. For Gandhi all hope for successful negotiation in London had faded. He decided to return to South Africa. Gandhi was convinced that as subjects of the British Empire all Indians were entitled to equal rights. He again accused Smuts of being unwilling to grant Indians equality in the eyes of the law.

The South African government introduced a new bill into Parliament in February 1911, which was to replace Act 2 of 1907. Smuts and Gandhi exchanged telegrams and letters. Gandhi went to Cape Town on 27 March and stayed there for virtually the whole of April. He tried his utmost to rally support for the modifications he had proposed to the bill, and on 19 April he met Smuts for an interview. Smuts was friendly towards Gandhi. Gandhi kept notes of this interview in which Smuts did most of the talking. Smuts *inter alia* said to Gandhi:

You as a lawyer will understand when I tell you that it is difficult to carry out your alternative suggestion ... Gandhi, my boy, I am sorry for you. You know I want peace ... Parliament will not pass such a bill, which I like and which I consider is fair. I shall try, but I may fail to pass it during this session. All the members want to go home. And the Free State members are still opposed to admitting any Asiatic.

You have a right to fight in your own way. But this country is the Kaffirs', where whites are a handful. We do not want Asia to come in. Now that Natal won't have immigration, I am hopeful of solving this question. But how can we hold out against you? I have read your pamphlet. You are a simple-living and frugal race, in many respects more intelligent than we are. You belong to a civilisation that is thousands of years old. Ours, as you say, is but an experiment. Who knows but that the whole damned thing will perish before long. But you see why we do not want Asia here.[60]

In October 1911 a new Immigration Bill was introduced in the Union Parliament. Although the bill was in some respects more satisfactory than the previous one, the Indians still resented it because in their opinion the bill did not fulfil Smuts' promise. Although the struggle was dropped temporarily, they made it clear that they would not submit to the Black Act. They would rather suffer the consequences brought about by their refusal.

In the meantime the governments of the Union and of India agreed in 1912 that G.K. Gokhale should go to South Africa to study the Indians' conditions. Gokhale was well received in South Africa by the white people as well as by the Indians.[61] On the eve of his return to India, Gokhale had constructive talks with the South African government. Early the next year the Union government introduced legislation into Parliament to transfer the regulation of Indian affairs from the provinces to the Union. The government wanted, at the same time, to rationalise and humanise the entire system. At long last the Transvaal's Black Act, which had been the great stumbling block, disappeared. Restricting Asian immigration was to be based explicitly and exclusively on economic and social grounds. All this was undoubtedly a significant step in the direction of removing conflict. But Gandhi would not admit it! His view was that the Union government was committing new aggressions towards the Indians. He mentioned the Indians in the Orange Free State who were, according to him, "left ... in precisely the same position as before". "But the Indians of the Free State were a mere handful," wrote Hancock, "and the legalistic argument which Gandhi advanced on their behalf was unlikely to arouse the masses."[62] He had to find a slogan that would appeal to mass emotion. Gandhi found it in the discriminatory £3 tax imposed upon the Indians of Natal nearly 20 years earlier.[63] Referring to Gandhi and the £3 tax Swan wrote: "Gandhi's position on the hardships of the £3 tax payers was less clear-cut however, and it seems unlikely that at this time he had any real understanding of the problems faced by Indian workers during the post-war depression."[64] He said that Smuts had again broken his promise, because he promised Gokhale that the £3 tax would be repealed.

By now Smuts was anxious to settle the Indian question. The Union government had reacted positively to Gandhi's demands. But Smuts told Gandhi that it was politically necessary that a recommendation regarding the demands should come from a properly constituted enquiry commission.[65] Gandhi could personally boycott the commission, Smuts told him, but he must not stand in the way of Indians who would want to appear before the commission. And, in addition, *Satyagraha* should be suspended. Gandhi held meetings at various places to persuade the Indians to accept the terms of the agreement. Smuts did his utmost to persuade the Union government to approach the problem "in a non-controversial spirit". Gandhi and Smuts finally exchanged letters on 30 June 1914 and in so doing they confirmed the terms of a complete agreement—the so-called Smuts-Gandhi Agreement.[66] Hereafter the document was incorporated into the Indian Relief Bill and submitted to the Union Parliament.[67] Referring to this *modus operandi* Fischer wrote:

> *The settlement was a compromise which pleased both sides. Gandhi noted that the Indians would still be 'cooped up' in their provinces, they could not buy gold, they could not hold land in the Transvaal, and they had difficulty in obtaining trade licences. But he regarded the agreement as the 'Magna Carta' of South African Indians.*[68]

Having won a battle, which lasted for almost 12 years, Gandhi boarded a ship for England on 18 July 1914.[69] Gandhi felt that he had finished his work in South Africa. He and his wife were now both 45 years of age. On Gandhi's departure Smuts wrote: "The saint has left our shores, I sincerely hope for ever."[70] While in prison Gandhi made a pair of sandals, which he asked Miss Schlesin and Polak to deliver to Smuts as a gift. Smuts wore the sandals every summer at his Doornkloof farm in Irene, near Pretoria. When Smuts and Gandhi met, many years later in London, they exchanged nostalgic memories of South Africa. "I did not give you such a bad time as you gave me," Smuts remarked to Gandhi with a twinkle in his blue eyes.[71]

Smuts visited London again during the Second World War. He and Churchill had dinner together. Smuts' opinion of Gandhi had changed considerably through the years. Gandhi's name came up during dinner. Smuts initially raised the subject. At first there was no reaction from the prime minister. Smuts hinted that big changes in the world were coming:[72]

P.M.   As I get older I begin to see a pattern of things.

SMUTS: There is a pattern in history, though it is not easy to see or follow.

SMUTS: (Of Gandhi) He is a man of God. You and I are mundane people. Gandhi has appealed to religious motives. You never have. That is where you have failed.

P.M.   (With a grin) I have made more bishops than anyone since St Augustine.

But Smuts did not smile. His face was very grave.

It was common knowledge that there was no love lost between Churchill and Gandhi. Churchill always referred to Gandhi as the "half-naked fakir".[73] From the time he became the King's first minister in 1940 to the day his party went out of office in 1945, Churchill was in conflict with Gandhi. Churchill once said: "Gandhism and all that it stands for must ultimately be grappled with and finally crushed."[74] Churchill's attitude towards Gandhi can be explained on the basis of India's struggle for independence. "I have not become the King's first minister," Churchill said on 10 November 1942, "in order to preside at the liquidation of the British Empire."[75] Churchill had made up his mind.

In 1939 Smuts was invited to contribute to a Gandhi memorial volume. Gandhi was 70 years of age. Smuts was then a world famous statesman and war leader. He wrote of Gandhi:

> *It was my fate to be the antagonist of a man for whom even then I had the highest respect. ... I must frankly admit that his activities at that time were very trying to me. Together with other South African leaders I was then busily engaged on the task of welding the old Colonies into a unified State. ... It was a colossal work which took up every moment of my time. Suddenly in the midst of all those engrossing preoccupations Gandhi raised a most troublesome issue. We had a skeleton in our cupboard....* [76]

After a Hindu fanatic assassinated Gandhi on 30 January 1948, Smuts sent a simple tribute: "A prince among us has passed."[77]

1. Louis Fischer, *The Life of Mahatma Gandhi,* 23 – 26.
2. W.K. Hancock, *Smuts, I. The Sanguine Years, 1870 – 1919,* 322.
3. *Ibid.*
4. *Ibid.,* 323.
5. *Ibid.*
6. *Ibid.*
7. *Ibid.*
8. K. Mahadevan, *The year of the Phoenix,* 24. Louis Fischer, *The Life of Mahatma Gandhi,* 57.
9. Surendrah Bhana, *Gandhi in South Africa.* South African Historical Journal, 18 (1986), 229. Hancock, 1, 324.
10. Brian Pottinger, *The Imperial Presidency. P.W. Botha, the first 10 years,* 161. Fischer, 57.

11. Sarah Gertrude Millin, *General Smuts.* Volume 1, 233.
12. Hancock, 324.
13. Trewhella Cameron, *A New Illustrated History of South Africa,* 222. Pottinger, 295.
14. *Smuts Papers,* Volume II, 14 May 1909, 569 – 573.
15. Cameron, 176. David Welsh, *The Roots of Segregation. Native Policy in Colonial Natal, 1845 – 1910,* 180.
16. Hancock, 1, 325. Fischer, 64.
17. Hancock, 326.
18. *Ibid.*
19. Pottinger, 161.
20. Hancock, 327.
21. Welsh, 229.
22. Hancock, 1, 327.
23. *Ibid.*
24. Cameron, 226, 232. Millin, 1, 237.
25. Cameron, 227.
26. Millin, 1, 234 – 235.
27. *Ibid.,* 237.
28. Hancock, 1, 328.
29. *Ibid.,* 329.
30. Fischer, 78.
31. Bridglal Pachai, *The South African Indian Question, 1860 – 1971,* 36.
32. Hancock, 329.
33. *Ibid.,* 331.
34. *Ibid.*
35. *Ibid.,* 332.
36. *Ibid.,* 330.
37. *Ibid.* Maureen Swan, Gandhi. *The South African Experience,* 168.
38. Fisher, 152.
39. Smuts Papers, Volume II, 9 December 1907, 368.
40. Smuts Papers, Volume II, 24 January 1908, 398.
41. Smuts Papers, Volume II, 3 January 1908, 395.
42. Kenneth Ingham, *Jan Christian Smuts. The Conscience of a South African,* 56.
43. Fischer, 105.
44. Hancock, 1, 333.

45. Fischer, 106.
46. Yogesh, Chadha, *Rediscovering Gandhi,* 128.
47. *Ibid.,* 129. Fischer, 106.
48. Fischer, 105.
49. Chadha, 130.
50. *Ibid.,* 131. Millin, 1, 244.
51. Chadha, 131.
52. Millin, 243 – 244.
53. Smuts Papers, Volume II, 10 September 1908, 516.
54. Hancock, 338.
55. Bhana, 1.
56. Mahaderan, 26 – 27. Bhana, 231.
57. Mahaderan, 27.
58. Swan, 270. Bhana, 233 – 234.
59. Chadha, 143 – 144.
60. *Ibid.,* 173.
61. Fischer, 139. Hancock, 341.
62. Hancock, 341.
63. Ingham, 71. D.W. Kruger, *The Making of a Nation. A History of the Union of SouthAfrica, 1910 – 1961,* 77.
64. Swan, 193, 196.
65. Chadha, 188. Fischer, 147.
66. Fischer, 150.
67. Kruger, 77. Ingham, 73.
68. Fischer, 150.
69. *Ibid.*
70. Hancock, 1, 345.
71. Chadha, 314.
72. *Ibid.,* 382. Lord Moran, *Winston Churchill. The Struggle for Survival, 1940 – 1965. From the Diaries of Lord Moran,* 52.
73. Larry Collins, *et al, Freedom at Midnight,* 81.
74. Fischer, 452.
75. Collins, *et al,* 71.
76. Hancock, 1, 346 – 347.
77. Collins, *et al,* 513.

Eamon de Valera. (Trustee of the Eamon de Valera Papers)

7

Eamon de Valera

"It is hopeless to identify Ireland with a mad fellow
like De Valera."
J.C. Smuts (Smuts Papers, V, 318)

"If any man could convince (me) of the advantages of
dominion status for Ireland, it was Smuts."
Eamon de Valera (Mansergh, *The Commonwealth
Experience*, 377 – 378)

At the end of the First World War there were numerous strong forces within the British Empire working towards fundamental changes in the basic constitutional structure of the Empire. As early as 1902, Jan Smuts foresaw a new imperial order. He was still uncertain at that early stage if Empire was the right name for the free and fraternal association that he envisaged. In the midst of the raging war Lionel Curtis, Alfred Milner and the *Round Table* were actively canvassing for the transformation of the Empire into a federation. They adopted a desperate now-or-never "Federate or Disintegrate" policy.[1] Smuts stood in opposition to this concept and this brought him in direct confrontation with

Premier Hughes of Australia who was an enthusiastic campaigner for a federation.

It was clear that Smuts saw beyond the demands of war. High up on his agenda were the national aspirations of the separate self-governing dominions—"scattered and various as they were". It was not strange that Smuts initiated a proposal brought forward by Sir Robert Borden, premier of Canada, to the effect that after the War a readjustment should be made in the constitutional relations of the component parts of the Empire. During that time it was put on record that any such readjustment "should be based on a full recognition of the dominions as autonomous nations of an Imperial Commonwealth."[2] Smuts emphasised the transformation of the British Commonwealth as well as the anomalous legal structure of former colonial subordination. "Too many of the old ideas," Smuts said, "still cling to the new organism which is growing. I think that although in practice there is great freedom, in actual theory the status of dominions is of subject character ... theory still permeates practice to some extent."[3] The "basis of freedom" of the dominion had to be assured. Naturally this meant that specific machinery for the basis of continuous consultation would have to be devised.

Smuts would play a significant role in the transformation of the British Empire. In addressing members of both Houses of Parliament at a banquet, given in his honour on 15 May 1917, Smuts considerably reinforced the anti-federalism cause:

> ... *we come to see the so-called dominions, a number of nations and states almost sovereign, almost independent, who govern themselves and who all belong to this group of this community of nations, which I prefer to call the British Commonwealth of Nations.... The man who would discover the real appropriate name for this vast system of entities would be doing a great service not only to this country, but to constitutional theory.*[4]

In 1921 Smuts presented a memorandum on constitutional relations of the British Commonwealth to L.S. Amery, British secretary of state.[5] Amery responded very positively to Smuts' memorandum. "I have read your draft memorandum," he wrote to Smuts, "with the greatest interest and with complete agreement on the main points."[6] Smuts wanted the British Empire to change its name to British Commonwealth. In this atmosphere of proposed change there were senior civil servants in London who did not regard Smuts in the same appreciative light as their political leaders. They saw Smuts as a danger to the British Empire, not because he did not care for it but because they were of the opinion that he did not understand it.[7]

With the foregoing as background, it is quite understandable why Smuts was considered a champion of national freedom for Ireland. He saw "national freedom" for Ireland as part of the constitutional evolution in the Empire, and he was eager to identify himself with it. "Smuts regarded the Irish question," wrote Sheila Lawlor, "in the context of the 'empire as a whole', and considered the present situation to be an 'unmeasured calamity' and a 'negation of all the principles of government which we have professed as the basis of empire'."[8] In his first major contribution to British politics, Smuts proposed a convention on the South African model—where the Irish should settle things for themselves. British prime minister, Lloyd George, and J. Redmond, chairman of the Irish Parliamentary Party, agreed with this in principle. This proposal did not materialise in the true sense of the word. On the eve of his return to South Africa, in July 1919, after two-and-a-half years of service in Europe, which gave him the status of an international statesman, he made it clear that he would be campaigning actively for that cause.[9] This was actually Smuts' first significant contribution to British politics. The convention could certainly not contribute to a settlement—it only bought time.[10] In his farewell address to the people of Britain he emphasised "that the Irish wound was poisoning their whole system". Smuts believed that freedom held the key to solving the acute problem. He reminded them that it was the remedy in his own country and also in other parts of the British Empire. "Unless," Smuts concluded, "that remedy were applied in Ireland, the British Empire must cease to exist."[11]

Smuts was disappointed and to a certain extent disturbed and disillusioned when he discovered that after a period of two years there was no sign of the British government moving in a clear and constructive direction to solve the political deadlock with Ireland. The whole situation was becoming increasingly worse. Amidst growing frustration, Dàil Eireann, the Irish Parliament, issued a declaration of Irish independence in January 1919. A Republican government was established with its own courts, executive departments and armed forces. This government took shape within the boundaries of the United Kingdom! The British government could not allow these constitutional developments to mature. In mid-1920 they showed their determination to destroy the new Irish state by force. Dàil Eireann denounced the Government of Ireland Act promulgated by the British government in December 1920. The act provided for limited Home Rule in Ireland—North and South. Dàil Eireann argued that the act was simply "a new British aggression against independent and united Ireland."[12] Tension and violence between Britain and Ireland increased rapidly.

In spite of all the hostilities earnest and serious attempts were made to solve the growing crisis, which had been building up to a most dangerous situation. In Ireland it was Sir Horace Plunkett, and his Irish Dominion League, who reached out with optimism to the concept of the Commonwealth as expounded by Smuts. Fortunately it materialised that a negotiated settlement could not be ruled out completely. In Britain there was strong opposition against the attempts to subdue Ireland by force. It was not only the Liberal newspapers that reacted. *The Times* and the *Round Table* also took a firm stance against British military force. Labour politicians and the Asquithian Liberals joined forces with Lord Robert Cecil and other prominent conservatives in denouncing any "British frightfulness in Ireland". King George V made it very clear to his ministers that he was severely opposed to a "policy of reprisals". In Britain and the dominions overseas public opinion showed an increase in dismay in the succeeding months. "If the British government can only be preserved by such means," declared the *Round Table,* "it would become a negation of the principle for which it has stood."[13] It is interesting to note that although the British government persisted in its Irish policy, it gradually started to explore the possibility of negotiation. This was kept a close secret, of course.

When Smuts arrived in London for the Imperial Conference of 1921, he was already regarded as an international statesman with high prestige (a member of Lloyd George's War Cabinet; offered the high command of the Allied Forces in Palestine during World War I; offered a seat in the House of Commons by the prime minister; and by drafting a memorandum on the constitutional relations of the British Commonwealth). His standing as statesman in the British Commonwealth was unprecedented. No wonder it proved inevitable that he would become involved in attempts to solve the Anglo-Irish problem. Apart from Smuts' international prestige, a kind of affinity had developed between the Afrikaners and the Irish since the end of the Anglo-Boer War in 1902. "Whenever England goes on her mission of Empire, we meet and we strike at her," wrote Patrick Pearce in 1914, "yesterday it was on the South African veldt, tomorrow it may be on the streets of Dublin."[14]

Smuts had quite a number of Irish friends. In early 1914, when the Home Rule crisis was at its height, Tom Casement wrote to Smuts: "It is a great pity you and General Botha are not in power (in Ireland)."[15] And on 18 April 1917 Mrs A.S. Green, 36 Grosvenor Road, Westminster, wrote to him:

> *My dear General Smuts, It will be delightful to see you on Thursday at five o'clock. Colonel Moore will be here, and a couple of Irish friends who are deeply concerned in the present movement to attempt an Irish settlement. They are George Russell, an ally for many years of Sir Horace Plunkett, and Editor of the Co-operative paper The Homestead; and Mr (J) Douglas, a very good representative of the young men, who ought now to be given their turn. All the counsels in Ireland have been of late years too much in the hands of the old, whose boast of forty years of service in the House of Commons ought to incline them to give a little way for the new and young spirit of the country.*[16]

Smuts advised Plunkett concerning the Irish Convention and while attending the Paris Conference in 1919, he warned that the survival of the Empire depended on the Irish issue being settled. In response to this warning Plunkett wrote to Smuts in April 1921: "Twice during the war you were kind enough to listen to my appeal for help in getting the Irish problem settled. Few pronouncements upon that old sore in recent times have had a more profound effect than your warning to the Empire, when you last left Europe, that an unsettled Ireland would prove its ruin."[17] Smuts was constantly informed about the growing violence in the country by George Russell, Colonel Maurice Moore, Tom Casement and Father T. Ryan—the latter being an Irish priest based in South Africa.

Smuts' involvement in the ongoing conflict between Ireland and the British government brought him in direct contact with Eamon de Valera—the man who later became the first president of the Irish Republic. De Valera, born in the United States, educated at Blackrock Intermediate College; University College, Dublin; the National University and Trinity College, Dublin, was one of the foremost fighters for Irish independence in the early 19th century. It was said that De Valera "spilled both English and Irish blood to found the Republic of Ireland."[18] Sir John Wheeler-Bennett wrote concerning De Valera:

> *Thus when Eamon de Valera completed his education and reached manhood, the stage was being set for the penultimate tragedy in Anglo-Irish relations, and the young man was ripe and eager to join the struggle for Irish freedom.*[19]

In 1905 Arthur Griffith, a political journalist, founded the Sinn Fein political movement in an attempt to canalise Irish nationalism. Conscription gave Sinn Fein such a "charge of wrathful energy" that it became the dominant political force in Ireland. De Valera later closely associated himself with Sinn Fein.

De Valera's political thoughts as a young man were initially more that of a Nationalist rather than that of a Republican. The latter only developed at a later and more mature stage in his life. De Valera was a founder member of the Irish Volunteers in January 1913. On 24 April 1916 the Irish experienced the Easter Rising against the British presence in Ireland. The rising was ill-conceived and extremely ill-prepared. De Valera was the last commandant to surrender. He was sentenced to death on 8 May 1916. The fact that he did not share the fate of his fellow commandants was perhaps, though this has never been confirmed, because he had been born, and still remained, a United States citizen. The American Consul in Ireland intervened on his behalf.

The entry of the United States into the First World War stimulated British efforts to solve Irish problems. Royal amnesty consequently freed Sinn Fein prisoners held in British gaols. De Valera returned to Dublin and eventually became Sinn Fein MP for East Clare. In 1917 De Valera was elected president of Sinn Fein and the Irish Volunteers. Later that year De Valera and other leaders were imprisoned in Lincoln Gaol because Sinn Fein activities had become a threat to the British government. On 11 June 1919 De Valera visited New York to gain recognition for the Irish government. Although he failed to do so, he nevertheless managed to raise funds for the Irish cause. De Valera returned secretly to Dublin on 23 December 1920. In the same month the Government of Ireland Act was promulgated, and it made provision for separate Parliaments in Dublin and Belfast, and for a joint Council of Ireland.

Various Irish factions were anxious about involving Smuts in their struggle for independence. Smuts symbolised, more than any other dominion prime minister, an alternative vision of a Commonwealth of Nations, which could be held together by sentiment. This was, as earlier indicated, in clear opposition to several Imperialists who wanted to centralise the Empire. During and after the War Smuts developed and established a standing, which resulted in his council being keenly sought. Plunkett assured Smuts that he would be more acceptable to the majority of the Irish people by assisting them with their constitutional problems than any other world statesman.

The Irish government commissioned Colonel Maurice Moore, shortly before the Imperial Conference of June 1921, to South Africa in order "to persuade General Smuts and the other South African ministers, who were expected to attend an Imperial Conference during the summer, to advocate the cause of Ireland and obtain a settlement between the two nations favourable to the complete independence of Ireland."[20] Later Moore reported to De Valera on his discussions with the concerned parties in South Africa. He brought it to De Valera's attention that the Smuts government abandoned the idea of an independent republic in South Africa and that it is therefore most unlikely that Smuts and his colleagues would be inclined to advocate an independent republic in Ireland. He was nevertheless of the opinion that "the most to be expected from them would be to press for independence from the British Parliament and a connection only by the Crown."[21]

Smuts arrived in England on Saturday, 11 June 1921. He made no pronouncement on Ireland but quietly brought himself up to date with the Irish news. It was at this stage, and already known to the British government, that he was *inter alia* opposed to the imprisonment of Eamon de Valera. Smuts was in favour of the release of the Sinn Fein leadership. He was clearly trying to create an atmosphere in which negotiations could proceed. "His Majesty is impressed," the King's secretary told Smuts, "with the belief that you of all men will be able to induce Mr de Valera to a settlement."[22]

Lloyd George's lack of enthusiasm was obvious regarding the negotiations with the Irish. "We have murder by the throat," declared Lloyd George at the Guild Hall Banquet in November 1920. And Sir Hamer Greenwood, chief secretary for Ireland, declared that the British government would not rest, "till we have knocked the last revolver from the last assassin's hand".[23] The King dissociated himself from this line of thinking. Two days after his arrival in London a situation suddenly emerged which gave Smuts the opportunity for action and consequent involvement in the Anglo-Irish question. He wrote to his wife at Doornkloof:

On Monday I was at Windsor Castle for lunch—Smartt, Mentz and I with the King, the Queen and Princess Mary. It was very sociable and pleasant. After lunch the other two went over the palace, but I sat talking with the King until

4.30, especially about Ireland. I am doing my best to do something about Ireland.[24]

The King was advised by his prime minister that it could prove to be advantageous if he opened the new Parliament in Belfast. Smuts found the King "anxiously preoccupied" with the idea. Naturally the King had his reservations regarding the whole issue. The King was unaware of the contents of his government's draft of the speech. He was afraid that his very presence in Belfast could appear as an insult to the vast majority of his Irish subjects. The King's private secretary, Lord Stamfordham, also had his doubts and reservations. Smuts on the other hand regarded the mission as an exceptional opportunity for bringing a message of peace and hope to the Irish people. It did not seem strange at all that the King hereafter requested Smuts to draft a speech for the opening of the Northern Ireland Parliament. The next morning the King received Smuts' draft and a copy of a letter, which Smuts had despatched to Lloyd George on this matter.

In five sentences Smuts submitted the essence of his political philosophy to the King. He was of the opinion that his political thinking at the time was directly relevant to the Irish situation. The King's approach to the Anglo-Irish problem was in complete harmony to that of Smuts', but the King was also aware that he could not take any official action in Belfast on Smuts' advice. It was the King's constitutional duty to act only on the advice of his government in all matters. Smuts' letter to Lloyd George was straight to the point. It was clear that Smuts regarded his own involvement as of the utmost importance and of extreme urgency:

I need not enlarge to you on the importance of the Irish question for the Empire as a whole. The present situation is an unmeasured calamity; it is a negation of all the principles of government, which we have professed as the basis of Empire.[25]

Lloyd George's Irish policy of aggressive and military confrontation was dismissed by Smuts' reconciliatory approach. He made it clear that the King's proposed visit to

Belfast would be fully justified if "it were made the occasion for declaring a new policy towards Ireland".[26] Smuts assured Lloyd George that all the dominion prime ministers would support him if he took the opportunity to announce a new practical acceptable policy towards Ireland.

Although the King's finally approved speech did not contain Smuts' five-sentence declaration, it nevertheless embodied the thoughts of Smuts on the matter. It was the King's desire that his visit to Belfast on that historical day be the first step towards the end of strife in Ireland. The King appealed to all Irishmen "to stretch out the hand of forbearance and conciliation, to forgive and forget ..."[27] Smuts in particular was extremely satisfied with the way the King's speech went. In essence it achieved all that Smuts had hoped for. No wonder the King, and several others concerned, thought that General Smuts would be able to tell Eamon de Valera that he himself had experienced very similar circumstances.[28] He could, therefore, most probably be of invaluable assistance in paving the way to an amicable Anglo-Irish treaty. Smuts was very aware of his indispensability in this matter and, true to his nature, this awareness gave him great joy. In a letter to the King, Lloyd George expressed his appreciation and deep thankfulness. "None but the King could have made that personal appeal," he wrote, "none but the King could have evoked so instantaneous a response."[29]

Lloyd George's peripeteia regarding his Irish policy was to a certain extent highly exceptional. He abandoned, almost overnight, the policy of violence and substituted one of negotiation. "No British government in modern times," commented Winston Churchill, "has ever appeared to make so complete and sudden a reversal of policy."[30] Smuts played no minor role in this unexpected change of policy. "In May," wrote Mansergh, "the whole power of the state and all the influence of the Coalition were being used to 'haunt down the murder gang'; in June the goal was a 'lasting reconciliation with the Irish people'—most extraordinary!" On the King's demand for prompt action, Lloyd George reported that the Cabinet had already decided to invite Mr de Valera to London, "as the chosen leader of the majority of Southern Ireland", and Sir

James Graig, as the "premier of Northern Ireland". The Cabinet had also decided that General Smuts would be their best intermediary with the Southern Irish. Smuts was willing to go to Dublin, and he made it abundantly clear that he would only go on a formal invitation from De Valera.[31] This was a most important and strategic move on the part of Smuts. This of course would give him an advantage and a dominant position in the negotiation process with the Irish leaders.

De Valera and Graig both responded to the invitation of the British government on 24 June. The former declined but the latter accepted. " ... Much as he desired a lasting peace between the English and the Irish," De Valera stated that "... (much) as he desired he could see no road leading to peace so long as the English denied Ireland's essential unity and her right of national self-determination."[32] The King was hoping that if De Valera would not go to London, then Smuts would go to Dublin. Smuts decided that the time had come to take action—but with extreme caution. On his own initiative Smuts was involved in talks with, *inter alia,* Lord Fitzalan, the newly-appointed first Roman Catholic viceroy of Ireland.[33]

Smuts was waiting patiently for the invitation from Dublin. It came towards the end of June. On 1 July Smuts informed Lord Stamfordham that he would be leaving for Dublin within days—"please inform His Majesty".[34] Smuts explained to Stamfordham what his objective at the meeting would be—"to ascertain his (De Valera's) views and try to establish with him some preliminary basis for an agreement, in order to reduce the risk of failure at the conference in London if and when it took place."[35] He undertook to report back to the King on his return from Dublin. Lord Stamfordham replied the same day:

> *The King desires me to say how delighted he is that you have accepted Mr de Valera's invitation to visit him in Dublin on Tuesday next. For His Majesty is impressed with the belief that you of all men will be able to induce Mr de Valera to be reasonable and to agree to a settlement.*[36]

But the whole venture would certainly be "a more complicated and time-consuming task" than every person involved, directly or indirectly, could have imagined in his or her wildest expectations. Smuts realised that Eamon de Valera would be an extremely hard nut to crack.

Smuts wanted to keep his visit to Dublin as secret as possible. "I may say," he wrote to Stamfordham, "that not more than half a dozen people are aware of my projected visit and I intend to keep matters as secret as possible."[37] He consequently travelled incognito as Mr Smith—but all in vain! News concerning his visit to De Valera was published in the *Manchester Evening Chronicle,* the *Morning Post* and the *Westminster Gazette.* Smuts met De Valera and three of his ministerial colleagues, Griffith, Barton and Duggan, at the Mansion House in Dublin on 5 July. It was a historic occasion—a South African premier trying to persuade the Irish "chosen leader" to accept the British prime minister's invitation to attend a conference in London to discuss the ongoing Anglo-Irish hostilities!

At Manor House, Smuts made it very clear to De Valera and his colleagues that he was from the outset determined not to come to Dublin unless officially invited by De Valera. He also emphasised, emphatically, the fact that he was not an emissary of the British government and that he, consequently, had no direct proposals from that government to lay before them. Smuts asked those present that day in Dublin to look upon him as a friend who was many years earlier confronted with a similar situation. He found it of the utmost importance to bring it to the attention of the Irish leaders "that an intense desire for peace existed in England; and that the King shared that desire."[38] In spite of Smuts' cautious approach, De Valera remained extremely suspicious. He had no problem accepting the goodwill of the King. Nevertheless, he was not sure if he could believe any form of sincerity on this matter from the King's government. He had reservations regarding his presence and that of Graig at a conference in London where Lloyd George would be in the position to play the two of them off against each other. Without any doubt, according to De Valera, the British prime minister would be able to benefit extensively from such a situation.

After listening with extreme patience to De Valera, Smuts made it clear that he would be making the mistake of his life by rejecting the invitation to the conference in London. Smuts argued that a refusal to attend would place him (De Valera) in the wrong in the eyes of the world, of America and even of Ireland. Smuts then brought forward a new and significant point: " ... Tell the prime minister that (you) came as the representative of South Ireland."[39] Smuts thought that Lloyd George and Graig would agree to such a proposal. Once again De Valera was not impressed by Smuts' suggestion. He was certainly not convinced because he regarded himself "as the lawfully elected president of Ireland one and indivisible ... ".

De Valera regarded it of extreme importance to put the "partition of Ireland" and therefore the Home Rule Bill on the table. Smuts believed that it was not a partition, but "merely that Ulster, which has always proved the obstacle, is now out of the way.... Both in Mr Gladstone's bill and in Mr Asquith's. The one stumbling-block had always been Ulster, with the result that Ulster, which did not want Home Rule, has got Home Rule, and the rest of Ireland is quit of Ulster but is left without the Home Rule she wants."[40] Back in London, Smuts wrote to De Valera on 4 August 1921: "My strong advice to you is to leave Ulster alone for the present, ... I know how repugnant such a solution must be to all Irish patriots, who look upon Irish unity as a *sine qua non* of an Irish settlement. But the wise man, while fighting for his ideal to the uttermost, learns also to bow to the inevitable. And a humble acceptance of the facts is often the only way of finally overcoming them."[41]

Smuts and the Irish representatives resumed their discussions in the afternoon. Smuts had high hopes that he could still persuade De Valera to go to London. During the morning's discussions he could see that Griffith was "evidently impressed" with what he had to say on the proposed conference in London. Although the others were silent, Smuts was "by their manner ... inclined to think that they also agreed with him." Smuts thought that it was time to ask De Valera straightforwardly what he ultimately wanted for Ireland. Promptly, without hesitation, De Valera replied: "A republic." Smuts was taken aback by such a prompt and provocative reply. He advised De Valera most strongly against demanding a republic—"As a friend I cannot advise you too strongly against a republic. Ask what you want, but not a republic."[42] De Valera responded by saying that eventually it would be up to the Irish people to say what form of constitutional government they wanted. De Valera was, however, prepared to be bound by a treaty with England. He admitted that Ireland would always chiefly be dependent upon England for her markets. He talked at length on self-determination, idealism, blood of martyrs and several topics of national interest to him. Smuts listened to De Valera with great patience and gave him the opportunity to talk himself out, before responding:

> *I can talk from experience as to Republics bound by Treaty, for I served as a Minister, Attorney-General, in the Transvaal Republic, under such conditions. The result was quarrelling day and night over breaches on our part of the Treaty, in which we very likely were to blame; but whoever were to blame the end was a three years' war, at the end of which our country was devastated.*[43]

Smuts was no Republican and it is understandable why he could not fully understand De Valera's insistence on a republic for Ireland. Late in the 1930s the National Party in South Africa would hijack De Valera and the Irish struggle for independence in order to strengthen their similar cause. Dr A.L. Geyer and Dr H.F. Verwoerd, respectively editors of *Die Burger* and *Die Transvaler* in the 1930s, regularly tried to prove a point in their editorials by putting De Valera and the Irish fight for independence as an example in the independent struggle of the Afrikaner. Eric Louw, later minister of foreign affairs in Dr D.F. Malan's Cabinet, published one of his speeches under the title—*Ierland toon die weg aan: Konstitusionele ontwikkeling sedert 1921.*

The Irish were always ahead of the Afrikaners in their struggle for independence. In 1937 Ireland broke off all formal links with Britain and in the Second World War they proclaimed Ireland's neutrality. This is what General J.B.M. Hertzog wanted for South Africa. On 18 April 1948 Ireland became a republic and left the Commonwealth. Smuts never identified himself with these developments in Ireland. He was a

Commonwealth man and according to him there was no place for a republic in the Commonwealth.

Eventually it seemed to Smuts that De Valera would ultimately support a decision on dominion lines. He was convinced that his visit to Dublin had had positive results and the Irish, despite their suspicions, would give the invitation to London favourable consideration. Smuts hoped that everything would turn out positively in the end. Events proved otherwise. Smuts left for London later that day.

Three days later, on 8 July, the Irish leaders accepted the invitation to London. De Valera, accompanied by Griffith and Collins, arrived in London on 10 July. The Irish leaders were back in Dublin in less than a fortnight. No agreement could be reached with the British on the basic principles of an Anglo-Irish settlement. Both parties became aware of the wide gap separating them. The British offered dominion status to Ireland, excluding Northern Ireland unless the six counties in the north should agree to join out of their own free will. The Irish, on the other hand, would agree to a dominion on condition that they could have the six counties—if not, they would only accept full independence for Southern Ireland.

Smuts had no part in the Anglo-Irish negotiations but he still kept in touch informally with both parties. Before he left for South Africa on 5 August he assured the King, in a short farewell letter, that he was convinced an agreement would ultimately be reached. It was Smuts' letter to Lloyd George, of which the contents were made public before the negotiations were finalised, that caused considerable displeasure in the Irish camp.[44] This unfortunately resulted in a breach of trust. It was argued that Smuts had no right to disclose any detail of the discussions between him and the Irish leaders while discussions with the British government were still in progress. Smuts also wrote a lengthy letter to De Valera the day before he left for South Africa. He emphasised the issues raised in Dublin during the discussions and once again tried to convince De Valera that the ultimate goal he, De Valera, had for Ireland, could only be achieved in successive stages. Smuts concluded: "At this stage I can be of no further use in this matter, and I have therefore decided to adhere to my plan of sailing for South Africa tomorrow. This I regret most deeply, as my desire to help in pushing the Irish settlement one stage further has been very great. But I must bow to the inevitable."[45]

On 5 August Smuts boarded for South Africa at Southampton. A telegram from the King awaited him in his cabin. The King conveyed his sincere appreciation for all Smuts' efforts during the past months "to break the Anglo-Irish log-jam". "It was," writes Hancock, "a fitting close to his work for Anglo-Irish reconciliation."[46] From this point on Smuts remained merely a spectator in the struggle to achieve permanent peace. "I have brought both mules to the water," he wrote later, "I have pushed their heads right into the trough; but the drinking is their own affair."[47] The news reached him later in Pretoria that after another attempt there emerged on 6 December 1921 a signature of Articles of Agreement for a treaty between Great Britain and Ireland—Michael Collins' choice for Ireland to achieve freedom. Smuts said in Pretoria: "The Irish question has been settled on the lines on which I advised last August."[48]

On 8 December 1921 Art O'Brien, representative of Dàil Eireann in Great Britain, wrote to the editor of the official organ of the *Irish Self-Determination* in Great Britain:

> *The time for rejoicing and thanksgiving will come when Ireland again enters the circle of sovereign and independent nations. But that time is not yet. Until then, dignity, calm and work.*[49]

These were wise words and they would soon crystallise in practical Anglo-Irish politics.

In South Africa Smuts' reference to parallels in South African history and especially his remark that, "in the recent election, a large majority of them (South Africans) had declared that they did not want a republic but free membership of the British Empire", did not go off well with General Hertzog and his National Party. Hancock rightly points out: "De Valera would not and could not accept South African history, in the Smuts version or in any other, as a copy book of wisdom for Irishmen."[50] Smuts' involvement in the Anglo-Irish dispute was the beginning of a process that would eventually lead to bitter strife among Irishmen. "Smuts might have been better prepared for that tragic anti-climax," wrote Hancock, "had he explored more deeply the temperamental and ideological roots of strife among his own people."[51] Smuts was anxious to gain personally, as statesman and as politician, from his Anglo-Irish intervention. This could have boosted his international standing.

In 1951 Dr A.L. Geyer, South African high commissioner to London, paid an official visit to Dublin. A visit to Eamon de Valera was a highlight for Geyer. The South African high commissioner was most impressed with De Valera—"a great man, a statesman and idealist, perhaps a dreamer".[52] De Valera regretted the fact that Ireland eventually had to leave the Commonwealth. He originally had suggested certain terms in 1921, which were the same as those granted willingly to India in 1947 when it became a republic and remained a member of the Commonwealth. He held Smuts responsible for the British government's rejection of his proposals at that time. Geyer tried to come to Smuts' rescue by reminding De Valera that Smuts had to sell the idea of a dominion in order to calm the English South Africans.[53] De Valera, as usual, could not be convinced.

Nicholas Mansergh had an interesting private interview with De Valera on 21 September 1965. Mansergh wrote:

Smuts, he (De Valera) thought a man of finer intellect and of greater depth than Lloyd George. But Smuts was 'slim' (clever). He knew from his own experience this was so. Smuts published private correspondence, which he must have known was private, in an attempt to appeal to the Irish people over or behind De Valera who was their leader. De Valera never forgave Smuts.[54]

Smuts and De Valera never met again.

1. D.W. Harkness, *The Restless Dominion. The Irish Free State and the British Common Wealth of Nations, 1921 – 1931,* 3. W.K. Hancock, *Smuts I, The Sanguine Years, 1870 – 1919,* 430.
2. Harkness, 3.
3. *Ibid.,* 4.
4. Nicholas Mansergh, *The Commonwealth Experience,* 22.
5. Jean van der Poel, *Selections from the Smuts Papers,* Volume V, 65 – 77. Hereafter referred to as Smuts Papers. See also D.0.: 117/33, X1/8945.
6. Smuts Papers, 78.
7. W.K. Hancock, *Smuts, II. The Fields of Force, 1919 – 1950,* 41.
8. Sheila Lawlor, *Britain and Ireland, 1914 – 1923,* 87.
9. Hancock, 11, 49. A.J.P. Taylor, *English History, 1914 – 1945,* 121.
10. Taylor, 121.
11. Hancock, 11, 49.
12. *Ibid.,* 50. John McColgan, *British Policy and the Irish Administration,* 1 – 2.
13. Mansergh, 201.
14. Quoted by Donal Lowrey, *The Alliance that dare not speak its name: Afrikaner and Irish nationalists and the British Empire/Commonwealth, 1902 – 1961,* 3.
15. *Ibid.,* 5.
16. Smuts Papers, Volume III, 18 April 1917, 476.
17. Smuts Papers, Volume V, 8 June 1921, 85.
18. Lord Longford, *et al,* (eds), *The History Makers.* See Sir John Wheeler-Bennett, *De Valera,* 274.
19. *Ibid.,* 275.
20. Franciscan Library, Killiney (hereafter referred to FLK), *Eamon de Valera Papers,* File 1462. *Colonel Maurice Moore to Eamon de Valera,* 22 Augustus 1921. Hereafter referred to as FLK.
21. *Ibid.*
22. Royal Archives, *Geo V Papers,* K1702/22 *Stamfordham to Smuts,* 1 July 1921. Hereafter referred to as RA.
23. Mansergh, 201.
24. Hancock, 11, 51.

25. RA, *Geo V Papers,* K1702/3, *Smuts to Prime Minister,* 14 June 1921.
26. Hancock, 11, 53.
27. *Ibid., 54 – 55.*
28. RA, Geo V Papers, K1702/23, *Memorandum by Lord Stamfordham,* 25th July, 1921.
29. *Ibid.,* 33. RA, Geo V Papers, K1702/1, *Grigg to Stamfordham,* 14 June 1921.
30. Mansergh, 201.
31. RA., Geo V Papers, K1702/27, *Memorandum of a Conversation between the King and General Smuts at Buckingham Palace, 7th July, 1921.*
32. Hancock, 11, 55.
33. RA, Geo V Papers, K1702/l, *Grigg to Stamfordham,* 14 June 1921.
34. RA, Geo V Papers, K1702/22, *Smuts to Stamfordham,* 1 July 1921.
35. *Ibid.*
36. RA, Geo V Papers, K1702/23, *Stamfordham to Smuts,* 1 July 1921.
37. RA, Geo V Papers, K1702/22, *Smuts to Stamfordham,* 1 July 1921.
38. RA, Geo V Papers, K1702/27, *Memorandum of a conversation between the King and General Smuts,* 7 July 1921.
39. RA, Geo V Papers, K1702/27, *Memorandum of a conversation between the King and General Smuts at Buckingham Palace,* 7 July, 1921.
40. *Ibid.*
41. RA, Geo V Papers, K1702/52, *Smuts to de Valera,* 4 August 1921.
42. Hancock, 11, 58.
43. RA, Geo V Papers, K1702/27, *Memorandum of a conversation between the King and General Smuts at Buckingham Palace,* 7 July 1921.
44. *Irish Bulletin,* 16 August 1921. *Letter of General Smuts.*
45. RA, Geo V Papers, K1702/52, *Smuts to de Valera,* 4 August 1921.
46. Hancock, 11, 60.

47. *Ibid.*
48. *Ibid., 61*
49. FLK, *Eamon de Valera Papers,* File 1309.
50. Hancock, 11, 60.
51. *Ibid.,* 61.
52. A.L. Geyer, *Vier jaar in Highveld: diplomatieke ervarings —soms sonder dorings—as Hoë kommissaris in Londen,* 70 – 71.
53. Lowrey, 23.
54. Diana Mansergh, 186.

Smuts relaxing in nature from serious international deliberations.
(Smuts House Museum)

Smuts with the British royal family in South Africa, 1947. (Smuts House Museum)

8

The Windsors

" ... it shows what faith the dear old King has in me
and how much he likes to look to me for help and
advice."
J.C. Smuts (Smuts Papers, V, 495)

"He (Smuts) is a very agreeable and interesting man."
King George V (Diaries, 02-11-1918)

Jan Smuts' close contact and friendship with the House of
Windsor has always been a topic of controversy and
criticism, not only from his own people but also from
leading political personalities in the Commonwealth. It was
King George V and Queen Mary who frequently invited Smuts,
when he was in England, to Windsor Castle to spend the
weekend with the royal family. Although several critics and
rivals had great respect and admiration for the general, they
were not at all enthusiastic about the special relationship
Smuts had with the royal family and in particular with the
King. King George V had a far better ongoing relationship with
Smuts than he ever had with any of his prime ministers during
his reign. While referring to Smuts in his diary as "a very sound

man" he referred at the same time to Lloyd George, his prime minister, "as usual ... impossible".[1]

The King attached great value to Smuts' advice and he consequently sought it even on matters concerning British politics. On one occasion Smuts wrote to his wife in South Africa:

> *While I was with him (Sir Graham Bower) there was a telephone call from the King who wished to know where I was. So I went to London this morning to see him. It then appeared that there was a big cabinet crisis yesterday; MacDonald was to resign, etc. And the King, as in the Irish difficulty of 1921, wished to have my advice about the whole matter. Fortunately for me the cabinet crisis was decided during the night and all was over when I arrived there this morning. But it shows what faith the dear old King has in me and how much he likes to look to me for help and advice. He looks well—not like an invalid.*[2]

Smuts was at this time not prime minister but leader of the opposition in the South African Parliament.

Smuts' real contact with King George V, and consequently with the House of Windsor, took place after the First World War. He had made a lasting impression on the British people during the War (a member of the Imperial War Cabinet; the only non-Brit to be a member of Lloyd George's British War Cabinet and an emissary on request of Lloyd George on various missions concerning the British war effort to Europe). "His political vision was, of course," wrote Lord Charles Chandos, "also wide and he ranged over the whole convulsive scene of world politics with a clearness, a simplicity and a penetration which are the stamp of superior intellects; he was one of the great men that I have met."[3] Smuts had become part and parcel of British politics and the British war effort. His position as an outstanding statesman in the British Commonwealth was unprecedented, unchallenged and recognised universally.

During the First World War, as already indicated in the previous chapter, Smuts became increasingly interested in the Irish question. He became known to his friends, including those in Ireland, as the champion of national freedom for Ireland.[4] Since the War, Lloyd George and his government had made little or no progress at all in solving the Irish question. Lloyd George and his ministers launched a well-motivated campaign in the mid-1920s on the independence declaration of Dáil Eireann. They wanted to destroy the Irish state by force. The King made it abundantly clear to his prime minister that he was most definitely not in favour of the Cabinet's "policy of reprisals".[5]

People started to look to Smuts for a solution to this very thorny political crisis. Tom Casement, the brother of Roger Casement, wrote to Smuts:

> *Privately, I have always felt that you would some day be a big factor in settling our question. I may be wrong, but I have pinned a lot of faith on you. You went through the mill years ago and see things quite differently from the narrow political point.*[6]

Smuts arrived in London on 11 June 1921 to attend the Imperial Conference.[7] He was extremely disappointed that nothing constructive had been done to solve the conflict with the Irish. He refrained from commenting on the issue and instead took time to bring himself up to date with the news in Ireland. He spent the first weekend with the Gilletts who took up a house in London for the duration of his visit. Two days after his arrival he was a guest at Windsor Castle. During a two-hour talk, according to Hancock, the King and Smuts "broke the Irish log-jam".[8] The King felt inclined from then on to involve Smuts in all stages of the Irish question. He was convinced that he could trust Smuts for sound and objective advice. A close friendship between king and subject was duly sealed. Smuts was from now on to become one of the monarch's most valued advisers for almost a decade. The King felt attracted to Smuts mainly because there was no love lost between him and his own prime minister, Lloyd George.[9] Smuts knew extremely well how to handle this special-growing relationship with the King. There were situations in which Smuts found it beneficial to listen, rather than to talk.[10] And this was undoubtedly a fact that the King appreciated.

Smuts greeting the Prince of Wales, June 1925. (Central Archives Repository)

The King was impressed when it became known that Smuts would go to Dublin in an attempt to persuade Eamon de Valera to accept Lloyd George's invitation to come to London for discussions on the Irish constitutional deadlock. He informed the King that he would be meeting De Valera in Dublin on Tuesday, 5 July. He also asked Lord Stamfordham, the private secretary of the King, to convey his apologies to the King and the Queen for being unable, due to his proposed trip to Dublin, to attend the state banquet hosted by the King.[11] Lord Stamfordham replied the same day. He wrote to Smuts:

> *Their Majesties are only sorry that this important mission will prevent your being present at Monday's state banquet.*
> *The King will be here till the 9th when he leaves for the Channel Islands and will be delighted to see you if you are back in London before that date.*[12]

Smuts was unable to report personally to the King on his return from Dublin. He was to leave for South Africa shortly. He consequently wrote to the King a most extraordinary letter, portraying the warmth and special friendship that existed between the two:

It was my intention to ask Lord Stamfordham to arrange an interview when I might have the opportunity of saying good-bye, but I regret that I have to leave London before Your Majesty returns. I embark from Southampton at 4 p.m. on Friday, 5th August.

Knowing the great personal interest that Your Majesty has taken in the projected Irish settlement, I think that I cannot do better than enclose for Your Majesty's information a copy of a letter I have written to Mr de Valera on the negotiations to date.

There is at the present time an apparent impasse but I cannot believe that public opinion will allow this golden opportunity to pass when the alternative is so grave. It is my earnest hope that Your Majesty will be able to keep in close touch with the progress of events and will use your great influence towards a settlement, which means so much to us all.

I take this opportunity of offering my respectful congratulations to Your Majesty on the success that is attending the Royal Yacht at Cowes, and I hope that both Your Majesties, the Queen and yourself, will enjoy a needed respite from your labours.

It was my intention to discuss with Your Majesty the possibility of His Royal Highness the Prince of Wales visiting South Africa on the conclusion of his tour in India. Perhaps if the contemplated visit to Japan falls through, His Royal Highness may be able to consider the possibility of a visit to the Union where the most cordial welcome awaits him, and where he will probably be able to find some rest and quiet from his all too strenuous labours.[13]

When Smuts boarded for South Africa at Southampton a telegram from the King awaited him in his cabin—"bidding him farewell and thanking him for all that he has done". Smuts must have felt this a very rewarding gesture on the part of the

King. Thereafter he was merely a distant spectator of the struggle for peace between Britain and Ireland.

Smuts was a regular and most appreciative guest of the royal family during his visits to London, even when he became leader of the opposition after the general election of 1924. "King George," wrote Kenneth Ingham, "repeatedly invited him to stay at Sandringham."[14] The King entered all Smuts' visits in his diary. On 6 October 1931 the King entered in his diary: "Genl. Smuts had luncheon with me & we had a very interesting conversation about the Empire etc." And on 5 November 1934: "Had a long talk with Smuts." Smuts frequently took the liberty of writing to the King and Queen Mary. The latter also enjoyed the general's company.

A striking example of the relation between Smuts and the Windsors is portrayed in a letter from Stamfordham to Smuts dated 12 April 1921:

> *The King desires me to thank you for the Cape grapes, which you so kindly sent for His Majesty's acceptance. They arrived in excellent condition and were much appreciated.*
>
> *All you wrote about Prince Arthur was most gratifying to the King, who is delighted that His Royal Highness is doing so well and gaining the confidence of all sections of the community.*
>
> *His Majesty is also interested in and values what you say of the Royal Family and the Dominions. I venture to think that the example of the Duke of Connaught and his son should be emulated by others of the Princes. They could not render better service, for, as I know you always hold, the Royal Family is the great and visible link of Empire. I trust that it may be possible for some of Their Majesties' younger sons at all events to visit the Dominions. I am glad to say they are evincing all those manly, virile characteristics, which invariably appeal to the British hearts.*[15]

Nevertheless, the good relationship he had with the royal family throughout his life never restrained him from criticism when it was due. Or perhaps it was for that reason that he permitted himself to criticise on a personal level. John Colville, private secretary to Winston Churchill, recalls in his diaries an almost unbelievable incident in which Smuts was directly involved. This incident occurred during a brilliant reception on 19 November 1947 at Buckingham Palace on the eve of the wedding of Prince Philip and Princess Elizabeth. The reception was, *inter alia*, attended by half a dozen crowned heads and their queens from Europe. Glittering tiaras and knightly orders, which had been tucked away for quite a long time, were taken from the cupboard and dusted for this special occasion. It was a magnificent scene of brilliant diamonds and rubies. Apart from the fact that an Indian Rajah was completely drunk, and assaulted the Duke of Devonshire who was incidentally completely sober, everything went off very well. There was though another incident, but quite different from the former. It involved Princess Juliana of the Netherlands. She was dancing with the Duke of Gloucester when she slipped and fell flat on the floor. And there she lay... "large and plump and gasping".[16] Everyone present, including the royal family, stood frozen. The duke unceremoniously helped the princess to her feet and the band continued.

The Queen Mother, Queen Mary, true to her custom, made a most tasteful impression at the reception with her exquisitely chosen jewellery. After all the initial commotion, Queen Mary was extremely taken aback by a remark made by Smuts as regards her appearance and the appearance of the other royal ladies present. By now Smuts must have been extremely bored with those around him. When the Queen Mother asked Smuts' opinion of her jewellery, he responded with all the presence of mind in the world: "You are the big potato; the other queens are all small potatoes."[17] It was an unsettled and displeased Queen Mary who heard this from the man she held with such high regard. No other person in the world would have had the courage and the boldness to say something of this nature to Queen Mary, who was at the best of times not an easy person.

Smuts also met the heir to the thrown, David, the Prince of Wales, eldest son of George V. Although he found the prince a "pleasant character", Smuts thought his father to be a stronger

Jan Smuts, King George V and Queen Mary. (Cape Times Supplement, 11 July 1933)

personality. He and the Prince of Wales were once guests at dinner in London in honour of the surviving leaders of the First World War. "The Prince of Wales was also there," Smuts wrote to his wife. "I sat next to him and we had a pleasant chat. We get on well although I like his father better than I do him."[18] On 5 November 1923 the King entered in his diary: "Genl Smuts came to see me at 10.00 & talked about Alge and Alice going to S.A. as governor general & also about David visiting S.A. next year."[19] Smuts also talked to the King about the possibility of the Prince of Wales visiting South Africa. The proposed visit was originally Lloyd George's idea. He had in mind a visit to Africa, including South Africa, and then South America. In the meantime, Lloyd George had fallen from power but his original idea for the visits by the Prince of Wales had not been abandoned. "The great South African premier, General Jan Smuts," wrote the Prince of Wales in his memoirs, "had also urged my father and the British government the wisdom of continuing with the project. However, in 1924 General Smuts had suffered the same fate as Mr Lloyd George."[20] There were doubts about the attitude of the Nationalist government towards the prince's visit to South Africa. But the South African prime minister, General J.B.M. Hertzog, reassured the British prime minister that the Prince of Wales would be most welcome. The prince consequently sailed for South Africa from Portsmouth on 28 March 1925.

On his return to Cape Town after travelling almost 16 000 kilometres as far north as the Rhodesians, and experiencing interesting as well as alarming incidents, Smuts asked the prince his impressions of the country. Years later the prince recorded this conversation in his memoirs:

My answer was that the tour had thrust me into so great a variety of communities that I hardly knew where to begin. But it had at last given me a comprehension of the unique and complex racial problems besetting the Union. And it had further given me a measure of the greatness of Smuts himself, who almost alone of the old Boer leaders worked ceaselessly and hopefully to hold South Africa within the Empire.[21]

If there was a good relationship between King George V and Smuts, there was an even better one between Smuts and King George VI. The Duke of York, second son of George V, succeeded his eldest brother, David, to the throne as George VI. When the Prince of Wales succeeded his father as Edward VIII in January 1936, his reign was to last less than a year. He abdicated in order to marry the twice-divorced American-born Wallis Simpson. King George V confided in his prime minister, Stanley Baldwin, before his death concerning his doubts about his eldest son: "After I am dead," the King said to Baldwin, "the boy will ruin himself within twelve months."[22]—it actually took approximately nine months! For the Duke of York the abdication of his eldest brother was to prove a great personal tragedy. The duke was completely unprepared for the burdens and responsibilities that had become such a vital and integral part to the throne. He was nervous, shy, completely lacking self-confidence, and a stutterer. In an article published in *Royalty Monthly* a contributor wrote of the duke:

> *Even though he was quite different from his elder brother,*
> *public affection also extended to Prince Albert, Duke of*
> *York, who was known in the family as 'Bertie'. Bertie could*
> *not have been a greater contrast to the dazzling heir to the*
> *throne. He, too, was handsome though in a more homely*
> *way, but he was also painfully shy, nervous, in fragile*
> *health and afflicted with an embarrassing stammer.*[23]

On top of all this the possibility of a devastating war in Europe was slowly but surely on the horizon. The Second World War was to prove an extremely burdensome and anxious event to the new King. "He had," wrote Denis Judd, "never fully recovered from the enormous strain imposed upon him during the Second World War."[24] It was actually the War, as it was with his father during the First World War, that brought King George VI and Smuts in closer contact with each other. The King, as in his father's case, attached great value to Smuts' opinion in Britain's war effort and he consequently consulted him frequently. The King followed the example of his father and invited Smuts to spend weekends with the royal family when he was in London. By now Smuts had become used to these invitations. Since the reign of King George V Smuts had actually become a dear and respected friend of the British royal family. Howarth wrote: "The King was fascinated by this ex-guerrilla leader, who became his country's prime minister and the principal architect of the League of Nations, and who found relaxation in reading the New Testament in Greek."[25] Churchill did not find it difficult to persuade the King to make Smuts a British field marshal. On 30 September 1941 Smuts received his Field-Marshal's Baton from the governor general of the Union. At the same time he was handed a letter from the King:

> *I was hoping to present your Field-Marshal's baton to you*
> *personally in England, but I well understand the reasons*
> *why you do not want to be away from South Africa for so*
> *long at the present time.*
>
> *I am, therefore, asking the Governor General as my*
> *personal representative to hand it to you on my behalf.*

*I would like you to know how proud my Field Marshals
are to count you among their numbers.*
With all good wishes believe me, yours very sincerely
George R.I.[26]

Howarth wrote that it was the talks on strategy in the
Mediterranean theatre that the King found most stimulating.[27]

A very important and decisive phase of the Second World
War developed when Churchill opposed and won the King and
Smuts over to his direction of thinking. Smuts was strongly in
favour of full British involvement in the Balkans as soon as
possible.[28] In this regard, he consequently sent two long
telegrams to Churchill in September 1943. Smuts was
extremely worried that the Russians were conveying the
impression in Europe that they were winning the War. He was
of the opinion that a possible shift in the world status of the
Allies might result in Russia becoming the "diplomatic master"
of the world.[29] Churchill was sympathetic, but American
opinion had to be taken into consideration. To be heard, Smuts
eventually turned to the King. He found the King less difficult
to convince. He even succeeded in sowing doubt in to the King's
mind regarding the desirability of making the main assault on
the German forces in north-west Europe.[30] The King wrote to
Churchill on 14 October:

*My dear Winston, I had a long talk with Smuts yesterday
about the Mediterranean theatre of war. He discussed this
with you, and wants us to go on fighting there and not to
switch over to a new front like 'Overlord'.*

*I was so impressed by what Smuts said that I felt I must
pass it on to you. I know there are many difficulties for a
change of plan at this late hour, but you, F.D.R. and Stalin
are to meet in the near future. I am alone for dinner
tonight, and if there is any possibility of Smuts and you
joining me, it would give us all a very good opportunity of
talking these things over undisturbed.*[31]

Churchill accepted the invitation to dinner but warned that any
major changes to Operation Overlord were completely out of

Top: Smuts and the Greek royal family. In front, from left to right, stands the present Queen Sophia of Spain and ex-King Constantine of the Hellenes. (Smuts House Museum)

Bottom: Smuts with Princess Frederika of Greece. (Central Archives Repository)

Insert top left: Princess Frederika of Greece. (Smuts House Museum) the question.[32] "There is no possibility," he wrote, "of going back on what is agreed. Both the US staff and Stalin would violently disagree with us."[33] Churchill was convinced that there were resources for "both theatres". Churchill revealed that he had already sent the King's letter advocating the conquest of Italy before Operation Overlord began to the chiefs of staff.[34] This advice was ignored, and the conquest of Italy was far from complete when the D-Day landings were eventually made on 6 June 1944.[34] The early months of 1944 were mainly taken up with the preparations for the Allied landings on the north coast of France.[35]

Smuts showed genuine concern for the restoration of the Greek monarchy that had suffered severe difficulties during the War.[36] Even today, Smuts' intense involvement in the Greek royalty situation is puzzling. Did he perhaps identify the possibility of personal gain, especially in the international politics of the day? In mid-1941 King George II of the Hellenes, who was a cousin of King George VI of Britain, arrived in South Africa via Crete and Egypt—a refugee from the Nazi invaders of Greece.[37] A large number of Greek royalty accompanied him, namely his younger brother—Crown Prince Paul and his wife, Crown Princess Frederika; and their two young children, Constantine and Sophia.[38] Ex-King Constantine is presently living in exile in London and Queen Sophia is married to King Juan Carlos of Spain. There were several other members of the royal family who accompanied him—as well as a large troupe of ladies-in-waiting, secretaries, valets and maids, an English nurse and a Greek nursemaid for the two children of the Princess Frederika.[39] The distinguished exiles were treated, shortly after their arrival in Cape Town, to lunch at Libertas, the official residence of the prime minister. Smuts found them pleasant guests. Both the King and the crown prince impressed him with their intelligence and their experience as commentators on European politics.[40] At a later stage the Smuts family received the Greek royalty for tea at Doornkloof. Major Piet van der Byl, minister without portfolio in the Smuts War Cabinet, was appointed by Smuts as minister of attendance to the Greek king.[41]

Shortly afterwards King George left for London. London remained his headquarters until victory was achieved in the

Mediterranean and the brightening prospects of Greek liberation made it advisable for him to establish himself in Egypt. The crown prince did not join his brother in London. He established himself in Egypt from where he had the opportunity, for the next two years, to frequently visit his family in South Africa. South Africa was to remain the abode of the crown prince's wife, Crown Princess Frederika and their family, the Princesses Marie, Katharine and Radziwell, for the next two years. "The friendship between Smuts and the royal ladies," wrote Hancock, "particularly the Crown Princess Frederika, continued to grow."[42]

"Smuts appreciated more acutely than the British government did," wrote Ingham, "that Britain's efforts to ensure that Greece should not be conquered by the Germans had involved supporting very disparate groups, not all of whom were fighting to restore the Greek monarchy."[43] Smuts wrote to Churchill a year later urging him to make it clear that Britain supported King George II of the Hellenes. He reminded him that the King supported the Allied cause all the way and at all times.[44] Smuts thought it of extreme importance that Allied military occupation of Greece should be maintained, until such time that the Greek people could choose the government they desired out of their own free will.[45]

In June 1943 Smuts wrote a very informative letter, with a certain personal touch, to the Greek monarch in Egypt. He stressed the role that the Greek monarchy had to play in Greece:

> *My interest in this matter is not merely personal but is partly due to my conviction that the royal house is essential to the stability of post-war Greece as well as to the vital Mediterranean interests of the British Commonwealth. Greek politics have been singularly unstable, instability, which has not grown less in wartime, and the royal house is the main hope for stability in future.*
>
> *The royal house and its members have therefore the duty cast on them to secure the maximum popularity in the national interest.*
>
> *I know from repeated talks with British statesmen how sincere is their support for Your Majesty and how*

conscious they are of the value to Britain of her loyal support for Your Majesty. They know that Greece must play an important part in Mediterranean policy after the war, and her friendship with Britain must be in no doubt. But their support for the Greek throne is not sufficient. Far better is it for the Greek people to stand unalterably behind their king.

I wish I had the opportunity to discuss these and other matters with Your Majesty in an unofficial way and in a spirit of friendship for the Greek cause. But I don't know how soon I shall be able to visit Egypt again, ... Greece may soon be called upon to put her house in order.[46]

Smuts took it upon himself to serve the royals with advice when he thought it to be necessary. Seeing that King George II of the Hellenes was related to the House of Windsor, he regarded it as a matter of course that he should advise the King on state affairs. But this was not the only reason why Smuts involved himself with the difficulties of the Greek monarchy. Some may argue that his involvement could be explained due to his friendship with the Princess Frederika. I think this is unlikely. It is more likely, as in the case of his involvement in the Irish question in 1921 when he opted for personal prestige internationally, that he tried again in this situation. This can surely not be ruled out.

The visit of King George VI, Queen Elizabeth and the two princesses to South Africa at the beginning of 1947 was a special event for Smuts. He had been planning this for a very long

Smuts with King George VI on Table Mountain, 1947. (Smuts House Museum)

time. Although he had invited the royal family to South Africa "so that they could have a holiday, and recover from the strains of the war years", it cannot be ruled out that the royal visit was actually a publicity stunt. "There was a political expediency behind the invitation," wrote Judd, "as Smuts, facing a general election in the fairly near future wished to consolidate support, particularly amongst English-speaking South Africans, for his United Party."[47] The King was anxious to assist in neutralising the secessionist agitation of the Nationalist Party under the leadership of Dr D.F. Malan. He wanted to help Smuts keep South Africa in the Commonwealth.[48] He was, therefore, prepared to make the visit to South Africa in spite of the extremely difficult circumstances in Britain at the time. He was even risking unfriendly suggestions that he and his family would be enjoying the South African sun merely to avoid "austerity and restrictions at home". The King was not comfortable at all about this. He was worried that he might be leaving Britain at the wrong time.[49] Britain was experiencing a severe winter, which caused extreme suffering and misery for the population.[50] In South Africa the King wrote to Queen Mary, his mother, in Britain: "I am very worried over the extra privations which all of you at home are having to put up with in that ghastly cold weather with no light or fuel. In many ways I wish I was with you, having borne so many trials with them."[51] Furthermore, the economic conditions at home were worse than ever. And in India there were threats to denounce the appointment of Lord Louis Mountbatten, a

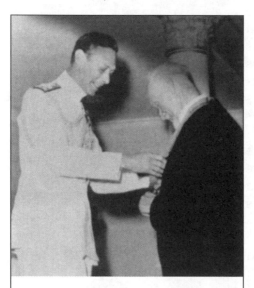

King George VI invests Smuts with the Order of Merit, *1947.* (Smuts House Museum)

close relative of the royal family, as viceroy to India.[52] This situation could easily erupt into widespread violence. In spite of all these misgivings, the King nevertheless decided to accept Smuts' invitation. The royal visit commenced on 17 February 1947. The HMS Vanguard arrived at the Cape Town harbour with all the attendant pomp and exitement.[53]

Friday, 21 February 1947, was a historic and memorable day as the King, for the first time in the history of the British Commonwealth, opened a Parliament outside Britain.[54] After delivering "The Speech from the Throne" he asked the president of the senate to read it in Afrikaans. He then declared the fourth session of the ninth Parliament of the Union of South Africa opened. The King invested Smuts with the Order of Merit. This was a most prestigious award—a distinction extended to no more than 24 people. Smuts responded to this in a letter to Margaret Gillett:

The King had mentioned it at Balmoral but somehow I never took him seriously ... it was only when the award came in published print that I began to realize that I had been greatly singled out for honour. I have really done or achieved little to deserve it, and usually only have the sense of how little I have really achieved of the dreams I have had through a long and busy life. So much chaff with so little corn in it.[55]

Due to ill health, Mrs Smuts could not attend the various functions in Cape Town. The Queen insisted that they must then all visit her at Doornkloof. Smuts responded to the Queen's decision with: "A Queen visiting a Queen!"[56] For Smuts the British monarchy had long since ceased to be merely an institution. He cherished the possibility that its "sheer humanness" was just what all South Africans so badly needed. In this regard Smuts wrote:

It is a good and sound people.... Our coloured people were specially pleased with the attention shown them.... This is just the sort of thing which Kings and Queens can do and which give them a blessed and fruitful function in our human society.... Nowhere is it more wanted than in this land of races and colours, and nowhere can it render a greater service. Politics runs too high with us, and as the King is above all politics he becomes the reconciler and peacemaker.[57]

Hancock rightly comments that this was a "wistful dream" of Smuts'. Keep in mind that Smuts' enthusiasm for the monarchy as an institution was surely not shared by the Afrikaner with his dream of a republic. One wonders if Smuts never realised this. His constant involvement in international affairs, with the interest of the British Empire and later that of the British Commonwealth preconceived, could have blurred his vision as regards the ideals of the Afrikaner.

An extremely strenuous timetable with numerous public functions and responsibilities was arranged for them. The royal family stayed for two months in South Africa and covered almost 16 000 kilometres. The Queen was well aware of her husband's anxieties. She wrote to Queen Mary: "This tour is being very strenuous as I feared it would be & doubly hard for Bertie who feels he should be at home."[58] Eventually the King

The royal family visits Isie Smuts at Doornkloof. (Smuts House Museum)

became restless at the intense security designed "to keep him away from his African subjects".

> *He was 'tired to death at being ordered about and sleuthed by Afrikaner policemen wherever they moved', and on one occasion, when he thought he was out of earshot, remarked to the Queen, 'We've shaken off the Gestapo at last'. One incident showed the extent of the King's irritation at the way he was being 'driven' on his visit to his South African Kingdom and, equally, Elizabeth's awareness and her attempts at damage limitation.*[59]

In Pretoria a state banquet was organised for the royal family. It was clear that the strain upon the King was taking its toll. Smuts delivered a short introductory speech and introduced the King to the guests. One of the officials forgot to switch of the microphone and consequently every word spoken at the head table could be heard.[60] Smuts asked the King to follow him:

> *The King replied crossly: I'll speak when I've had my coffee and the waiters have left the room.*
>
> *Smuts urged him: They're waiting for you now in England, Sir.*
>
> *The King, answered mutinously: Well, let them wait. I have said I will speak when the waiters have left the room.*
>
> *Elizabeth (intervening anxiously): Can't we be heard?*
>
> *The intervention of his daughter must have changed the King's stubbornness. He stood up and made his speech.*
>
> *Finished, he sat down: Well, I suppose I may now have my coffee.*

Smuts was more than satisfied with the royal visit. He had been looking forward to it for a long time and with so much excitement. He later wrote to Margaret Gillett:

> *The royal family have had a wonderful reception everywhere, and enjoy their visit to the full, in spite of it being strenuous, as all these functions must be. Every section of our population has played their part magnificently and even politics has retired before this*

triumph. The queen has captured all hearts, and the king has also been very good. The princesses are full of fun and jollity. All have made the greatest and best impression.[61]

The Windsors returned to Britain towards the end of April 1947. At the farewell luncheon on the 24th, Smuts gave the King 399 diamonds for mounting in his Star of the Order of the Garter. The Queen received a gold tea service and Princess Margaret, 35 bracelet stones.[62] The King found the South African tour "both exhilarating and tiring".[63] During the return journey, on board HMS Vanguard, he had to spend a week in bed. He nevertheless wrote Smuts a farewell letter on 2 May:

Now that we are on our homeward voyage from our never to be forgotten visit to SA I feel I must write and tell you how sorry we were to leave Cape Town last week; we all wept as the Vanguard went out of Duncan Dock, after our very pleasant stay with you.

I am so glad that our long projected visit has been successfully accomplished & I thank you so much for all the help you gave in every way to make the visit both possible & such an interesting one.

I regret that it was all too short....[64]

Smuts attended the wedding of Princess Elizabeth and the Duke of Edinburgh on 20 November 1947. Field Marshal Smuts was especially welcome among the dominion prime ministers—he was after all a special friend of the family!

Smuts died unexpectedly on 11 September 1950. In his letter of tribute, King George VI wrote:

In peace or in war, his counsel and his friendship were of inestimable value ... while the force of his intellect has enriched the wisdom of the whole human race.[65]

Smuts was always extremely concerned that the image and the prestige of the monarchy would come into dispute. When it was time in South Africa to appoint a new governor general, Colonel C.H. Hore-Ruthven, secretary to governor general Lord

Clarendon from 1933 – 1936, had an interview with Smuts on the issue. Hore-Ruthven entered in his diary on Wednesday, 29 January 1936:

> *Smuts seemed considerably perturbed at the idea of having to consider the question of the next Governor-General. He still seemed doubtful as to whether it would be necessary to have a South African or another Englishman. He said the Athlones had so enjoyed being here and might have stayed even longer but for a small misunderstanding by General Hertzog of what Athlone had said to him. He (Smuts) would like to have another Royalty, but he did not want a Royal Prince unless he was sure he was a good one as he feared if a Royal Prince made any mistake it would be highly detrimental to the Royal House, whereas if a commoner makes a mistake it does not much matter. He was, therefore, against asking for one of the King's brothers.*[66]

Never before and never since Smuts' death has a South African leader had such close contact with the British royal family over such a long period.

1. Royal Archives, *Diaries of King George V,* 6 October 1931. Hereafter referred to as RA.
2. Jean van der Poel (ed), *Selections from the Smuts Papers,* Volume V, 6 October 1931, 495. Hereafter referred to as Smuts Papers.
3. O. Lyttelton, *The Memoirs of Lord Charles Chandos,* 244.
4. W.K. Hancock, *Smuts, II. The Fields of Force, 1919 – 1950,* 49.
5. *Ibid.,* 50.
6. Smuts Papers, Volume V, 30 May 1921, 84 – 85.
7. Hancock, 51.
8. *Ibid.*
9. Lord Beaverbrook, *Men and Power, 1917 – 1918,* 409.

10. *Ibid.*
11. RA, Geo V Papers, K1702, *Smuts to Stamfordham,* 1 July 1921.
12. Smuts Papers, Volume V, 4 August 1921, 94.
13. *Ibid.,* 100.
14. Kenneth Ingham, *Jan Christian Smuts. The Conscience of a South African,* 165.
15. RA, Geo V Papers, L1688/4, *Stamfordham to Smuts* 12 April 1921.
16. Charles Higham, *et al, Elizabeth and Philip. The Untold Story,* 148 – 149.
17. John Colville, *The Fringes of Power. Downing Street Diaries.* Volume Two: 1941 – April 1955, 271. Higham, 148.
18. Smuts Papers, Volume V, 6 October 1931, 494.
19. RA: *Diaries, King George V,* 5 November 1923.
20. Windsor, Duke of, *A King's Story. The Memoirs of H.R.H. the Duke of Windsor, K. G.,* 204.
21. *Ibid.,* 208.
22. Howarth, Patrick, *George VI,* 55.
23. *Royalty Monthly,* November 1988, 23.
24. Denis Judd, *King George VI, 1895 – 1952,* 238.
25. Howarth, 151.
26. Crafford, 307 – 308.
27. Howarth, 151.
28. *Ibid.*
29. *Ibid.,* 152.
30. *Ibid.*
31. Howarth, 152, Martin Gilbert, *Road to Victory, Winston S. Churchill, 1941 – 1945,* 530.
32. Gilbert, 530.
33. Howarth, 153. Gilbert, 531.
34. Judd, 205.
35. *Ibid.* Gilbert, 697.
36. Ingham, 227.
37. Piet van der Byl, *Top Hat to Velskoen,* 200. Hancock, 11, 402.
38. Ex-King Constantine and his family are currently living in exile in England and Queen Sophia is married to King Juan Carlos of Spain.

39. Hancock, 11, 402.
40. *Ibid.*
41. Piet van der Byl, *Top Hat to Velskoen*, 200. Hancock, 402.
42. Hancock, 11, 403.
43. Ingham, 227. Harold Macmillan, *War Diaries. The Mediterranean, 1943 – 1945,* 612 – 613.
44. Ingham, 227.
45. Anthony Eden. *The Eden Memoirs. The Reckoning,* 497. Ingham, 227 – 228.
46. Smuts Papers, Volume VI, 9 June 1943, 434 – 435.
47. Judd, 223.
48. *Ibid.* Howarth, 199 – 200.
49. Judd, 224.
50. Howarth, 200.
51. Judd, 224.
52. Higham, 135.
53. Piet van der Byl, *The Shadows Lengthen*, 17.
54. *Ibid.,* 19.
55. Cameron, Trewhella, *Jan Smuts and Illustrated Biography*, 171.
56. Hancock, 11, 495.
57. *Ibid.*
58. Judd, 224.
59. Sarah Bradford, *Elizabeth: A Biography of Her Majesty the Queen,* 118 – 119.
60. *Ibid.,* 119.
61. Smuts Papers, Volume VII, 16 March 1947, 127.
62. Higham, 140.
63. Howarth, 204.
64. RA, *George VI Archive.* Original draft of letter from King George VI to Smuts.
65. Trewhella Cameron, *Jan Smuts. An Illustrated Biography,* 189.
66. Imperial War Museum, Diary, Colonel C.H. Hore-Ruthven, Secretary to the Governor-General of South Africa, the Earl of Clarendon, 1933 – 1936, Wednesday, 29th January 1936.

Charles de Gaulle. (South African Museum of Military History)

9

Charles de Gaulle

"His limitations as a public man were very great, but he did an immortal service in helping France to get going again, and to recover her soul."
J.C. Smuts (Smuts Papers, VII, 38)

"The fact that he (De Gaulle) was possessed by an all-consuming and uncontrollable passion, transcending all other cravings, for France."
Lord Longford, et al (*The History Makers*, 365)

There was not much love lost between Smuts and the French. To a certain extent Smuts was really a thorn in the flesh to the French. George Clemenceau's remark after the First World War regarding Smuts—*le saboteur du Traité de Versailles*[1]—is proof of this tension, which lasted over a long period. This extremely uncomfortable situation, especially to Smuts' colleagues in the Allied Forces, can only be explained partially. The French did not approve of Smuts' involvement in European affairs, even though he was a distinguished Commonwealth statesman. It was most probably Smuts' arrogance, which surfaced from time to time, that provoked the French. The tension between the two parties became apparent for the first time during the First World War.

The British prime minister, Lloyd George, sent Smuts on several fact-finding missions to Europe during the First World War. He had to report to the prime minister and it is not clear if he was always impartial in his conclusions, especially as far as France was concerned. Sir Henry Wilson criticised Smuts on his comments regarding the situation in France during the War. On 3 July 1917 Wilson entered in his diary: "I explained the situation in France and finished by saying that, although not desperate, it was undoubtedly serious. I was struck by the tone of the committee, except Smuts who seemed rather to revel in the idea that the situation was desperate and impossible. Of course this is nonsense."[2] The French prime minister, Georges Clemenceau, was far harsher in his criticism of Smuts. When Smuts went on another mission, this time to Switzerland under the name of Mr Ashworth, Clemenceau, as pointed out in a previous chapter, criticised Lloyd George severely on his choice. "Lloyd George is a fool," Clemenceau said to Sir Henry, "and an extra fool for sending Smuts, who doesn't even know where Austria is."[3] In spite of days of negotiations, as in the case later between Smuts and Eamon de Valera in Dublin, Smuts accomplished nothing on this particular mission.

It was actually Smuts' attitude towards the peace negotiations in Paris after the First World War that really enraged the French and caused the long-lasting rift. The French of course had cause to be annoyed with Smuts. They wanted to avenge themselves on Germany for the great embarrassment caused by Otto von Bismarck during the Franco-Prussian War (1870 – 1871). The French had never forgiven the Germans for crowning the new German Emperor, Wilhelm I, as Emperor of the United Germany in the Hall of Mirrors in the Palace of Versailles. And now, after the First World War, revenge was beckoning. "What Germany had done since 1870," wrote S.F. Crafford, "must be undone. The destruction of this country was a fitting end to what had been a veritable jehad... he (Clemenceau) was determined to break Germany."[4] Smuts, on the other hand, had an open approach to the dawning post-war era. He wanted to restore permanent peace and prosperity to a devastated Europe. While France's approach towards the peace negotiations was based firmly on nationalistic introspective principles, Smuts on the other hand had a more global international approach.

The Allies won the War. Smuts was determined that peace should be won as well. At the Peace Conference in Paris, Smuts was not, as pointed out earlier, a representative of the British government but a representative of the South African government.[5] This really made a big difference! Prime Minister Louis Botha also attended and Smuts was therefore only second in command. He was not a member of the Council of Four—Lloyd George, Clemenceau, Wilson and Orlando were.[6] Smuts could not directly influence the decisions taken. On the other hand it was clear that Clemenceau was determined to have his own way. "From the outset," wrote Crafford, "Clemenceau was determined to dictate a peace of his own making or precipitate a bloody anabacis."[7] Clemenceau's attitude was actually building an extremely difficult road for his successors in the international arena. By now France was branded as a thorny partner. Smuts predicted this and foresaw severe problems ahead. Churchill also, in later years, joined Smuts in his gloomy outlook. "The Almighty in His infinite wisdom," Churchill said, "did not see fit to create Frenchmen in the image of Englishmen."[8]

Smuts saw great difficulty ahead for Europe and the free world if Clemenceau was allowed a free hand. "To destroy Germany completely as a leading force in Europe," Smuts said, "would undoubtedly result in a vulnerable Europe." On this basis he regarded the peace negotiations as the forerunner of another devastating war in Europe. Smuts wrote to Lloyd George on 14 May 1919:

> *Democracy is looking to you who have killed Prussianism —the silent masses who have suffered mutely appeal to you, to save them from the fate to which Europe seems now to be lapsing.*[9]

Smuts maintained throughout the peace negotiations that destroying Germany would ultimately lead to the destruction of

Europe. If the Allies were earnest in saving Europe they would not be able to do it without the help of Germany. Clemenceau consequently regarded Smuts to be in the opposite camp and therefore argued that he could not be a friend of France. Furthermore, an enemy of France had to be neutralised! He viewed Smuts to be a traitor and a man not to be trusted. He said to Marshal Pétain: "Tell the Marshal that there is only one thing he can do to redeem his treachery. That is to die very quickly."[10]

Against this background Charles de Gaulle entered the scene. Charles André Joseph Marie de Gaulle was born on 22 November 1890. Both his father's and mother's family belonged to the conservative Catholic *bourgeoisie*. His father, Henri de Gaulle, could claim aristocratic descent from the year 1210.[11] Henri de Gaulle was undoubtedly a Royalist and consequently anti-Republican. He claimed to have been a personal friend of Charles Maurras. Charles de Gaulle's own books pose one central question—"To what extent are these history, and to what extent are they merely an *apologia pro vita sua*?"[12] De Gaulle was educated at *École Militaire* and at *St Cyr*. The education he received was the typical classical training of his time. The curriculum included a good portion of mathematics but, above all, Latin and Greek.[13] At school De Gaulle had to work very hard to pass his examinations. Crozier wrote that De Gaulle's intelligence was fully recognised in his youth, "but his fixed ideas of grandeur were generally ascribed to overweening vanity".[14]

De Gaulle's father was the headmaster of the fashionable *Jesuit College of the Immaculate Conception*. He taught Latin, Greek, philosophy and literature. Henri de Gaulle had to restrain his son's interest in literature and philosophy in case he should not acquire the necessary proficiency in mathematics and other subjects to enable him to pass the examinations for *St Cyr*.[15] It is interesting to note that De Gaulle was an excellent classical scholar. While a prisoner during the First World War in 1916 he could repeat long passages from Greek tragedy and Xenophon. He retained a familiarity with Latin all his life. He wrote his first adult literary works in the '20s and early '30s. These works throw interesting light on his adolescent development.[16] The writings clearly represented a young man who was familiar with the great French writers of the 17th century as well as the ancient. "They are the works of an intellectual," wrote Ashcroft, "and not merely of a soldier with intellectual leanings."[17] De Gaulle was greatly influenced by Nietzsche and Bergson—two philosophers from the period of his youth. As a matter of fact Bergson was a friend of his father and a regular visitor to De Gaulle's Paris home. It was Bergson who in 1938 listened to and approved Charles de Gaulle's advocacy of armoured forces.[18]

De Gaulle's determination to become a soldier was typical of his family milieu. "Aged ten," wrote Crozier, "Charles de Gaulle had already formed his 'certain idea of France'; at 13, he had chosen a military calling."[19] De Gaulle had a romantic view of history, which he most probably inherited from his grandfather. The reading of Nietzsche singularly aided the formation of the military side of his character.[20] "As a child," wrote Ashcroft, "he had identified himself with great historical figures; as an adolescent whose ambition it was to serve France he consciously prepared himself to be a leader of men."[21] De Gaulle's career was indeed an extraordinary one. The fact that a man of his "exceptional ability, character and sense of purpose, with so enormous a faith in himself" remained for so long so relatively unknown in France is difficult to understand. It was not until the age of 49 that De Gaulle came to the attention of the majority of his countrymen.[22] Crozier wrote of De Gaulle as a military man: "Although always known as *mon général*, when in the highest civilian office of the French Republic, his military career was honourable rather than distinguished, the fortunes of war having denied him the opportunity of ultimate fame."[23]

After the First World War Pétain did not forget the young officer. He had a very high regard for De Gaulle's intellectual qualities. He consequently appointed him to his staff. De Gaulle's first task was the compilation of a history of the French army. Nevertheless, there was never real warmth in the relationship between De Gaulle and Pétain. There were several confrontations between them in the '30s and Pétain was to bear De Gaulle considerable antagonism.[24] De Gaulle's army career was, despite Pétain's patronage, actually far from spectacular.[25] He remained a captain for nine years. It was only in 1927 that he became a major; lieutenant colonel in 1932 and a colonel in 1938. Alphonso Juin, who was a fellow-graduate at *St Cyr*, was by this time already a general. "The most important insight into the Major de Gaulle of those years," wrote Werth, "is provided by his own writings, and, above all, by his extraordinary book, *Le Fil de Lépee,* published in 1932."[26] In 1940 Pétain complained to Spears that Reynaud had made a great mistake in taking De Gaulle into his Cabinet. "He thinks the art of war has no secrets for him," Pétain said, "and he is terribly ambitious."[27] On the other hand Pétain had done much to encourage this ambition. Werth wrote:

> *So de Gaulle is certainly not a 'typical' general. But is he a 'typical' Frenchman? The question has often been asked, and it is not an easy one to answer. For what is a 'typical Frenchman'? He himself has often said that he does not fit into any 'category'. It might, indeed, be argued that de Gaulle is without precedent. If one takes earlier 'saviours' of France—whether Clemenceau, Pioncaré, Doumerque, or even Pétain—each in his own way, was a 'typical Frenchman': the ruthless, sarcastic 'Jacobin' Clemenceau; the humourless, hardworking, drearily legalistic Poincaré; Doumerque, the average politician with his false bonhomie; Pétain, the traditional general, suddenly called upon to play the Father Figure.*[28]

It was during the Second World War that Smuts and De Gaulle met for the first time. Smuts was part of Churchill's inner-circle advisers—the so-called *privileged trio*—as Brian Crozier called them. They were Smuts, Ernest Bevin and Sir Hastings Lionel Ismay.[29] A constant hostile attitude existed between the war leaders and De Gaulle. Werth describes the relationship between Churchill and De Gaulle as a "love-hate relationship".[30] And Joseph Stalin once said of De Gaulle: "De Gaulle is a simple man."[31] Werth refers to De Gaulle's 'paranoia' as "anti-British and anti-American".[32] He placed the accent on "De Gaulle's attitude towards the United States (after the War) ... and the 'de-satellization' of France and, if possible, of the whole of Western Europe (as) one of his principal aims".[33] Taking into account Smuts' role in the Commonwealth at that time and his personal history of animosity towards France, it was obvious that he would side with Churchill in every aspect of his policy towards De Gaulle. Nevertheless, Smuts regarded it of utmost importance that the Allies cooperate in order to achieve their common goal—the defeat and destruction of Nazi Germany.

Smuts and De Gaulle grew up in completely different environments. Smuts lived on a farm in the Cape Colony; his father was a farmer and a member of the Cape Parliament. "His boyhood," wrote Hancock, "made him a hard-headed farmer's son; an authentic Boer."[34] De Gaulle grew up in Paris and his father was a headmaster and an intellectual. Smuts went to Victoria College, Stellenbosch and Christ's College, Cambridge, to qualify as a lawyer. De Gaulle entered *St Cyr* in order to prepare himself for a military career. Nevertheless, these two extraordinary men had interesting and several common characteristics. Smuts did not have a wide circle of friends—only a few intimate friends but he did have a horde of acquaintances throughout his public life as a politician. He often lived "in a world of his own". Crozier wrote of De Gaulle: "De Gaulle had a few intimates, but no friends."[35] Both were intellectually above average but Smuts was intellectually far superior to De Gaulle. Smuts, with his *Holism and Evolution,* pioneered into the field of philosophy. In his *Le Fil de Lépee* and *Vers l' Armée de Métier* De Gaulle pleaded for a mechanised professional army and suggested a strategic plan.[36] De Gaulle is the author of various historical and diplomatic studies, among which are *The European Idea (1967)* and *Europe after de Gaulle* (1970). He published his memoirs in 1972. Smuts and De Gaulle both had a great interest in the classics, philosophy and literature. And they both pledged their patriotism to their fatherland on more than one occasion. Smuts once said: "I am an Afrikaner and my soul is with my people. In no person's breast does the flame of dedication burn higher than mine."[37] And: "South Africa my first love, my only love."[38] De Gaulle wrote in his diary: "An anxious concern about the fate of our country came as second nature to my three brothers, my sister and myself."[39] Lord Gladwyn wrote:

> *The fact was that he (De Gaulle) was possessed by an all-consuming and uncontrollable passion, transcending all other cravings, for France. It was a love-affair with an abstraction which took the physical form of 'mingling' whenever possible, with a crowd of loyal supporters. 'All the sentimental side of my nature', he tells us himself, 'inclines me to picture France as a sort of fairytale princess or as a madonna in a fresco for whom some wonderful and exceptional future is in store. I instinctly feel that Providence has decreed that she must either be completely successful or utterly unsuccessful'. For France, 'mediocrity' he continues, is an 'absurd anomaly'. France is only herself if she is in the front rank ... 'In short, as I see it, France cannot be France without grandeur'.*[40]

In spite of this exulting patriotism, their fellow countrymen did not accept both Smuts and De Gaulle. Smuts had to fight these prejudices all his life and De Gaulle only made his debut as a national leader at the age of 49, and then in a time when France was in a severe crisis.

Upon the outbreak of the Second World War in September 1939, De Gaulle commanded a brigade of tanks attached to the fifth army in Alsace. On 6 June 1940 the new French premier, Paul Reynaud, appointed De Gaulle under-secretary of state for war.[41] It proved to be an unpopular appointment. German forces invaded Poland on 1 September 1939.[42] Denmark and Norway were occupied in April 1940. Adolf Hitler and his High Command secretly worked towards greater triumph—the ultimate defeat of France and Great Britain. On 10 May 1940 an impressive German offensive was launched. The massive German force consisted of 89 divisions, with 47 divisions in reserve. The neutral Low Countries of Luxembourg, the Netherlands, and Belgium were the ultimate aim in the third phase.[43] The invasion of Belgium and Holland on 10 May 1940 opened the period of "lightning war" (*Blitzkrieg*). German tanks complemented by air power encompassed the fall of the

Netherlands within four days and Belgium within three weeks.[44] Leaving the British to be dealt with later, Hitler turned to the task of finishing off Germany's ancient foe—France. This he accomplished within seven weeks.[45] The German offence swept over France, from Brittany and Normandy to the Swiss border.[46] The Maginot Line was encircled and its garrisons captured. On 14 June German troops entered Paris. With drums beating, German troops marched past the *Arc de Triomphe*. Paris fell to the enemy on 14 June 1940—scarcely one shot was fired in its defence.[47] The French prime minister, Paul Reynaud, resigned. The aged Marshal Pétain, who soon thereafter asked the Germans for an armistice, replaced him. "In 1940," wrote Werth, "the 84-year-old Marshal H.P. Pétain was expected to rescue what could still be rescued after the fearful military defeat France had suffered."[48] In response to Pétain's request for an armistice De Gaulle broadcasted a strong appeal to the French to continue to fight. In July – August 1940 a Free National Committee came into existence. It was headed by De Gaulle and its headquarters were in London. It directed the French forces, which continued the War against the Axis powers in opposition to the French government at Vichy.[49]

During the War, friction continued between De Gaulle and the British and between De Gaulle and the Americans. In an extraordinarily personal letter to De Gaulle, which Smuts had written on 16 September 1942, Smuts welcomed "this opportunity once more to come in touch with" De Gaulle.[50] Smuts took the liberty to point out the futility of petty trivialities that may block the way for constructive cooperation among the Allies. Only Smuts could approach leaders of this capacity in this way. Does this *modus operandi* of Smuts simultaneously project his symptomatic meddlesomeness and his arrogance? Colonel Pechkoff, De Gaulle's representative in South Africa, delivered the letter in person to De Gaulle. Smuts got the impression that things were not going well between De Gaulle and the British authorities in Syria, Cairo and London. He told De Gaulle in the letter that he regretted this situation most deeply. There was alarming friction from time to time between De Gaulle and Churchill. Churchill could not always hide the irritation De Gaulle caused him. "Through no fault of his own," Churchill wrote, "he (De Gaulle) has not been of any important help to us. Indeed, his Movement has created new antagonism in French minds."[51] However Smuts assured De Gaulle of British goodwill towards him. "I know," Smuts wrote, "that British leaders have repeatedly used their influence in Washington to be helpful to you."[52] Despite the fact that Smuts acknowledged the important role the United States was playing in the War, he nevertheless had no regard for the Americans. John Colville entered in his diary: "Smuts said the Americans were certainly very powerful, but immature and often crude."[53]

The friction between De Gaulle and the Americans was genuine. Smuts recalled in his letter to De Gaulle a meeting between him and the general. The latter told Smuts that Washington did not see eye-to-eye with him concerning the full recognition of the National Committee.[54] With so much at stake it seems as if Smuts thought it his responsibility to explain British policy to De Gaulle and to establish goodwill between the two parties. He asked De Gaulle to appreciate Britain's special concern and anxiety about, *inter alia,* Syria. "Their attitude in Syria," wrote Smuts, "is and can only be dictated by this governing consideration which I would beg you to keep constantly in mind when difficulties arise. They can have no *arrière pensée* in reference to French interests."[55]

It was Smuts' ultimate goal to establish a good working relationship between De Gaulle and Churchill. Surely not an easy task at all! He urged De Gaulle to accept without any delay Churchill's invitation to return to London to discuss matters with him personally. He earnestly assured De Gaulle of Churchill's constant goodwill. Smuts was confident that a personal talk "between two big men" would neutralise the atmosphere of misunderstanding regarding the common problems all parties had to deal with. Smuts seemed to be the champion of reconciliation in the interest of the big task that lay ahead. He wrote to De Gaulle:

We are comrades together; we are comrades in the greatest cause and in the most dangerous phase of history. No human differences or weaknesses should be allowed to

*interfere with our utter devotion to our great task. Here the
spirit of comradeship is the highest statesmanship and the
best strategy. Between two such men as you and Mr
Churchill there should in this crisis be the utmost
frankness and mutual confidence, and any little
differences should be thrashed out in personal exchanges.*[56]

Smuts told De Gaulle that he spoke to Churchill in exactly the
same way in which he was now writing to him. Smuts felt that it
was very urgent that De Gaulle and Churchill should meet as soon
as possible in order to discuss frankly the tension between them.
Smuts told De Gaulle that the sooner he and Churchill met, the
sooner the way could be paved for creating an atmosphere of trust
and understanding between them. Smuts concluded:

*I would have invited you to visit us in the Union on this
occasion, but I think the call of London on you must have
priority, and therefore I will only wish you a safe journey to
London, and a successful solution of all pending questions.
Whatever I can do to promote the best feeling and the
happiest solutions I shall most gladly do so.*[57]

It was abundantly clear that Smuts enjoyed this self-imposed
role as peacemaker between De Gaulle and Churchill.

The fall of France and especially the way in which they
surrendered to the Germans distressed Smuts immensely. At
this time his nerves awoke in him a fighting mood. He was
forced to observe how the French gave free passage to Germans
through Tunis to supply Erwin Rommel. He could not contain
himself—it was simply too much to bear! "If God would only
send them a woman," Smuts cried out, "another Joan of Arc,
for her men have failed her."[58]

Three months after Smuts' letter to De Gaulle, Churchill
found himself in an extremely difficult situation. The House of
Commons was disturbed by and deeply suspicious of Vichy
France. There was considerable Parliamentary dislike of
Admiral Jean Francois Darlan's mastery in French North
Africa, and of General Dwight Eisenhower's support for
Darlan. They did not approve of Eisenhower entrusting such

authority to Darlan. Knowing full well the value of the United States as an ally, Churchill addressed a Secret Session of the House of Commons on 10 December 1942 in order to explain the situation. "In war," Churchill told the House of Commons, "it is not always possible to have everything go exactly as one likes. In working with allies it sometimes happens that they develop opinions of their own."[59] Churchill told the Secret Session that he supported Eisenhower in entrusting Darlan with authority. He pointed out that Vichy France had maintained for most of its existence "a legal and even fairly intimate" relationship with the United States. This, according to Churchill, placed Britain in a strategic and privileged position to obtain insight in matters she would otherwise not have been able to obtain.

Martin Gilbert pointed out that the most remarkable section of Churchill's Secret Session speech concerned not Darlan, but actually De Gaulle. Churchill told the House of Commons:

I have tried to work as far as possible with General de Gaulle, making allowances for his many difficulties, for his temperament and for the limitations of his outlook. In order to sustain his Movement at the moment of the American occupation of French North Africa and to console him and his friends for their exclusion from the enterprise we agreed to his nominee, General Legentilhomme, being proclaimed as High Commissioner for Madagascar, although this adds somewhat to our difficulties in pacifying that large island, which oddly as it seems to us would much prefer Darlan. We are at the present time endeavouring to rally Jibuti to the Free French Movement. Therefore I consider that we have been in every respect faithful in the discharge of our obligations to De Gaulle, and we shall so continue to the end.

However now we are in Secret Session the House must not be led to believe that General de Gaulle is an unfaltering friend of Britain. On the contrary, I think he is one of those good Frenchmen who have a traditional antagonism engrained in French hearts by centuries of war against the English.

I continue to maintain friendly relations with General de Gaulle and I help him as much as I possibly can. I feel bound to do this because he stood up against the Men of Bordeaux and their base surrender at a time when all resisting will-power had quitted France. All the same, I could not recommend you to base all hopes and confidence upon him, and still less to assume at this stage that it is our duty to place so far as we have the power, the destiny of France in his hands.[60]

These were harsh words and to a certain extent a vote of non-confidence in General de Gaulle. No wonder Smuts was extremely upset. He turned his mind to occupied France and it seemed as if Smuts started to lose confidence in France's ability to handle her own affairs. Smuts had to now show his real colours very distinctly. The time for diplomacy had run out. Churchill always tried to get Smuts to London and, once there, tried to keep him at his side as long as possible. "When Smuts came to England," Colville entered in his diary, "Churchill would drop all else and listen attentively to the accented words of wisdom, spoken in high staccato tones, which poured from the South African patriarch on all the issues of present and future policy."[61]

Towards the end of 1943, at Churchill's insistent invitation, Smuts made his second wartime visit to London.[62] This visit was to be one of great significance and it would lead to a commotion as far as De Gaulle and the Movement were concerned. Smuts was invited to address a large meeting of the Lords and Commons under the auspices of the *Empire Parliamentary Association* on 25 November.[63] As usual he had a global approach to his topic. He concentrated on basic principles on which world peace could be restored and maintained. He pointed out that the League of Nations had failed in its purpose, because the leaders, including him, had shut their eyes to the realities of power. Smuts was now thinking of a new world organisation. He believed that effective peace-keeping authority would have to be vested primarily in the Great Powers. Who were these Great Powers he was thinking about? He recognised, for the present, only three:

> *Great Britain, the United States, and Russia now form the trinity at the head of the United Nations fighting the cause of humanity. And as it is in the new international organisation the leadership remains in the hands of these great trinity powers.*[64]

And then he produced the explosive stuff when he referred to France's place, *inter alia,* in the New World he envisaged after the War. Smuts was informed that he would be addressing a closed meeting. Consequently he did not expect to be reported in the press. Smuts told his audience:

> *Just look for a moment at what is happening, and what will be the state of affairs at the end of the war. In Europe three of the great Powers will have disappeared. That will be quite a unique development. We have never seen such a situation in the modern history of this Continent. Three of the five Great Powers will have disappeared. France has gone, and if ever she returns it will be a hard and long upward pull for her to emerge again.*
>
> *A nation that has once been over-taken by a catastrophe such as she has suffered, reaching to the foundations of her nationhood, will not easily resume her old place again. We may talk about her as a Great Power, but talking will not help her much. We are dealing with one of the greatest and most far-reaching catastrophes in history, the like of which I have not read of. The upward climb will be a bitter and a long one. France has gone, and will be gone in our day and perhaps for many a day.*[65]

The French were in general, to put it mildly, most upset about Smuts' unfriendly remarks towards France and De Gaulle. De Gaulle's many clashes with Churchill and Roosevelt, and now this, seemed to him to be a kind of conspiracy. But, on the other hand, De Gaulle was at loggerheads with literally all the Allied leaders, including General Eisenhower.[66] "It took De Gaulle a long time to be taken seriously," wrote Werth, "Churchill, Roosevelt, Stalin persistently refused to do so, and it was not perhaps till 1958, or even 1962 – 3, that De Gaulle, through sheer persistence, attained the world stature of a major statesman. It was a long and arduous climb."[67] De Gaulle surely did not appreciate the fact that Churchill had established a *privileged trio*—Smuts, Ernest Bevin and General Sir Hastings Lionel Ismay—to which he could turn for advice.[68] Smuts was present at most of the meetings Churchill had had with De Gaulle from time to time.[69] Referring to a meeting between Churchill and De Gaulle on 4 June 1944, a few months after Smuts' notorious speech, Crozier wrote: "De Gaulle found Smuts rather embarrassed. Not long before, he had made some widely reported remarks to the effect that France was no longer a Great Power and might as well join the Commonwealth."[70]

Taking into consideration the complex and divergent personalities of Smuts and De Gaulle, one can see that there could not have been any kind of real affinity between them—in any case not the type of relationship that existed between Smuts and Churchill. Smuts and De Gaulle met in a war situation and Smuts would have done anything in his power to support Britain's role in the War. Undoubtedly the main reason for Smuts' contact with De Gaulle must be seen as a clear attempt to serve this role. It is certainly not far-fetched to accept that De Gaulle associated Smuts with the other Allied leaders with whom he himself had had an ongoing struggle for recognition. At the same time Smuts, who achieved the stature of a major statesman at a fairly early stage, always regarded himself to be De Gaulle's senior. The only factor they really had in common was the downfall of Adolf Hitler and the consequent dismantling of Nazi Germany.

1.   Nigel Nicolsen (ed), *Diaries and Letters, 1939 – 1945,* 334.
2.   F.S. Crafford, *Jan Smuts. A Biography,* 151.
3.   *Ibid.,* 153.
4.   *Ibid.,* 162.

5. W.K. Hancock, *Smuts, I. Sanguine Years,* 505.
6. *Ibid.,* 513.
7. Crafford, 162.
8. Martin Gilbert, *Road to Victory. Winston S. Churchill, 1941 – 1945,* 275.
9. Jean van der Poel (ed), *Smuts Papers,* Volume IV, 14 May 1919, 158. Hereafter referred to as Smuts Papers. Hancock, 1, 522.
10. Nicolson, 334.
11. Alexander Werth, *De Gaulle, a political biography,* 63.
12. *Ibid.,* 63.
13. Edward Ashcroft, *De Gaulle,* 25.
14. Brian Crozier, *De Gaulle. The Warrior,* 5.
15. Ashcroft, 25.
16. *Ibid.*
17. *Ibid.*
18. *Ibid.*
19. Crozier, 17.
20. Ashcroft, 26.
21. *Ibid.*
22. Werth, 54. Crozier, 9.
23. Crozier, 3.
24. Ashcroft, 29.
25. Werth, 77.
26. *Ibid.* Lord Longford (ed), *The History Makers,* 362.
27. Ashcroft, 29.
28. Werth, 56.
29. Crozier, 281. Don Cook, *De Gaulle. A Biography,* 210.
30. Werth, 68.
31. Ashcroft, 19.
32. Werth, 314.
33. *Ibid.*
34. Hancock, 1, 9.
35. Crozier, 9.
36. Longford, 362.
37. Anthony Trowbridge, *Holism and Evolution, 1926 – 1986.* In *Veld Trust,* December 1986, 14.
38. T.J. Haarhoff, *Smuts the Humanist,* 2 – 3.
39. Ashcroft, 23.

40. Longford, 365.
41. *Ibid.*, 362.
42. Peter Young, *World War II,* 23.
43. William Shirer, *World War II. Readers Digest Illustrated Story,* 47.
44. *Ibid.*
45. Shirer, 47.
46. *Ibid.*, 48.
47. Werth, 53.
48. Werth, 53.
49. *Ibid.*, 110 – 111.
50. Smuts Papers, Volume VI, 16 September 1942, 386.
51. Gilbert, 10.
52. Smuts Papers, Volume VI, 16 September 1942, 386.
53. John Colville, *The Fringes of Power. Downing Street Diaries.* Volume Two. 1941 – April 1955, 227.
54. Smuts Papers, Volume VI, 16 September 1942, 386.
55. *Ibid.*
56. *Ibid.*, 386 – 387.
57. *Ibid.*, 387.
58. W.J. Hancock, *Smuts, II. The Fields of Force, 1919 – 1950,* 362.
59. Gilbert, 274 – 275.
60. *Ibid.*, 277. Cook, 166 – 167.
61. Colville, 397.
62. Hancock, 11, 408.
63. *The Times,* 03.12.1943.
64. *Ibid.*
65. *Ibid.*
66. Crozier, Chapters V & VI. *De Gaulle versus his Allies,* 144 – 182.
67. Werth, 63.
68. Crozier, 281.
69. Cook, 210. Ashcroft, 139.
70. Crozier, 281.

Top left: Smuts in Berlin, October 1931. The Brandenburg Gate is in the background. (Central Archives Repository)

Top right: Adolf Hitler.

Bottom: Smuts in Germany, 1946. (Central Archives Repository)

10

Adolf Hitler

**"Adolf Hitler is personally friendly towards the
British Empire and has repeatedly declared himself
for a rapprochement with us."**
J.C. Smuts (Smuts Papers, VI, 431)

**"It is said that Hitler laughed when he was told that
South Africa had declared war on Germany."**
F.S. Crafford (*Adolf Hitler*, 305)

Since his early years as a student at Stellenbosch and
Cambridge, Smuts had had a high regard for the
Germans and their culture. "I looked on the Germans,"
he once said, "as the most cultivated race in the world. The
French hated me for my belief in them."[1] It was Isie, his future
wife, who actually introduced Smuts to Goethe and Schiller
while they were students at Stellenbosch. He decided to learn
German and in later years he frequently quoted Goethe and
Schiller in his numerous letters. Isie could still remember in her
old age a translation Smuts made in 1896 of Schiller's *Das Ideal
und das Leben*.[2] "In the evenings," wrote Hancock, "she and
Jan use to often sing together. German lieder became their

favourites, for she had fallen in love with German literature and was bent on making him a Goethe lover."[3] As a student at Cambridge he considered it unthinkable not to visit Germany. He went to Strasbourg in 1894 and studied literature, Hegelian philosophy, and English conveyancing. He returned to London in October and entered the Middle Temple. But four decades later, in the months before the outbreak of the Second World War, he wrote, most probably much against his innermost conviction, that Nazism had changed the Germans. "I see now," he wrote, "that Prussianism underlay all their learning and sentimentality. They've thrown over Goethe and Schiller for Nietzsche."[4]

Smuts' attitude was quite positive towards the Germans between the two World Wars. He was extremely appalled by the Allied Forces' ill treatment of Germany at the Paris Peace Conference in 1919. He was convinced that the peace, towards which the Allies were working, would eventually turn out to be an impossible peace. In this regard he wrote to his wife from Paris:

I have fought and worked for a different peace—a peace of reconciliation and recovery among the nations, whereas this is a peace of hatred and bitter estrangement. Sometimes it seems to me as if poor old Europe were under sentence of death, and as if she had reached her zenith and will from now on slowly decline. Conditions everywhere are terrible and will perhaps become still worse. My wish, my ardent wish, is to get out of it as soon as possible and to return to home and country.[5]

In Britain there was, between the two wars, "a residual sense of guilt that Germany had been unjustly treated under the post-war Treaty of Versailles".[6] However, many Britons were extremely impressed by the Nazi's health programmes' activities for the young, their unemployment benefits and their social security. It seemed that all this had given back to the Germans the pride they had lost in defeat and humiliation at the end of the First World War in 1918. In Britain there was a great appreciation for this. Many people in Britain envied the

Germans' new initiatives in social upliftment because they themselves were suffering in Britain in the '30s from appalling poverty, filthy living conditions, bad health and unemployment. All this blighted the lives of the working classes in Britain. The Prince of Wales embarrassed the Baldwin government in the first half of the 1930s with his promise that he would do his utmost to improve these conditions. In the light of this, Smuts was not at all out of step with his initial positive remarks regarding Hitler and his Nazi regime.

Smuts was convinced that the peace, negotiated in Paris, was conceived on a wrong basis. He was of the opinion that the Germans would not accept the Peace Treaty and even if they did accept it, it was bound to be an unstable peace.[7] "Germany," Smuts said, "was being destroyed—Germany was bound to remain the dominant factor in Europe."[8] Smuts truly believed that the Peace Treaty, if not drastically amended, would certainly lead to another big war in the very near future. He consulted General Louis Botha to determine how they could bring it to the attention of Lloyd George. Should Britain get involved in another such war she could no longer count upon South Africa to come to her aid in whatever form.

Smuts and General Von Lettow Vorbeck, 1929. (Central Archives Repository)

In the late 1930s, leading up to the Second World War, Smuts was deputy prime minister in Hertzog's Coalition government. Naturally he was watching and following developments in Europe very closely. Undoubtedly one of Smuts' greatest wishes was to be part and parcel of all the events in Europe. While Hertzog went to London to attend the Imperial Conference of 1937, Smuts had to stay at home. From the time of Munich to the outbreak of the War, Smuts kept his friends informed from week to week about his views on the international situation. "His letters," according to Hancock, "expressed

Smuts, deputy prime minister and General J.B.M. Hertzog, prime minister, 1938. (Central Archives Repository)

two intermingling moods: the mood of an observer, trying to understand events in the outer world and their significance for South Africa; the mood of a participator, trying to discover his own duty."[9]

From London Hertzog wrote to Smuts on his birthday: "That there is little sympathy for Germany and Germans in government circles here was clearly to be seen from a few words added by Mr Baldwin to those of Eden after the latter had finished his 'general review of the situation'."[10] Hertzog pointed out that there was actually no reason for Eden to disapprove of Germany's behaviour—besides her move into the Rhineland and her rearmament with Hitler's dictatorial power.

Baldwin was, in turn, alarmed by Germany's "immoral and incalculable form of government".[11] This was of course in great contrast to English democracy. On this matter Hertzog concluded that neither Eden nor Baldwin could explain why the world situation could be regarded as "deterioration"—going from bad to worse due to Germany's actions. How Smuts wished to be in London at this time! Conflict between Hertzog and Smuts was unavoidable. Hertzog saw Hitler as the champion of European freedom, while Smuts saw him as its destroyer.

Apart from his constant correspondence with friends and colleagues in London in which he emphatically expressed his views on events in Europe, Smuts also had friends in other parts of the world. In October 1937 he wrote to Thomas Lamont, an American banker, and assured him that South Africa was "most anxious to keep American good will ... I personally look with you upon closer economic cooperation between the two great countries as possibly the best prospect we have at present for world security and peace in future". He turned to world events:

I had hoped to have an opportunity of discussing these and cognate problems with British statesmen personally. You know how little you do by correspondence and how much you get by personal suasion and pressure. I know that British statesmen are overwhelmed with European troubles and that it may be most helpful for them to come into contact with those who see world events from a wider angle, and for this reason I had wished to go to London after the session of our parliament concluded in June. However the absence of the prime minister and some other of my colleagues at the imperial conference and the necessity for me to remain at the helm in South Africa, made it impossible to leave the country, and even yet I see no prospect of getting into personal contact with the British leaders. This I deeply regret but I cannot help myself. My first duty is here, however deeply I may feel the importance of what is happening abroad. Perhaps in the not distant future some opportunity may occur for me to get to grips with our friends in London, and to endeavour to push some of the causes which I have at heart.[12]

Smuts had a much better in-depth understanding of current European affairs than Hertzog. In spite of the fact that Smuts was not prime minister or for that matter minister of foreign affairs he, apart from studying international affairs intensively, kept in close contact throughout with those he knew so well in government circles in White Hall. His regular correspondence, for instance, with Lord Amery, Lord Lothian and various other personalities provide interesting reading matter. Smuts tried very hard to influence these people in high positions and press upon them his ideas regarding the rising Adolf Hitler.

Smuts was extremely puzzled by events in Germany. His own analysis could not really satisfy him. Soon after the "bloodbath at Nuremburg" in June 1934, he wrote:

It was always said that the Germans were too highly cultured to imitate the Bolshevists. But Nazi Germany seems to me even more repulsive in her methods than Russia or Fascist Italy ever was. I am deeply puzzled over this, as it fills me with doubt and misgiving for the future. We can continue to cultivate the good life in our private circle, but what is to become of the world if this sort of madness continues to grow in public life.[13]

Smuts' opinion was that Germany's "inferiority complex" contributed greatly to her aggressive mood. He believed that this mood could probably be neutralised by treating her as an equal. Smuts was concerned about Hitler's "mind and motives". To a certain extent he regarded Hitler's unpredictability as a menacing factor. It was time to return to the term *appeasement*. It was a concept coined by Smuts 15 years earlier at the Paris Peace Conference.[14] At that time *appeasement* signified, for him, a policy of magnanimity and the application of extreme restraint from the stronger party's side towards the weaker party. Gradually Smuts realised that in the '30s the whole situation had changed considerably. It moved in just the opposite direction—"a policy of propitiation pursued by the stronger party towards the weaker party".[15] But, due to the fact that he strongly believed that the victors in the First World War remained the stronger party, he still used the term in its original sense.

Smuts knew that it was no use preaching *appeasement* without practising it. He was prepared to state whom he wanted to *appease* and with what. He was, furthermore, prepared to state which countries he would exclude from his *appeasement*—namely Italy and Japan. Naturally their elimination left Germany as the only European power who qualified for Smuts' *appeasement*. "My own view," he wrote in March 1935, "is that the colonial question as settled in Paris should be reopened and that some real effort should be made to satisfy Germany."[16]

Smuts remained extremely critical towards the French. He did not regard the French as an effective ally and was most suspicious about their diplomatic and negotiating abilities. He viewed Britain as the strongest partner in the Allied camp. To him it was Britain that would have to set the pace and the direction in European affairs. He wrote to Lord Lothian:

I agree very much with Hitler where he says that no progress will be made by Franco-German conversations. The French are either too suspicious, or their government is too weak to come to any arrangement which requires courage and foresight. French policy has consistently queered the pitch ever since the peace. If any advances are to be made, it will have to be made by direct talks between England and Germany. It is only after a careful exploration of a possible settlement between these two, that a strong line can be taken with France, and she can be induced to acquiesce in a settlement. England has the advantage of support by Italy in any firm line that she might take, and I cannot believe that once there is the possibility of an advantageous settlement agreed on between England, Italy and Germany, that France will really stand out. Any lead today will have to come from the British government.[17]

But developments in Europe did not go the way Smuts would have liked them to go. He started to doubt the successful outcome of it all in an attempt to defuse the developing tension. To him France remained a weak and unpredictable partner in European affairs. When he wrote to A.B. Gillett there were signs of despair:

> *The fat is of course in the fire, and the position is very bad. When this reaches you the crisis will have gone one way or the (other) way. I think it will be peace. But at the moment the French seem to have lost their heads, and one cannot say what will happen. I hope Simon will persuade Hitler partly to retrace his steps. It may be that the French plan to frighten Hitler into such a course by their violent attitude. But with Germany in the mood of nationalistic exultation in which she has been for some time, the outcome of the Simon mission is in doubt. I have spoken some words backing up a peaceful settlement which express the sentiment of South Africa. But of course that does not amount to much. It is almost unthinkable that we should once more be precipitated into war. But the impossible sometimes happens when people are not normal, and people today are not normal on the Continent. The English have only one role and that is to be the peace-maker in this sad and dangerous development.* [18]

Smuts became more critical of Britain's handling of the growing European crisis, especially her handling of the Italian dictator, Benito Mussolini. Smuts realised that what he had said earlier, of the possibility of Italy assisting Britain in solving European problems and defusing the growing tension in Europe, would and could not come into practice. Smuts now warned that success for Mussolini in Abyssinia would undoubtedly encourage Hitler to follow the same path in order to boost his prestige in Europe. The Italians were extremely proud of the extension of their territory by the annexation of Abyssinia. "If Italy gets away with it," he wrote later, "Germany or rather Hitler will follow suit within five years and the world will once more be convulsed from end to end." [19] Smuts was extremely upset with Britain's handling of Mussolini as well as Mussolini's defiance of the League of Nations. When frustrated he would always put his thoughts on paper:

> *The cowardly surrender of the British government to Mussolini has come as a grievous disappointment to me, and I don't know on what issue they could now be counted to stand firm.... My confidence is deeply shaken, and I do not know at the moment where a solid foundation for hope and confidence remains..... If Britain had stood firm and faced up to Mussolini, the world would have caught new hope and faith and would have rallied to the British standpoint. The world was waiting for a sign, for a lead. But what leadership has been here?*[20]

His friend Lord Lothian inspired Smuts by visiting Berlin. He returned with the news that Hitler certainly did not want war. He reported that Hitler believed in self-determination. Lothian's opinion was that Hitler could be trusted to keep the peace for at least the next ten years. But there was certainly a specific provision to this. Britain had to negotiate with Hitler in "a spirit of frankness, firmness and respect for Germany's equal rights". Smuts accepted Lothian's diagnosis of Hitler's attitude. If only the British would pursue "a resolute policy of appeasement and reconstruction of the Peace". He was convinced that this could have far-reaching effects.[21]

Hitler reoccupied the Rhineland on 7 March 1936. He went beyond his earlier defiance of the Versailles Treaty. He did this in spite of the fact that the previous October he declared that Germany would continue to accept neutralisation of the Rhineland. Hitler acknowledged Germany's obligation under the freely negotiated Locarno Treaty. Smuts ranked Hitler at this stage equal to Mussolini as a disturber of the peace. It was therefore expected that he would certainly demand equal treatment for both alike. But strangely enough, he did just the opposite. For Mussolini he thought coercion the most effective treatment and for Hitler conciliation. The Italians qualified for a thrashing, but Smuts thought the Germans should rather, as an investment for the future, be persuaded into peaceful behaviour.[22] Smuts took a strong stand against Mussolini. "He is unfriendly," he wrote to L.S. Amery, "he is mischievous, he has done his best to humiliate the British government successfully for the last four years, and his menace to our Empire communications and to those of France across the Mediterranean is probably the most serious danger that we have to face at the moment."[23]

Smuts knew, however, that he was acting contrary to his own better judgement. He thought it a curse that, for the sake of European peace, Hitler's villainous policy should be supported. It simply went against the grain of Smuts' temperament. In March 1936 he wrote:

> *Hitler's general election is over and once more the inevitable 100% majority has been recorded. And now the negotiations will be resumed. It is a cursed spite that we have (for the sake of European peace) to support the ruffianly policy of Hitler. That is to say we have to maintain peace with him and keep France in check, although we hate the internal policy of Hitler. Fate makes strange company, and we cannot always choose ours.*[24]

Smuts was referring to Hitler's scoundralist policy in his own country:

> *Nazism ... destroys the very soul of our civilization.... I have not taken the same grave view of Bolshevism, for it never was clear to me that Bolshevism, in spite of its brutalities and cruelties, really threatened the essentials of our ethical civilization. And after all it was a revolution of a semi-barbarous people against a rotten government and an effete church. But Nazism in highly cultured Germany is a very different affair.*[25]

Smuts found Hitler's policy detestable in spite of his positive approach towards other countries. "From the point of view of the Commonwealth," wrote Hancock, "he saw a distinction between the Fascist and Nazi dictatorships: Italy, the friend of yesterday, had become a deadly and dangerous enemy;

Germany, the deadly enemy of yesterday, wanted to be friendly."[26] Nevertheless Smuts remained puzzled, but he continued concentrating on possible positive aspects. He recognised the vital importance of keeping the peace. Some thought that Smuts was grasping desperately at grass-blades in an atmosphere of aggressiveness and mistrust. But he nevertheless thought it to be worthwhile.

Smuts welcomed Hitler's offer of peace negotiations. He recalled the years of Germany's peaceful neighbourliness with the countries in Europe, and of course Germany's return to the League of Nations. All this convinced him that there was a real chance to rebuild. It could develop into a positive outcome and this could lead to a genuine desire amongst European statesmen to opt for lasting peace in Europe.

In spite of all that had happened since Hitler came to power in 1933, Smuts still believed that the British Empire had nothing to fear. "Hitler is personally friendly towards the British Empire," he wrote in December 1937 to Lord Amery, "and has repeatedly declared himself for a *rapprochement* with us. Publicly and privately he has expressed his view that the cardinal mistake of imperial Germany was to menace the British Empire and he is not going to repeat that mistake."[27] But Smuts still resented Mussolini and branded him as an extreme menace. He was most concerned about Mussolini's threat to the Mediterranean. He regarded this as a most serious danger to be faced presently.[28] Smuts predicted that the Mediterranean would replace the North Sea and most probably become the prospective scene of severe trouble for the Empire and its Allies. With this in mind Smuts believed that the British diplomatic talks with Hitler were justified. "There is this to be said in addition, that if an understanding with Hitler is possible, Mussolini could not stand out, and the same cannot be said for the reverse situation."[29] In spite of mistrust and disappointments Smuts remained convinced that the current European system should continue at all cost! While the League of Nations was functioning effectively, Smuts thought that it should be used in order to secure universal peace.

Smuts was extremely worried that the League could lose its effectiveness as a peace-preserving organ internationally, especially in the light of the ever-increasing tension in Europe. Remember that the League was one of his creations! Smuts thought the developing set-up of the League a disadvantage for its survival. He pointed out that the Great Powers were not always present at discussions, and therefore a completely different *modus operandi* would have to be developed.

Although continually puzzled by Hitler's actions, Smuts constantly tried to put these actions into perspective. In Germany a strong movement developed, supported by Dr Hjalmar Schacht, a prominent German banker, for the restoration of the former German colonies.[30] To Smuts it was certainly not necessary to take this seriously. He ignored it as cheap German propaganda. "No doubt Hitler wants to save his face," Smuts said. "He is a dictator who must constantly be able to deliver the goods."[31] Significantly, Smuts suggested that Hitler was probably forced in this direction by a pressure group in Germany and that, due to this fact, "we may have to meet him a little way in order to save his face".[32] Smuts' opinion was that Hitler would not try to repeat Mussolini's "madness" in North Africa in an attempt to "strike their luck" to regain South West Africa and Tanganyika. "They know how keen we are to keep both," Smuts concluded, "and I do not think that they will attempt to force the pace as far as these territories are concerned."[33] Mussolini's colonisation of Ethiopia boosted his image in Italy as well as the morale of the Italians. Mussolini ignored international condemnation of this aggressive act. The League of Nations simply made no impression on him.

Since 1933 the local Germans in South West Africa had run a well-organised Nazi propaganda campaign. This was operated in such an aggressive way that D.G. Conradie, the administrator of SWA, ordered Erich von Lossnitser, leader of the Hitlerjugend, and Major Heinrich Weigel, leader of the NZDAP, to leave the country between July – October 1934. The German/Italian press launched a vicious attack abroad on the South African government. The political situation in SWA became extremely tense and developed into a very delicate international diplomatic issue. The Nazis now indulged in an underground *modus operandi*. The South African government appointed a commission to investigate the developments in SWA. The

Top: Smuts pointing out to Isie the position of troops in East Africa. (Smuts House Museum)

Center: Smuts and his family during World War II. Seated, left to right: Kathleen Mincher (née de Villiers, foster daughter); Isie Smuts; Jan Smuts; Dr Louis McIldowie (née Smuts); Sylma Coaton (née Smuts). Standing, left to right: Jan Smuts Jnr; Jack Coaton (son-in-law); Japie Smuts. Inserts, top left: Daphne, Smuts (née Webster, wife of Jan Smuts Jnr). top right: Santa Weyers (née Smuts). Absent: Cato Clark (née Smuts). (Smuts House Museum)

Bottom: Smuts and sons, Japie and Jannie. (Central Archives Repository)

Germans and the Italians continued their attacks from abroad. On 7 April 1937 *The Cape Argus* in Cape Town warned that these vicious attacks on the South African government from abroad could ignite a world conflict. On Hitler's birthday, 20 April 1939, the British government warned the South African government that the Germans in SWA could start a revolt. On 17 April Smuts decided to send a police force of 363 men to SWA. The commissioner of police reported that the force arrived just in time to prevent a *coup d' état*.

In his analysis of Hitler's *modus operandi*, Smuts was anxious to maintain the stance that Hitler's policy in Europe involved expanding economically into Central and Eastern Europe. Smuts argued that this was indeed the theme of Hitler's *Mein Kampf* and there were, according to him, just too many indications that economics was the real objective of German foreign policy.[34] Smuts was of course totally wrong in this assumption. Smuts had no further illusions about the difficulty in deciding how far Britain and her Allies should fall in line with, or acquiesce to, Germany's current politics. It was an important matter and there were considerations to be made both ways. According to Smuts, Germany should have been given an outlet to the East to divert her from the West and from her colonial ambitions. Smuts made it abundantly clear to Amery that he found it very difficult to come to any balanced conclusion on this matter. It was of the utmost importance for Smuts, in order to prevent the outbreak of a full-scale war in Europe, to control those forced measures, which might just easily precipitate a conflict of a dangerous nature. He thought it advisable in those circumstances to gain time and let the current situation develop as normally as possible. By doing so the natural forces, which governed the European situation, would be given the opportunity "to find their way to the future".[35] "With the disappearance of the Austro-Hungarian Empire," Smuts argued, "Germany was certainly given a great opportunity for aggrandisement." This was the result of the situation in which the remnants of the former Empire suddenly found themselves. Although it was extremely difficult to predict how the general situation in Europe would really develop, Smuts nevertheless thought that it would most probably favour Germany. He concluded:

But whatever the evolution of the future may be, we should take every precaution that it develops peacefully, and that Germany is kept in check and prevented from embarking on policies that must inevitably lead to a general war. Our game is to play for time and for peaceful developments, and I think that if we are on good terms with the German government, we are more likely to succeed in this policy and in maintaining the peace of Europe, than we would be by dealing with her at arm's length.[36]

Smuts did his utmost to convince his friends in government circles in London that there was no other option left than to win Hitler over with diplomacy and a great amount of patience and self-discipline. There was simply too much at stake.

Smuts was convinced that no future conflict in Europe, should it come to that, could be handled without a close association with the United States.[37] He believed that a strategy should be embarked upon so that the United States would consider the British Empire her concern. Smuts realised that Great Britain's position in Europe was becoming increasingly more difficult and certainly more precarious.

Smuts blamed the non-enthusiastic attitude of the German middle classes for the rise of Adolf Hitler and his Nazi regime. He made the point that the middle classes in Germany did not play the role that was expected from them in the economic society and therefore they did not do their duty to the republic.[38] Smuts wanted to "go all out", by means of political action and if necessary by fighting, in order to preserve the democratic principles of the Western world. He was convinced that the totalitarians were certain to win "and reduce our civilization to a confirmed servitude", if something radical was not done. And this was naturally unacceptable. He would rather die in action than become totally passive. Smuts stated that if the latter became the option—being passive—the downfall of Western civilisation was inevitable. In March 1939 Smuts wrote:

If fighting is at all justified for self-defence, indeed if self-defence is under any circumstances justified, we

*should be prepared to fight for ultimate principles. These
principles I think are at stake in the present conflict of the
ideologies. Nazism is a form of what is called Anti-Christ. I
am prepared to fight against that.*[39]

In March 1939 events in Europe moved extremely fast. In a
pessimistic mood, Smuts mentioned in a letter to Margaret
Gillett that events had moved even faster than he had ever
expected. While the newspapers reported that conditions were
improving in the tension in Europe, and while both
Chamberlain and Hertzog were talking about the prospects of a
long era of peace, Hitler once again delivered a stunning
surprise—the invasion of Czechoslovakia without any
resistance whatsoever.[40]

Smuts was sharp in his denouncement of Chamberlain's
speech in the House of Commons after the invasion. He
referred to the speech as a "feeble performance". He was
wondering if any previous British prime minister had ever
made such a feeble show. He really pitied the prime minister.
"His whole effort for peace," Smuts said, "has simply been set
aside without further ado, and the naked reality stares him in
the face. I have no doubt that his intention was good and first
results (in securing peace last September) all to the good. But
how can one deal with these people if one genuinely wishes to
avoid war? Must force be the last word, on our side also?"[41]

On Friday, 1 September 1939, Britain and France heard that
the armed forces of the *Third Reich* had invaded Poland. They
proclaimed general mobilisation and gave their ambassadors in
Berlin instructions to deliver identical messages to the German
Foreign Ministry: Germany must halt her invasion of Poland
and withdraw her troops from Polish territory immediately.[42] If
she did not, Britain and France would "fulfil their obligations to
Poland without hesitation".[43] When her ultimatum expired,
Great Britain declared war on Germany on Sunday, 3
September 1939.[44] In the South African Parliament a dramatic
debate was conducted on the issue of South Africa's
responsibility as a dominion and member of the British
Commonwealth to Britain. Hertzog proposed neutrality and
Smuts active involvement. Eventually, the speaker rose and

said: " ... those who supported General Hertzog's original motion take seats to his right and those against to his left." From his place beside Hertzog, Smuts rose and, followed by his supporters, crossed the floor; Dr Malan and his followers crossed and sat behind Hertzog. This was the moment of final parting between these two great leaders.[45] Hertzog got 67 votes and Smuts 80. Hertzog's motion was thus defeated. Smuts wrote to his wife on 6 September: "Whereas I thought when I came here that I would soon be out of the government, I am now, or shall be tomorrow, prime minister."[46] Major Piet van der Byl, minister in Smuts' War Cabinet, wrote:

How well I remember my feelings at the time. I realised fully what a colossal military power we were up against; and what our fate as a country and as individuals would be if we lost, I felt very small and humble. But I honestly believed that there was no other course open. It was obvious to me that, with our strategic position at the tip of Africa ... we would be forced to take sides one way or the other....[47]

On 6 September Smuts, having completed his Cabinet the day before, called his first Cabinet meeting. He was in high spirits and started by saying, "Well, gentleman, we must now declare war on Germany."[48] It was said that when Hitler learned about South Africa's declaration of war on Germany, he laughed![49] The new prime minister received a telegram from Winston Churchill[50]:

> TO: General Smuts
> FROM: First Lord of the Admiralty
> DATED: 7 September 1939
>
> I rejoice to feel that we are once again on commando together

But to Smuts war was a serious business. During this time his correspondence to friends portrayed a gloomy outlook on the future of Europe. He wrote to Margaret Gillett on 21 September:

> *... there is no turning back. This war may go on until*
> *Britain and France are utterly exhausted and Germany*
> *also is utterly exhausted ... and Russia, the looter, strides*
> *on to the desolate scene to collar the spoils. I hate to think of*
> *a Hitler Europe, but no less to think of a Stalin Europe: it is*
> *a choice between the Devil and Beelzebub. Our hope is there*
> *will be an early internal collapse of Germany and that this*
> *devastating struggle will not continue till Europe sinks*
> *down in utter exhaustion and despair.*[51]

Amid the dramatic developments of those past few days Smuts
thought about all the tragedies of the First World War. He
wrote to W.T. Lamont:

> *Shall we never learn our lesson? There is no solution*
> *through war. This war, whatever the ultimate issue, will be*
> *followed by another peace which may be no peace, for after*
> *a devastating conflict there is no mood for a real and wise*
> *peace, as you and I found at Paris in 1919. Meanwhile*
> *civilisation is falling back, and the light of the spirit is*
> *being dimmed.*
>
> *The outcome no man can foresee. I hope for the best and*
> *pray that Human Personality may triumph against the*
> *overwhelming forces threatening to submerge it.*
>
> *And so the caravan passes once more into the night. May*
> *God be with us and take the hands of His erring children.*[52]

As Europe moved rapidly into a state of total war, and Smuts
finally realised that nothing could be done to avert it, his attitude
towards Adolf Hitler changed radically. In a letter to Lord Brand
he referred to Hitler as "a scourge of God, like Attila the Hun".[53]
Smuts found it extremely difficult to come to terms with a Nazi
Germany that had vigorously replaced the Germany he, Smuts,
admired for her traditions and culture. It is doubtful whether he
ever came to terms with it at all! Once again he wrote, *inter alia*,
to Margaret Gillett to relieve his troubled mind:

> *I don't hate Germans, and I feel deeply for Europe of which*
> *Germany remains an integral, if not a dominant part. I*

know how dangerous the predominance of any one power can be, and how liable such dominant power is to abuse. I remember British jingoism and the Boer War; and I know Russia has even less experience and human wisdom than the British. And so my faith in man does not extend to faith in Russia, with no check on her in Europe and Asia, and mistress of the continent of Europe. Such a position is too much of a temptation even to the wisest, let alone to an upstart power such as Russia. Our position in the world is therefore a very dangerous one, and one which permits of no mere optimism and exultation in victory.... [54]

Smuts was not present at Yalta and Potsdam where the fate of Germany was decided.[55] As in the case of the Peace Conference in Paris after the First World War, Smuts was very concerned about the treatment of Germany by the victorious Allies. He still thought, as was the case in Paris 26 years ago, that the destruction of Germany would ultimately mean the destruction of Europe. Clement Attlee, the new British prime minister who replaced Churchill in the first general election after the War, wrote in response to a letter he received from Smuts:

I have given much thought to the message which you sent me through the South African high commissioner here in reply to my personal telegram of 1 August supplementing the final report of the Berlin conference. Needless to say, I welcome this expression of your views on a subject on which you are so well qualified to speak, and I am glad that you have given us such a clear exposition of the anxieties which you feel and which, to some extent, we naturally share.

It is of course true that to depress the level of Germany's industry and standard of living below a certain point would do harm to Europe as a whole and to ourselves. We shall do everything in our power to prevent this, but any suspicion—and the Russians are not slow to form suspicions—that we were trying to deal softly with Germany, or to build her up, would be such an obvious threat to Russia that we could thereby harden the Soviet government's present attitude in eastern Europe and help to give actual shape to our fears.

I am sorry you cannot come to London during the meeting of foreign ministers. Your great experience in these matters and the reliance which we have always been able to place on your advice lead me to hope that you may find an opportunity during the next few months to pay us a visit here, giving us the benefit of your counsel.[56]

Smuts' anxiety is quite understandable. With Franklin D. Roosevelt and Winston S. Churchill not present at the peace negotiations, the inexperienced Harry S. Truman and Clement Attlee were to face the experienced Josef Stalin. Would they be up to it?

1. Gertrude Millin, *General Smuts,* 1, 94 – 95.
2. *Ibid.,* 36.
3. W.K. Hancock, *Smuts, I. The Sanguine Years, 1870 – 1919,* 16.
4. Millin, 95.
5. Jean van der Poel (ed), *Smuts Papers,* Volume IV, 10 June 1919, 225.
6. Royal Monthly, Volume 8, no. 7, April 1989, 42.
7. Hancock, 1, 510.
8. *Ibid.,* 511.
9. W.K. Hancock, *Smuts, II. The Fields of Force, 1919 – 1950,* 308.
10. Smuts Papers, Volume VI, 24 May 1937, 82.
11. *Ibid.*
12. Smuts Papers, Volume VI, 21 October 1937, 98.
13. Trewhella Cameron, *Jan Smuts. An Illustrated Biography,* 132.
14. Hancock, 11, 271.

15. *Ibid.*, 272.
16. Smuts Papers, Volume VI, 23 March 1935, 16.
17. *Ibid.*, 20 February 1935, 8.
18. *Ibid.*, 23 March 1935, 15. Sir John Simon was then foreign secretary.
19. Hancock, 11, 275.
20. Smuts Papers, Volume VI, 27 June 1936, 46.
21. Hancock, 11, 271.
22. *Ibid.*, 275.
23. Smuts Papers, Volume VI, 9 December 1937, 110.
24. Smuts Papers, Volume VI, 30 March 1936, 32.
25. Hancock, 11, 358.
26. *Ibid.*, 276.
27. Smuts Papers, Volume VI, 9 December 1937, 110.
28. *Ibid.*
29. *Ibid.*
30. *Ibid.*, 111.
31. *Ibid.*
32. *Ibid.*
33. *Ibid.*
34. *Ibid.*
35. *Ibid.*
36. *Ibid.*, 111 – 112.
37. Hancock, 11, 379. Ingham, 212, 221.
38. Smuts Papers, Volume VI, 10 March 1939, 153.
39. *Ibid.*, 154.
40. Smuts Papers, Volume VI, 17 March 1939, 154.
41. *Ibid.*, 156.
42. E. Bauer, *The History of World War II. The full story of the world's greatest conflict*, 33.
43. *Ibid.*
44. *Ibid.*
45. Piet van der Byl, *Top Hat to Velskoen,* 159. F.S. Crafford, *Jan Smuts. A Biography*, 304.
46. Smuts Papers, Volume VI, 5 September 1939, 189.
47. Van der Byl, 163.
48. *Ibid.*
49. Crafford, 305.
50. Smuts Papers, Volume VI, 7 September 1939, 191.

51. Smuts Papers, Volume VI, 21 September 1939, 193.
52. Smuts Papers, Volume VI, 6 September 1939, 189.
53. Smuts Papers, Volume VI, 13 November 1939, 199.
54. Smuts Papers, Volume VI, 4 March 1945, 527.
55. A.J.P. Taylor, *English History, 1914 – 1945,* 315 – 316, 720 – 721.
56. Smuts Papers, Volume VII, 31 August 1945, 6 – 7.

Top: Smuts addressing the San Francisco Conference, 1945.
(Central Archives Repository)

Bottom: Smuts signing the United Nations Charter. (Central Archives Repository)

Smuts, Isie and their six children, 1919. Left to right: Sylma, Isie, Santa, Japie, Louis, Cato, Smuts, Jannie. (Smuts House Museum)

Smuts with two of his grandchildren. (Smuts House Museum)

Top left: *Part of the ceremony during the presentation of the Freedom of the City of Aberdeen, October 1930.* (Central Archives Repository)

Top right: *Smuts' inauguration as chancellor of Cambridge University, June 1948.* (Central Archives Repository)

Bottom: *The installation of Smuts as rector of St Andrews, the oldest university of Scotland, October, 1934.* (Central Archives Repository)

Serue
15 Nov. 1926

Liewe Mrs Steyn

My was te my dat U
haar on Holism gekmywe het.
Ik voel waarlik baie gevleid
dat U belangstel in die werk, en
said U een copie, nie met
die doel om U lastig te val om
dit te lees nie, maar meer as
een blyk van die ou bande

wat ons so lang aan mekaar
bind, en wat sans ook
maar sveear bij ons al
die verskille in die land!
Maar het soos my van
voel en weerdes ek altyd
baie U liefde en hartelikheis.
En van ons kant is daar
ook een gevoel wat baie dieper
gaat as woorde of ander
uitinge.

Holism was my een gud
om mee besig te wees, ondat dit een
wereld behandel van vrede en eenheid
in die groote dinge van die gees. It is
nie gemaak vir twis en haat, a wel
my altyd rgelukkig in daardie omgewing.
Maar in Holism is daar die gees wat
alles na mekaar trek met bande
wat nederhand sterker is as enige
krag ter wereld.

Dit was my baie aangenaas
wees ader toe ek vind te Bloemfontein te
wees. Die herinnering wat as die mekaar
bind is tot maar die groothe en diepte van
die lewe. Baie hartelik groet
J. Smuts.

Smuts' letter in November 1926 to Mrs Rachel Steyn, wife of President M.T. Steyn, President of the Orange Free State, regarding his Holism and Evolution. (M.T. Steyn)

Top left: *Smuts on Table Mountain, 1924.* (Central Archives Repository)

Top right: *Smuts identifying a specimen.* (Smuts House Museum)

Bottom: *Smuts botanising with Margaret Gillett and her son Jan. The latter was named after Smuts.* (Smuts House Museum)

Smuts and Isie at Groote Schuur among the chrysanthemums. (Smuts House Museum)

Smuts and his close friend and confidant Louis Esselen. (Central Archives Repository)

Smuts staring into the future at San Francisco. (Central Archives Repository)

SELECT BIBLIOGRAPHY

I. ARCHIVAL SOURCES
1.   UNITED KINGDOM
1.1   PUBLIC RECORD OFFICE (London)
1.1.1   Colonial Office
   C.O. 532
   C.O. 551
1.1.2   Dominion Office
   D.O. 13
   D.O. 35
   D.O. 114
   D.O. 116
   D.O. 117
1.1.3   Cabinet Office
   CAB 32: Minutes of Meetings of British Cabinet
1.2   PUBLIC RECORD OFFICE (Edinburgh)
   G.D: Papers of Philip Kerr, 11th marquess of Lothian, 1882 – 1940
1.3   INSTITUTE OF COMMONWEALTH STUDIES, UNIVERSITY OF LONDON
   Diary: Lt. Col. H. Birch Reynardson. Military Secretary to Earl of Athlone, Governor General of South Africa. (4 volumes)
1.4   IMPERIAL WAR MUSEUM, London
   Diary: Colonel C.H. Hore – Ruthven, Secretary to the Governor General of South Africa, Earl Clarendon, 1933 – 1936.
1.5   ROYAL ARCHIVES (Windsor Castle)
   George V Papers
   Diaries of George V
1.6   COLLINDALE PRESS LIBRARY
   Various English newspapers as indicated in footnotes
2.   REPUBLIC OF IRELAND
2.1   NATIONAL LIBRARY OF IRELAND (Dublin)
   M.S 10, 581: Col. Maurice Moore Papers

2.2   FRANCISCAN LIBRARY (Killiney)
        Eamon de Valera Papers
2.3   NATIONAL ARCHIVES (Dublin)
3.   SOUTH AFRICA
3.1   CENTRAL ARCHIVES (Pretoria)
        J.C. Smuts Collection

II. CONSULTED WORKS

Adamthwaite, *The Making of the Second World War*. London, 1980.

Albrecht-Carrie, René, *The Meaning of the First World War*. New Jersey, 1965.

Alhadeff, V., *South Africa in Two World Wars*. London, 1979.

Aronson, Alice, *Princess Alice of Athlone*. London, 1981.

Aschcroft, Edward, *De Gaulle*. London, 1962.

Attlee, Clement, *Empire into Commonwealth. The Chichele lextures of May 1960*. London, 1961.

Barnard, S.L., *et al, Die Verenigde Party. Die groot eksperiment*. Pretoria, 1982.

Bauer, E, *The History of World War II. The Full Story of the World's Greatest Conflict*. London, 1979.

Beaverbrook, Lord, *Men and Power, 1917 – 1918*. London 1956.

Beukes, Piet, *The Holistic Smuts. A Study in Personality*. Pretoria, 1989.

Blackwell, L., *Blackwell Remembers*. Cape Town, 1971.

Bradford, Sarah, *Elizabeth: A Biography of Her Majesty the Queen*. London, 1996.

Brink, André, P, *Heildronk*. Cape Town, 1981.

Brockway, Lord, *Britain's Anti-Colonial Campaigner in the British Empire*. Volume 8. Part 89. London, 1980.

Calvocoressi, Peter, *et al, Total War. Causes and Courses of the Second World War*. Harmondsworth, 1974.

Bullock, Alan, *Hitler: A Study in Tyranny*. Harmondsworth, 1974.

Cameron, Trewhella, *Jan Smuts. An Illustrated Biography*. Cape Town, 1994.

Cameron, Trewhella (ed), *A New Illustrated History of South Africa*. Cape Town, 1991.

Campbell, A., *Smuts and Swastika*. London, 1943.

Carter, V.N., *Winston Churchill. As I knew him*. London, 1965.

Chadha, Yogesh, *Rediscovering Gandhi*. London, 1997.

Chalfont, Alan, *Montgomery of Alamein*. London, 1976.

Chamberlain, Austen, *Politics from Inside. An Epistolary Chronicle, 1906 – 1914*.

Churchill, Winston, S., *My Early Life*. London, 1972. Ninth Impression.

Churchill, Winston, S., *The World Crisis, 1916 – 1918*. London, 1927.

Churchill, Winston, S., *The Second World War*. Volumes 1 – 12. London, 1948.

Churchill, Winston, S., *The Second World War and an Epilogue on the years, 1945 – 1957*. London, 1959.

Churchill, Winston, S., *My Early Life*. London, 1972.

Churchill, Winston, S., *The Boer War*. London, 1989. The Cooper edition.

Churchill, Winston, S., *The Boer War. London to Ladysmith*. London, 1990.

Clomer, William, *Cecil Rhodes*. Cape Town, 1984.

Collins, Lorry, *et al, Freedom at Midnight*. London, 1977.

Colville, John, *The Fringes of Power. Downing Street Diaries. Volume One: 1939 –October 1941*. London, 1985.

Colville, John, *The Fringes of Power. Downing Street Diaries. Volume Two: 1941 – April 1955*. London, 1987.

Colville, John, *Footprints in Time. Memories*. London, 1976.

Coogan, Tim, Pat, *De Valera. Long Fellow, Long Shadow*. London, 1993.

Cook, Don, *Charles de Gaulle. A Biography*. New York, 1983.

Crafford, F.S., *Jan Smuts. A Biography*. London, 1946.

Cross, Colin, *The Fall of the British Empire*. London, 1968.

Cross, Colin, *Adolf Hitler*. London, 1974.

Crozier, Brian, *De Gaulle. The Statesman*. London, 1973.

Crozier, Brian, *De Gaulle. The Warrior*. London, 1973.

Danziger, C., *Jan Smuts. 'n Blik op Suid-Afrikaanse Geskiedenis*. Cape Town, 1978.

Davidson, Apollon, *Cecil Rhodes and his time*. Moscow, 1984. Translated from the Russian by Christopher English.

Eddy, John, *The Rise of Colonial Nationalism*. London, 1988.

Eden, Anthony, *The Eden Memoirs. The Reckoning*. London, 1965.

Engelenburg, F.V., *General Louis Botha*. Pretoria, 1929.

Everett, Susanne, *World War II.* London, 1980.

Felix, Gross, *Rhodes of Africa.* London, 1956.

Fest, Joachim, C., *The Face of the Third Reich.* Harmondsworth, 1970.

Fischer, John, *The Afrikaners.* London, 1969.

Fischer, Louis, *The Life of Mahatma Gandhi.* London, 1952.

Friedlander, Z., *Jan Smuts Remembered. A Centennial Tribute.* Cape Town, 1970.

Friedman, B., *Smuts. A Reappraisal.* Johannesburg, 1975.

Galpin, G.H., *There are no South Africans.* London, 1941.

Gilbert, Martin, *Winston S. Churchill, Volume III, 1914 – 1916.* London, 1971.

Gilbert, Martin, *Winston S. Churchill, Volume IV, 1917 – 1922.* London, 1975.

Gilbert, Martin, *Finest Hour. Winston S. Churchill, 1939 – 1941.* London, 1983.

Gilbert, Martin, *Road to Victory. Winston Churchill, 1941 – 1945.* London, 1986.

Grant, R.G., *Winston Churchill. An illustrated biography,* London, 1989.

Griffiths, Percival, *Empire into Commonwealth.* London, 1969.

Grigg, J., *Lloyd, George. From Peace to War, 1912 – 1916.* London, 1985.

Gross, Felix, *Rhodes of Africa.* London, 1956.

Gwynn, Denis, *The Life of John Redmond.* London, 1932.

Haarhoff, T.J., *Smuts the Humanist.* Oxford, 1970.

Hall, H. Duncan, *Commonwealth. A History of the British Commonwealth of Nations.* London, 1971.

Hamilton, Nigel, *Monty. Master of the Battlefield, 1942 – 1944.* London, 1987.

Hancock, W.K., *Smuts, I. The Sanguine Years, 1870 – 1919.* Cambridge, 1962.

Hancock, W.K., *Smuts, II. The Fields of Force, 1919 – 1950.* Cambridge, 1969.

Hancock, W.K., *Smuts. Study of a Portrait.* Cambridge, 1965.

Harkness, D.W., *The Restless Dominion. The Irish Free State and the British Commonwealth of Nations, 1921 – 1931.* London, 1969.

Harris, Peter, *The Commonwealth.* London, 1975.

Headlam, Cecil (ed), *The Milner Papers. South Africa, 1897 – 1905*. Two volumes, 1897 – 1899 and 1899 – 1905. London, 1931 and 1933.

Higham, Charles, *et al, Elizabeth and Philip. The Untold Story*. London, 1991.

Howarth, Patrick, *George VI*. London, 1987.

Hyam, Ronald, *The Failure of South African Expansion, 1908 – 1948*. London, 1972.

Ingham, Kenneth, *Jan Smuts. The Conscience of a South African*. Johannesburg,1986.

Joseph, J., *South African Statesman. Jan Christian Smuts*. Folkestone, 1970.

Judd, Denis, *King George VI, 1895 – 1952*. London, 1982.

Keppel-Jones, A., *When Smuts goes: a history of South Africa from 1952 – 2010*. Pietermaritzburg, 1950.

Kierman, R.H., *General Smuts*. London, 1943.

Krause, R., *Old Master: the life of Jan Christian Smuts*. New York, 1944.

Kruger, D.W., *Paul Kruger, Volume II, 1883 – 1904*. Johannesburg, 1963.

Kruger, D.W., *The Age of the Generals*. Johannesburg, 1958.

Kruger, D.W., *The Making of a Nation. A History of the Union of South Africa, 1910 – 1961*. London, 1969.

Lawlor, Sheila, *Britain and Ireland, 1914 – 1923*. Dublin, 1983.

Lawrence, James, *The Rise and Fall of the British Empire*. London, 1994.

Levi, M., *Jan Smuts: being a character sketch of General Hon. J.C. Smuts, Minister of Defence, Union of South Africa*. London. No date mentioned.

Lewsen, Phyllis, *Selection from the Correspondence of John X. Merriman*. Cape Town, 1969.

Lloyd, T.O., *The British Empire*. London, 1984.

Lockhart, *et al, Rhodes A new biography based, for the first time, on unrestricted use of the Rhodes Papers*. London, 1963.

Longford, Elizabeth, *Winston Churchill*. London, 1974. An authorised biography.

Longford, Lord (ed), *The History Makers*. London, 1973.

Lyttelton, O., *The Memoirs of Lord Charles Chandos*. London, 1962.

Macmillan, Harold, *Tides of Fortune, 1945 – 1955*. London, 1969.

Macmillan, Harold, *War Diaries. The Mediterranean, 1943 – 1945*. London, 1984.

Mahadevan, T.K., *The year of the Phoenix. Gandhi's Pivotal Year*. New Delhi, 1982.

Malherbe, E.G., *Never a Dull Moment*. Cape Town, 1981.

Mansergh, Diana, (ed), *Selected Irish Papers by Nicholas Mansergh*. Cork University Press, 1997.

Mansergh, Nicholas, *Documents and Speeches on British Commonwealth Affairs, 1931 – 1952*. Volumes I & II. London, 1953.

Mansergh, Nicholas, *et al, Commonwealth Perspectives*. London, 1958.

Mansergh, Nicholas, *The Commonwealth Experience*. London, 1969.

Marlowe, John, *Milner. Apostle of Empire*. London, 1976.

McColgan, John, *British Policy and the Irish Administration*. London, 1983.

McIntyre, W. David, *Colonies into Commonwealth*. London, 1974. Revised Edition.

McIntyre, W.D., *The significance of the Commonwealth, 1965 – 1990*. London.

Menzies, Robert, *Afternoon Light. Some memories of men and events*. Melbourne, 1968.

Meiring, Piet, *Jan Smuts. Die Afrikaner*. Cape Town, 1974.

Miller, J.D.B. *The Commonwealth in the world*. London, 1965.

Millin, Sarah, Gertrude, *General Smuts*. Volumes I & II. London, 1936.

Montgomery, Lord, *The Memoirs of Field-Marshal the Viscount Montgomery of Alamein*. London, 1958.

Moorhead, Alan, *Churchill. A Pictorial Biography*. London, 1960.

Moran, Lord, *Winston Churchill. The Struggle for Survival, 1940 – 1965. From the diaries of Lord Moran*. London, 1960.

Morgan, Kenneth, O., *British Prime Minister, Lloyd George*. London, 1974.

Newhouse, Julia, *Spotlight on Winston Churchill*. London, 1981.

Nicolson, Nigel (ed), *Diaries and Letters, 1939 – 1945*. London, 1968.

Nimocks, Walter, *Milner's Young Men. The "kindergarten" in Edwardian Imperial Affairs*. London, 1970.

Pachai, Bridglal, *The South African Indian Question, 1860 – 1971*. Cape Town, 1971.

Pakenham, Thomas, *The Boer War*. London, 1979.

Palmer, A.W., *A Dictionary of Modern History, 1789 – 1945*. Harmondsworth, 1964.

Paton, Alan, *Hofmeyr*. Cape Town, 1971.

Paton, Alan, *Save the Beloved Country*. Melville, 1987.

Pearson, Lester, *Memoirs, 1897 – 1948. Through Diplomacy to Politics*. London, 1973.

Pearson, Lester, *Memoirs, 1948 – 1957. The International Years*. London, 1974.

Plomer, William, *Cecil Rhodes*. Cape Town, 1984.

Rhoodie, Denys, *Conspirators in Conflict. A Study of Johannesburg Reform Committee*. Cape Town, 1967.

Rose, Kenneth, *King George V*. London, 1984.

Rose, Norman, *Churchill. An unruly life*. London, 1994.

Roskill, Stephen, *Churchill's Admirals*. London, 1977.

Ryan, Cornelius, *The Longest Day. The D-Day Story*. London, 1960.

Scholtz, G.D., *Hertzog en Smuts en die Britse Ryk*. Kaapstad, 1975.

Shirer, William, L., *The Rise and Fall of the Third Reich*. London, 1972.

Shirer, William, L., *The Rise and Fall of the Third Reich. Illustrated and Abridged*. London, 1987.

Smuts, J.C. *Holism and Evolution*. London, 1926.

Smuts, J.C. (jnr), *Jan Christian Smuts*. London, 1952.

Soames, Mary, *Clementine Churchill*. London, 1979.

Soames, Mary, *A Churchill Family Album. A personal anthology*. London, 1982.

Sulzberger, C.L., *World War II*. New York, 1970.

Swan, Maureen, *Gandhi. The South African Experience*. Johannesburg, 1985.

Taylor, A.J.P., *The Origins of the Second World War*. Harmondsworth, 1963.

Taylor, A.J.P., *English History, 1914 – 1945*. Oxford, 1970.

Taylor, A.J.P. (ed), *Lloyd George. A Diary by Frances Stevenson*. London, 1971.

Young, Peter, *World War II*. London, 1980.

Van der Byl, Piet, *Top Hat to Velskoen*. Cape Town, 1973.

Van der Byl, Piet, *The Shadows Lengthen*. Cape Town, 1973.

Van der Poel, Jean, *Selections from the Smuts Papers*. Volumes I – VII. Cambridge, 1966 – 1973.

Van Thal, Herbert (ed), *The Prime Ministers*. Volume Two: *From Lord John Russell to Edward Heath*. London, 1974 – 1975.

Van Wyk, At, *Vyf Dae. Oorlogskrisis van 1939. 'n Spannings-verhaal uit Suid-Afrika se Geskiedenis*. Kaapstad, 1985.

Walker, Eric, A., *W.P. Schreiner. A South African*. London, 1937.

Walker, Patrick, Gordon, *The Commonwealth*. London, 1962.

Watson, J.B., *Empire to Commonwealth, 1919 – 1970*. London, 1971.

Welsh, David, *The Roots of Segregation. Native Policy in Colonial Natal, 1845 – 1910*. London, 1971.

Werth, Alexander, *De Gaulle, a political biography*. Harmondsworth, 1965.

Williams, B., *Botha, Smuts and South Africa*. London, 1946.

Wilmot, Chester, *The Struggle for Europe*. London, 1952.

Windsor, The Duke, *A King's Story. The Memoirs of H.R.H. the Duke of Windsor, K.G.* London, 1951.

Wilson, John, *A Life of Sir Campbell-Bannerman*. London, 1973.

III. UNPUBLISHED THESES

Bester, M.L.C., *Die opvatting van Generaal Smuts oor die demokrasie*. Universiteit van Pretoria, 1960.

Du Plessis, L.J.P., *Generaal J.C. Smuts se bydrae tot die ontwikkeling van die Statebondsidee, 1907 – 1917*. Universiteit van Pretoria, 1973.

Grimbeek, M.J., *Politieke verhoudinge tussen generaals J.B.M. Hertzog en J.C. Smuts gedurende die tydperk 1933 – 1939*. UOVS, Bloemfontein, 1978.

Janeke, J., *Generaal J.C. Smuts as Oorlogspremier*. UOVS, Bloemfontein, 1993.

Meyntjies, E.A., *Generaal J.C. Smuts en die Vrede van Versailles.* P.U. vir C.H.O., 1973.

Pyper, P.A., *Generaal J.C. Smuts en die Tweede Vryheidsoorlog, 1899 – 1902.* P.U. vir C.H.O.,1960.

Snyman, J.J., *'n Histories-kritiese studie van die Smuts-Onderwyswet van 1907.* P.U. vir C.H.O., 1951.

Trümpelmann, M.H., *Generaal J.C. Smuts as premier van die Unie van Suid-Afrika, 1919 – 1924.* Universiteit van Pretoria, 1978.

Index

A

A Churchill Family Album 101

A.W. Lloyd *see Lloyd, A.W.*

Abyssinia 210

Act 2 131

Active Citizen Force 99

Admiralty *Lord Selborne, first lord of,* 53; *Churchill, first lord of,* 102, 219; *telegram from first lord of,* 104

Adolf Hitler *see Hitler, Adolf*

Africa 3, 13, 33, 40; *expansion into,*7 *see also Central Africa, East Africa, North Africa, South Africa*

Afrikaner 1, 16, 27, 39 42-44, 75, 178-179, 191; *Cape,* 28; *republic,* 31; *rising,* 36; *and Irish,* 143, 152

Afrikaner Bond 3-4, 6-9, 11, 17; *Hofmeyer leader of,* 2; *Smuts member of,* 6; *headquarters of,* 7; *leaders of,* 9

Afrikanerdom 11, 16, 24-25, 40, 43, 66

agraha 126 *see Satyagraha*

Albert *see King Albert, Prince Albert*

Alfred Milner *see Milner, Alfred*

All Souls 75

alliance *Rhodes and Bond/ Hofmeyer,* 6, 9; *mine magnates and governor,* 43; *Het Volk and Nationalists,* 64

Allied *Forces,* 143, 185, 204; *landings,* 173; *cause,* 174; *military occupation,* 174; *leaders,* 198-199; *camp,* 209

Allies 85-88, 171, 187, 191, 193, 204, 213, 216, 221

Alsace 192

ambassador 218; *Austro-Hungarian,* 85

amend *Lyttleton Constitution,* 56-57; *Hertzog's neutrality motion,* 103; *Peace Treaty,* 205

America 86, 151, 171 *see United States*

American Consul 145

Americans 86, 193-194, 196

Amery, L. S. (British secretary of state) 45, 80-81, 140, 208, 212-213, 216

Anglicise 39

Anglo-Boer War 41, 51, 96, 122-123, 143, 221; *Peace Treaty concluding,* 53, 60, 86 *see also War*

appeasement 208-209, 211

appendicitis 99-100

Arc de Triomphe 193

archbishop *of Canterbury,* 75; *of Armagh* 81

Armagh 81

armoured 189

Arthur Oliver Russell *see Russell, Arthur Oliver*

Article 7 53

Ashcroft, Edward *see endnotes*

Ashworth, Mr *see Mr Ashworth*

Asiatic/s 115, 123, 127-129, 131

Asiatic Act 128-129, 131

Asiatic Law Amendment Ordinance 123

Asquith (a British prime minister) *member of Cabinet committee* 57, 59, 62; *Lord,* 98; *Bill,* 151

Asquithian Liberals 142

Asquith, Mrs 75

Astor, Lady 75

Attlee, Clement 109, 221-222
attorney general *W.P. Schreiner*, 13; *Sir Richard Solomon*, 34; *J.C. Smuts*, 53; *Jacob de Villiers*, 124
Auchinleck, General 105 (photo); 109
Australia 140
Australian Commonwealth 97
Austria 85, 90
Austro-Hungarian *ambassador to London*, 85; *Empire*, 90, 216
Axis 193

B
Baldwin, Stanley (a British prime minister) 169, 205-207
Baldwin government 205
Balkans 171
Balliol College 24
Balliol Kindergarten 38 *see also kindergarten, Milner*
Barnes, George Nicoll 82
Baron of Ampthill 131 *see also Russell, Arthur Oliver*
barrister 116, 118
Barton 150
Bechuanaland 9
Belfast 148; *Parliament in*, 145, 147
Belgians 85
Belgium 85; *is invaded*, 106, 192-193
Bergson 189
Berlin *Smuts in*, 202 (photo); *Lord Lothian's visit to*, 211; *ambassadors in*, 218; *conference*, 221
Bertie 170, 178 *see also Prince Albert*
Bevin, Ernest *privileged trio*, 190, 199
Beyers 57
Bhana, Surendra 117
Black Act 124-125, 128-129; *repealed in*, 132

Black Ordinance 123-124 *see also Black Act*
Blackrock Intermediate College 144
Blitzkrieg 192
Bloemfontein 28
Bloemfontein Conference 28, 30, 32
Boer War *see Anglo-Boer War*
Boer/s 4-5, 8, 25, 29, 33-37, 51, 53, 56-57, 59, 61-63, 68; *commandos*, 33, 36; *leaders*, 34, 57; *delegates in Vereeniging*, 35-36; *republics*, 39, 96; *pro-*, 56; *states*, 68; *Churchill captured by*, 94 (photo)
Bolshevism 212
Bolshevists 208
Bonar Law *see Law, Bonar*
Bond *see Afrikaner Bond*
Borden, Sir Robert (prime minister of Canada) 77, 140
Botha, General Louis 36, 57, 60, 73-74, 82, 84, 128, 143, 205; *part of five-man negotiation team*, 33; *and Smuts*, 41-42, 45; *leader of Het Volk and prime minister*, 64-65; *differences with Smuts*, 66-68; *advises Smuts on Palestine command*, 81; *at Paris Peace Conference*, 88, 187; *in London*, 96, 131; *election speech*, 124
Brand, Lord 220
Brandenburg Gate 202 (photo)
Brassey, Lady 75
Bright, John 61
Bristol 76
Britain 12, 25, 59, 68, 80, 173, 176-177, 180; *interest in South Africa*, 26-28, 39; *negotiations with Boers*, 34; *war with Transvaal*, 37; *Milner's disrepute in*, 44; *Unionist government*, 51, 53; *War Cabinet in*, 82; *debt*, 90; *declare war on Germany*, 102, 105; *and Indians*,

115, 118, 121; *and Irish affairs*, 141-142, 152, 154, 166; *war effort*, 170, 174-175, 199; *in Second World War*, 192, 218, 220; *and De Gaulle*, 194, 196; *a Great Power*, 198-199; *post-war*, 204-205; *and the European crisis*, 209-211, 216-217;

British 3, 17, 26, 29, 33-34, 37, 56, 59, 80, 83, 104,118, 122, 145, 153, 166, 171, 193-194, 211, 221; *imperialism*, 14, 68; *policy*, 23, 194; *government*, 25, 31, 37, 57, 74, 81, 86-87, 105, 121, 123, 142, 144, 146, 148-150, 153, 155, 187, 209, 211-212; *people*, 25, 97, 123, 162; *Nationalist*, 26; *agent in Pretoria*, 30; *South Africa*, 31, 39-40; *Cabinet*, 33; settlers for the Rand, 38; and Dutch, 38; high commissioner, 38, 44, 109, 124; Transvaal, 38; *politicians*, 41, 61; *War Cabinet*, 45, 82, 88, 97-98, 162, 204; *dominion*, 63; *prime minister*, 75, 90, 102, 104, 108-109, 141, 150, 186, 218, 221; *politics*, 80, 83, 90, 98, 141, 162; *war effort*, 82, 86, 162; *generals*, 84; *air power*, 85; *newspapers*, 96; *Crown*, 97; *war strategy*, 97; *general election*, 99; *troops*, 106; *constitution*, 116-117; *colonies*, 121; *colonial secretary*, 122; *military force*, 142, *royal family*, 160 (photo), 174, 181; *field marshal*, 170; *monarchy*, 177; *leaders*, 194, 207

British Commonwealth 140, 143, 177; *name changes to*, 141; *Smuts' position in*, 162, 178; *Mediterranean interests of*, 174; *South Africa a member of*, 218 see also Commonwealth

British Empire 45, 58, 68, 74, 79-80, 99, 154, 178; *consolidation of the*, 24; *expansion of the*, 25; South Africa part of, 26, 39, 41; *Indians in*, 119-120, 131, 135; *transformation of the*, 139-141; *and Adolf Hitler*, 203, 213, 217

British Guiana 120

British Parliament 84, 146

British War Cabinet *Milner/Smuts in*, 45, 82-83, 88, 98, 104, 162; *members of*, 82; *in political crisis*, 97

Britons 204

Brittany 193

Bryce 57

Buchan, John 38 see also *Balliol Kindergarten*

Bulgaria 98

Burger, Schalk (acting president) 36-37

burghers 33-34

Burns, John 62-63

Butler, Sir William (commander-in-chief in South Africa) 28

C

Cabinet of Governments 77

Cairo 193; *Smuts and Churchill in*, 94 (photo); *Smuts at British Embassy in*, 105 (photo)

Calvinist 116

Cambridge 5-6, 81; *Christ's College in*, 10; *Smuts' lodgings in*, 81; *University*, 98, 116, 119, 191, 203-204 see also Smuts

campaign 41, 163; *general election*, 57, 163; *East African*, 73; *in Norway*, 105; *Nazi propaganda*, 214

Campbell-Bannerman, Sir Henry 50 (cartoon), 51, 54-57; *Liberal government of*, 55, 96; *and Smuts*, 59-61, 67-68, 96; *letter to the King*, 61; *gives responsible government to Boers*, 62-63, 68

Canada 97; *governor general of*, 38; *prime minister of*, 77, 140

Cannes 99

Cape 6, 34, 39, 166; *politics*, 2, 6, 13; *government*, 3; *Assembly*, 6; *newspapers*, 6; *Dutch*, 7; *English*, 7; *prime minister*, 14; *politician*, 17; *Afrikaners*, 28; *Crown Colony*, 32; *Loyalists*, 33; *Parliament*, 191 *see also Cape Colony, Cape Town*

Cape Colony 7, 25, 36, 191; *prime minister*, 2, 17, 27; *schools in*, 4; *superintendent of education for*, 6; *attorney general*, 13; *governor of*, 23

Cape Town 10, 23, 25, 28, 99, 131, 169, 216; *headquarters of the Bond*, 7; *Greek monarchy's arrival in*, 173; *Windsors' visit to*, 177, 180

capitalist 8, 11, 66

Cardiff 76; *Smuts receives the Freedom of the City of Cardiff*, 75 (photo)

Carlos, King Juan *of Spain*, 173

Carrington, Lord 63

Carson, Lord 82

Cartwright, Albert *editor of the Transvaal Leader*, 127; *mediator*, 129

Casement, Roger 163

Cecil John Rhodes *see Rhodes, Cecil John*

Cecil, Lord Robert 163

Central Africa 11

Chalfont, Alan 109

Chamberlain, Joseph 41, 53, 61; *new colonial secretary in London*, 24; *on the Jameson Raid*, 25-26; *policy*, 25; *and the Transvaal*, 26, 30-31, 34-35; *succeeded by Lyttelton*, 52

Chamberlain, Neville 106-107; *British prime minister*, 102, 106; *resigns*, 106; *and Gandhi*, 122; *speech*, 218

Chamberlain School 3

Chanak Crisis (1922) 91

chancellor *of the exchequer*, 24; *lord*, 57

Chandos, Lord Charles 162

Charles de Gaulle *see De Gaulle, Charles*

Chartwell *Churchill's residence*, 100

Chinese labour 39, 43

Christians 118

Christ's College 10, 98, 191

Churchill, Winston 33, 58, 148, 167, 221-222; *writes to Smuts*, 55; *new under-secretary*, 57; *and Smuts*, 59, 75, 83, 170, 174, 187, 191, 194-195, 197, 199, 219; *announces proposals for South Africa*, 63; *Smuts and Churchill*, 113 (photo); *regarding Indian immigration*, 127; *and Gandhi*, 134-135; *and the Irish*, 148; *Operation Overlord*, 171, 173; *and De Gaulle*, 190-191, 193-199; *addresses Secret Session*, 196

citizenship *Indians denied*, 120

Claredon 181

Clarks 58

Clause II 35

Clemenceau, Georges (French prime minister) 85, 87, 89-90, 186-187, 190; *member of Council of Four*, 88, 187; *views of Smuts*, 187-188

Clement Attlee *see Attlee, Clement*

Clementine, Lady 100, 113 (photo)

Clivedon 75

Clomer, William 6,

Coalition government *fall of Lloyd George's*, 91, 99; *Hertzog's*, 206

coercion 211

Collins, Colonel W.R. 103

Collins, Michael *Irish leader*, 153-154

Colonial Home Rule 3
Colonial Office 24, 35, 38, 44, 52, 55-57, 131
colonial secretary 25; *in Britain – Chamberlain*, 9, 122; *in South Africa – Jan Smuts*, 65
Colonialism 3
colonisation *of Ethiopia*, 214
colony 31, 56
Colville, John *writes about Smuts*, 104, 108-109; *private secretary to Churchill*, 167; *diary entries*, 167, 194, 197104, 108-109, 111-112, 167, 182, 194, 197, 201
commandos 33, 36
commission 26, *investigates developments in SWA*, 214
Commission on Austrian Reparation 90
commissioner of police 216
committee 34, 54, 63, 85, 87, 186; *of enquiry*, 17; *Cabinet*, 57-58
Commonwealth 16, 41, 85, 139, 140, 161, 174, 177; *Imperial*, 79, 140; *envisaged by Smuts*, 80, 85, 141-143, 178; *Australian*, 97; *prime ministers in*, 108; *Smuts' involvement in*, 143, 162, 178, 185, 191; *Ireland leaves the*, 152-153, 155; *South Africa in*, 176, 218; *and France*, 191, 199; *and Hitler*, 212
Commonwealth of Nations 45, 140, 145
Companion of Honour 76
concentration camps *Boer War*, 32, 36
concessions *for South Africa*, 27-28; *for Asiatics*, 131
conciliation *through Boer War*, 44, 60; *Irish*, 81, 148, 154; *between Britain and India*, 115; *Smuts the champion of*, 194; *between the World Wars*, 204; *with Hitler*, 211

conference 28-29, 74, 76-78, 149, 151, 207; *a peace*, 34; *Berlin*, 221 *see also Bloemfontein Conference, Imperial War Conference, Paris Peace Conference*
Conradie, D.G. *administrator of SWA*, 214
Conservative government *formed by Bonar Law*, 99
Conservative Party 100
Constantine 173
Constantine, King *see King Constantine*
Constantinople 97-98
constitution *South African*, 62; *British*, 116-117
constitutional 76, 78-79, 83, 139-141, 143, 145, 147; *reform*, 45; *development*, 68, 142; *candidate*, 100; *government*, 152; *Irish deadlock*, 164
Continent, the 24, 210
convention 80, 84, 104, 141
corps *at Spioenkop*, 122
council 78; *Smuts'*, 145
Council of Four 88, 187
Council of Ireland 145
coup d' état 216
Crafford, F.S. *see endnotes*
Crew, Lord 131
Cripps, Sir Stafford 109
Cronjé, General Piet 14
Cronwright, Samuel 7-10
Cronwrights 8
Cronwright-Schreiners 8-9, 14
Crown Colony 39; *government*, 32, 64
Crown Prince Paul 173
Crozier, Brian *see endnotes*
Curtis, Lionel 38, 139
Curzon, Lord 74; *member of War Cabinet*, 82
Czechoslovakia 90, 105; *invasion of*, 218

D

Dàil Eireann *declares Irish independence*, 142; *representative in Great Britain*, 154

Daily Mail 106

Dardanelles 97

Darlan, Admiral Jean Francois 195 -196

David Lloyd George *see Lloyd George, David*

Dawson, Geoffrey 38 *see also Balliol Kindergarten*

D-Day 173

De Beers Mines Political and Debating Society 9-10

De Gaulle, Charles 184 (photo), 185; *early life*, 188-189; *early career*, 189; *army career*, 189-190; *and Smuts*, 190-192, 194-195, 198-199; *during Second World War*, 192-193; *appointed under-secretary of state*, 192; *friction with Churchill*, 193-198; *friction with Americans*, 193-194, 198

De Gaulle, Henri 188

De la Rey, General 36. 41; *part of negotiation team*, 33

De Valera, Eamon 138 (photo), 139, 141, 143-144, 146-159, 164-165, 186; *and Smuts*, 144, 146, 148-153, 155, 164, 186; *association with Sinn Fein*, 144; *founder of Irish Volunteers*, 145; *sentenced to death*, 145; *invited to London*, 148, 150-151, 164; *on national self-determination*, 150, 152; *wants a republic*, 151-152; *Anglo-Irish negotiations*, 153, 155

De Wet, General *chosen for five-man negotiation team*, 33-35; *signed peace agreement*, 37; *launches reconstruction campaign*, 41

delegates 28; *selected*, 33; *to ratify*

peace terms, 35-36; *vote*, 37

democracy 207

democratic 12; *principles in South Africa*, 12, 13; *principles in United States*, 12; *principles of Western world*, 217

denationalisation 43

dictator *Mussolini* 210 *see also Mussolini, Benito*

dictatorial 66; *Hitler*, 206 *see also Hitler, Adolf*

dictatorships *Fascist and Nazi*, 212

Die Burger 152

Die Transvaler 152

dominion/s 79, 108, 140, 142, 145; *status in South Africa*, 63, 218; *representatives of*, 76; *growing nationalism in*, 79; *status for Ireland*, 139, 153, 155; *prime minister/s of*, 145, 147, 180

Doornkloof 60, 76, 86, 134, 146, 173, 177; *Smuts writes to his wife at*, 86, 146; *The royal family visits Isie at*, 178 (photo)

Doornkop 14

Downing Street 16, 42, 59, 62, 105, 111, 182, 201

Dublin 143, 145, 149, 153; *University College in*, 144; *National University and Trinity College in*, 144; *Smuts invited to*, 149-150, 153, 164, 186; *Dr A.L. Geyer visits*, 155

Duchess of Rutland 75

Duggan 150

Duke of Devonshire 167

Duke of Edinburgh 180

Duke of Gloucester 167

Duke of York 169-170

Duncan, Patrick 103; *governor general of South Africa*, 38; *member of Balliol Kindergarten*, 38; *member of the new Union Cabinet 1939*, 103 (photo); *accepted Hertzog's resignation*, 104

Dundee 99

Durban 118, 130

Dutch 6, 29, 38-39, 40, 42, 63; *and British union*, 3; *equality with English*, 4, 7, 11, 38, 97; *Cape*, 4, 7; *anti-*, 33; *and English conflict*, 40, 42, 55

Dwight, Eisenhower *see Eisenhower, Dwight*

E

Eamon de Valera *see De Valera, Eamon*

Earl of Selborne 53

East *and West*, 116, 119 *see also Near East*

East Africa 73, 127, 215; *position of troops in*, 215 (photo)

East Clare 145

Eastern Africa 216

Easter Rising 145

École Militaire 188 *see also De Gaulle*

economic/s 14, 100, 122; *factors*, 4; *expansion*, 5; *ties*, 25, 207; *action*, 30; *servitude in Germany*, 89; *Austria*, 90; *Indian threat*, 121, 132; *conditions in Britain*, 176; *German*, 216-217

Eden, Anthony *member of War Cabinet*, 107 (photo), 206-207; *succeeded Churchill*, 95

Edinburgh 76 *see also Duke of Edinburgh*

education *religious school*, 3; *superintendent of*, 6; *Milner's*, 24; *minister of*, 65, 103; *De Valera's*, 144; *De Gaulle's*, 188

Egypt 173; *Milner in*, 24; *Greek Monarch in*, 174-175

Eighth Army 109

Eisenhower, General Dwight *in support of Darlan*, 195-196; *De Gaulle at loggerheads with*, 198

election 57, 64, 99-100, 154, 221; *Rhodes wins*, 3; *1905 Great Britain general*, 51-52, 58; *Transvaal general*, 64; *1922 British general*, 99; *1924 British general*, 100; *1924 South African general*, 100, 166; *1939 South African general*, 103; *speech*, 124; *South African general*, 176; *Hitler's general*, 212 *see also campaign*

electorate 104

Elgin *Cabinet committee member*, 57-58, 62

Empire *see British Empire*

Empire Parliamentary Association 197

empiricist 13

England 6, 25, 28, 41, 53-54, 62, 74, 96, 127, 170, 179, 209; *Milner returns to*, 24, 51; *Rhodes in*, 31; *Milner and Smuts in*, 45; *conquered Boer republics*, 58; *of John Bright*, 61; *Smuts in*, 75, 79, 82-83, 86, 104, 108, 146, 161, 197; *Smuts returns from*, 91; *Gandhi in*, 116-117, 134; *and Ireland*, 143, 150, 152 *see also Britain*

English 116, 122, 144, 173, 204; *people*, 16, 23, 27, 36, 55, 68, 181, 187, 196, 210; *equality with Dutch language*, 4, 7, 11; *language*, 6, 8, 39; *Cape*, 7; *Nationalist*, 26; *paper*, 65; *government*, 119; *and the Irish*, 149; *South Africans*, 155, 176; *democracy*, 207

Esselen 99

Ethiopia 214

Europe 13, 41, 43, 88-90, 98, 162, 167, 198, 204, 207, 210, 213-214, 217, 219, 221; *Smuts in*, 85, 87, 141, 144, 186; *war in*, 162, 170-171, 187-188, 218-220; *Western*, 191; *Central and Eastern*, 216, 222

European Powers 11
Europeans 122, 125
executive 31, 142
Executive Council 28
expansion *economic and territorial,*
5, 7; *into Central Africa,* 11

F
Fascist *Italy,* 208, 212
Father T. Ryan 144
Federal State 45
Federalists 79
'Federate or Disintegrate' pol-
icy 139
federation 45, 140; *Smuts envis-
ages,* 6; *Empire into a,* 139
Field Marshal 171; *Jan Smuts,*
101, 109, 170, 180; *Montgomery,*
109; *baton to Smuts,* 170; *Pétain,*
185
fifth army 192
First World War 86, *Smuts and the
Air Council during,* 108 (photo);
139, 162, 168, 170, 185, 189; *War
Cabinet during,* 45; *Churchill and
Smuts during,* 100, 104; *United
States entry into,* 145; *Irish question during,* 162; *Smuts and the
French during,* 186; *De Gaulle a
prisoner during,* 188; *Germany after,* 204, 221; *victors in,* 209; *tragedies of,* 220
Fischer, Lord *admiral of the fleet,*
97
Fischer, Louis *see endnotes*
Fitzalan, Lord *first Roman viceroy
of Ireland,* 149
foreign policy 79; *German,* 216
France 185, 189, 196-197, 209-210,
212, 220; *Smuts to,* 85, 186; *Churchill stays in,* 100; *declares war on
Germany 1939,* 102; *preparations
for Allied landings in,* 173; *approach to peace negotiations,* 187;

and Smuts conflict, 188, 191,
198-199, 210; *'de-satellization' of,*
191; *and De Gaulle,* 188-193,
197-198; *defeated by Germany,*
193, 195; *proclaims general mobi-
lization,* 218
franchise *in New Zealand,* 12; *in
the Transvaal,* 28, 37; *for
Uitlanders,* 29; *bill in Natal,* 118
Franchise Act 4
Franchise Bill 121
Franco-German 209
Franco-Prussian War 186
Franklin D. Roosevelt see Roosevelt, Franklin D.
Free National Committee 193-194
Free State *see Orange Free State*
freedom 55, 76, 140, 207; *of British
action,* 37; *war of,* 41-42; *fight for,*
61; *principles of,* 80; *for Indians,*
123; *for Ireland,* 141, 144, 154,
163
Free French Movement 196
French 86, 186-187, 190, 193-195,
198; *president,* 85; *Smuts and the,*
185-186, 203, 209-210; *great writers,* 189; *Republic,* 189; *prime
minister,* 186, 192-193
French Republic 189

G
Gallipoli Peninsula 97
Gandhi, Mahatma 66, 114 (photo);
Smuts' dealings with, 115-117,
119, 122, 126-129, 131, 133-135;
early life of, 115-116; *comes to
South Africa,* 117; *returns to India,* 117, 122; *experiences social
inequality,* 118; *founded the Natal
Indian Congress,* 118; *fights for
Indian cause,* 118, 120-125, 129,
131-133; *and Satyagraha,* 120,
122, 125-127, 130; *imprisoned,*
126-128, 130; *released from*

prison, 128, 130; *arrives in England*, 131, 134; *Smuts-Gandhi Agreement*, 133; *and Churchill conflict*, 134; *assassinated*, 135
Gandhism 134
General *Piet Cronjé*, 14; *Louis Botha*, 33, 57, 64, 128, 143, 205; *De Wet*, 33; *De la Rey*, 33, 36; *Jan Smuts*, 51, 65, 77, 103 (photo), 104, 129, 145, 148-149, 168, 219; *Murray*, 81; *Auchinleck*, 105 (photo), 109; *Wavell*, 105 (photo); *Gott*, 109; *J.B.M. Hertzog*, 152, 154, 169, 181, 206 (photo), 219; *Dwight Eisenhower*, 195, 198; *Charles de Gaulle*, 196-197; *Legentilhomme*, 196; *Sir Hastings*, 199; *Von Lettow Vorbeck*, 205 (photo)
general election *see election*
Geoffrey Robinson *see Robinson, Geoffrey*
German/s 206, 208, 211, 217, 220; *Kaiser*, 34, 50 (photo); *East Africa*, 73; *Milner*, 74; *defeated*, 88; *peace negotiations*, 88-89; *Reich*, 103; *minister*, 104; *forces*, 171, 192; *Emperor*, 186; *offensive launched*, 192; *troops*, 193; *France surrenders to*, 195; *Smuts high regard for*, 203 204; *Smuts learns*, 203; *lieder*, 203; *literature*, 204, *und Nazism*, 204; *in SWA*, 214, 216; *press*, 214; *foreign policy*, 216
German Foreign Ministry 218
Germany 11, 25, 88, 109, 174, 187-188, 205-208, 210-211, 213-214, 216-217, 220-221; *Milner born in*, 23; *and peace negotiations*, 88-90; *invades Poland*, 102; *France and Great Britain declare war on*, 102; *Nazi/Nazism*, 102, 191, 199, 208, 212, 218, 220; *invades Denmark and Norway*, 105,

192; *invades Holland and Belgium*, 106, 192; *tension concerning*, 186; *attacks France*, 193; *Smuts in*, 202 (photo), 204; *ill-treatment of*, 204, 221; *and Smuts' appeasement*, 209; *imperial*, 213; *to restore colonies*, 214; *at Yalta and Potsdam*, 221
Geyer, Dr A.L. *editor of Die Burger*, 152; *South African high commissioner to London*, 155
Gilbert, Martin *see endnotes*
Gillett, A.B. *Smuts visits*, 163; *Smuts' letters to*, 210
Gillett, Margaret *Smuts' letters to*, 58, 177, 179, 218, 220
Gladstone, Mr 151
Gladwyn, Lord 192
Glasgow 56
Goethe 203-204
Gokhale 122, 132-133
goldfields 3
Goschen, G.T. *chancellor of the exchequer*, 24
Gott, General 109
Government of Ireland Act 142, 145
governor 43; *of the Cape Colony*, 23; *of the two conquered republics*, 38 *see also Milner*
governor general 103, 168, 180-181; *for Transvaal and Orange River Colony*, 44, 51, 57; *Sir Patrick Duncan*, 103 (photo); *of the Union*, 170
Graham, Secretary 57
Graig, James 149-151; *premier of Northern Ireland*, 149
Great Powers 88, 197-198, 214
Greece 174; *Princess Frederika of*, 172 (photo); *Nazi invaders of*, 173; *Greek monarchy in*, 174
Greek 188; *royal family*, 172 (photo); *monarchy*, 173-175; *king*,

173-174; *liberation*, 174; *people*, 174-175; *politics*, 174
Green, Mrs A.S. 143
Greene, Conyngham *British agent in Pretoria*, 30; *negotiates with Smuts*, 30-31
Greenwood, Sir Hamer *chief secretary for Ireland*, 146
Grey, Lord Edward 57, 59
Griffith, Arthur *founded Sinn Fein movement*, 144
Grobler, Pieter 30, 150-151, 153
Guild Hall 146
Guild Hall Banquet 146

H
Haarhoff, T.J. *see endnotes*
Habib, Sheth Haji 131
Haig, Sir Douglas 85
Haldane, Viscount 56
Hall of Mirrors 186
Hamilton, Colonel Ian 32-33
Hancock, W.K. *see endnotes*
Harlech, 109
headquarters *of the Bond*, 7, 9; *in Pretoria*, 37; *in Johannesburg*, 38, 99; *in London*, 173
Hellenes *ex-King Constantine of the*, 172 (photo); *King George II of the*, 173-175
Henri de Gaulle *see De Gaulle, Henri*
Henri Campbell-Bannerman *see Campbell-Bannerman, Henri*
Hertzog, J.B.M. 36, 103, 154, 181, 207-208, 218; *Judge*, 33; *member of negotiation team*, 33-34,36; *opponent of Milner*, 39; *in conflict with Smuts*, 66, 207; *as prime minister*, 100, 169, 206; *neutrality motion of*, 102-103, 152, 218-219; *vote of non-confidence in*, 103; *resignation of*, 104, 219; *welcomes British royalty*, 169; *Smuts and*,

206 (photo); *Coalition government of*, 206; *at Imperial Conference 1937*, 206
Het Volk Party 53, 64
High Command 192
high commissioner 221; *Sir Herculus Robinson*, 9; *Sir Alfred Milner*, 22 (photo), 23-24, 28, 38, 44, 51, 57, 123; *Lord Selborne*, 57, 124; *Lord Harlech*, 109; *Dr A.L. Geyer*, 155; *General Legentilhomme*, 196
Hindu 116, 118, 135
Hinduism 116
His Excellency 29
His Majesty 146, 149, 166
Hitler, Adolf 199, 202 (photo), 203, 205, 207-209, 211, 213-214, 219; *during WWII*, 192-193, 211, 218-220; *and France*, 193, 210; *dictator*, 206, 214; *expansion of*, 210; *reoccupies the Rhineland*, 211; *a disturber of the peace*, 211; *and Nazism*, 212; *policies of*, 212, 216; *in peace negotiations*, 213; *birthday*, 216; *rise of*, 217; *invades Czechoslavakia*, 218
Hitlerjugend 214
HMS Vanguard 177, 180
Hobhouse, Emily *Smuts writes to*, 39-40, 53, 56; *writes to Smuts*, 76
Hodgson *Smuts' chauffeur*, 99
Hofmeyer, Jan 9, 17
Holism and Evolution 191, 200
Holland *invasion of*, 106, 192
Hollanders 6
Home Rule *in Ireland*, 142-143, 151 *see also Colonial Home Rule*
honorary fellow 76
Hore-Ruthven 181
House, the 65, 103, 107; *Royal*, 181 *see also Manor House*
House of Commons 82, 97, 143, 218; *Churchill in*, 57-58, 63, 196,

218; *Norwegian debate in*, 106; *suspicious of Vichy France*, 195; *in war*, 196

House of Lords 12; *member of the*, 131

House of Windsor 175; *Smuts' contact with the*, 161-162

Houses of Parliament 45; *Smuts speaks to both*, 80, 140; *Lloyd George introducing*, 84 (photo); *Smuts in*, 84 (photo)

Howarth, Patrick *see endnotes*

Hughes, Premier *of Australia*, 140

Hungary 90

I

Ibn Saud, King 95

immigration 6; *Indian*, 125, 127, 132

Immigration Act 127, 131

Immigration Bill 132

imperial 2-5, 24, 38, 82, 139; *supremacy over South Africa*, 32, 63; *Germany*, 213

Imperial Commonwealth 79, 140 *see also British Commonwealth*

Imperial Conference *March 1917*, 73, 76, 79; *June 1921 Smuts at*, 143, 145-146, 163; *1937 Hertzog at*, 206-207

Imperial Federation 79

Imperial General Staff 81

Imperial Parliament 39 *see also British Parliament*

Imperial War Cabinet 72 (photo), 76; *Milner and Smuts members of*, 45, 162; *Smuts speaks at*, 78; *dissolved*, 82 *see also British War Cabinet*

imperialism 2, 14, 39; *Milner's ardour for*, 24; *Lord Selborne for*, 53; *Smuts and*, 68

Imperialist 76, 145; *Milner an*, 24, 26; *anti-*, 51, 76; *Liberal*, 56

independence *Boer/Transvaal*, 4, 29, 96; *India's struggle for*, 134; *Irish*, 142, 144-146, 152-153, 163

Independent Party 64

India 79, 117, 121, 127, 132, 165, 176; *reconciliation with Britain*, 115; *Gandhi in*, 116-117, 122; *viceroy of*, 121, 131, 177; *government of*, 132; *struggle for Independence*, 134; *a republic*, 155

Indian/s 117-119, 121-125, 127-133; *Gandhi an*, 116; *attitudes to*, 118,132; *rights of*, 66, 118, 120, 123, 130-131; *labour*, 120; *population*, 120; *debarred*, 120; *trading licence holders*, 121; *ambulance corps*, 122; *in Transvaal*, 122-124, 129; *immigration*, 125, 127, 132; *imprisoned*, 126, 128; *in Orange Free State*, 133; *taxes*, 133; *Rajah*, 167 *see also Natal Indian Congress, Indian Relief Bill*

Indian Opinion 129

Indian Relief Bill 133

Ingham, Kenneth *see endnotes*

inland revenue 24

international 34, 54, 104, 175, 187, 198, 206; *statesman*, 41, 141, 143, 155; *affairs and Smuts*, 73, 84, 98, 178, 208; *government*, 80; *politics*, 98, 173; *condemnation of Mussolini*, 214

Ireland 56, 59, 80, 139, 141-148, 151-154, 166; *national freedom for*, 141; *and Smuts*, 141, 144, 163; *Britain in deadlock with*, 142, 144; *limited Home Rule in*, 142; *Republic of*, 144; *Sinn Fein in*, 144; *British presence in*, 145; *American Consul in*, 145; *independence of*, 146; *chief secretary for*, 146; *Roman Catholic viceroy in*, 149; *president of*, 151; *dependent on England*, 152; *a republic for*, 152; *neutrality*, 152;

dominion status to, 141, 153; *leaves Commonwealth*, 155 *see also Government of Ireland Act, Northern Ireland, Northern Ireland Parliament, Southern Ireland*

Irene *Earl of*, 76; *Smuts' farm in*, 134, 141

Irish 80, 141-148, 151-155, 162-163, 165; *problem*, 80, 144, 147; *and Smuts*, 81, 143, 145, 151, 153; *reconciliation*, 81; *question*, 141, 147, 154, 162-163, 175; *independence*, 142, 144; *Britain and the*, 143-144, 146-150, 153-155, 163-164; *policy*, 143, 147-148; *nationalism*, 144; *government*, 145; *leaders*, 149-150, 153

Irish Dominion League 142

Irish Parliament 141-142

Irish Parliamentary Party 141

Irish Volunteers 145

Isie Smuts *see Smuts, Isie*

Ismay, General Sir Hastings Lionel *part of privileged trio*, 190, 199

isolationism 6

Italians 210-211, 214, 216; *propoganda*, 86; *dictator*, 210; *annex Abyssinia*, 210; *press*, 214

Italy 210, 214; *a Fascist dictatorship*, 208, 212; *conquest of*, 173

J

Jamaica 120

Jameson, Dr Leander Starr 14, 39

Jameson Raid 3, 8, 14, 16, 25-26; *failure of*, 14; *Rhodes' involvement in*, 15

Jan Christiaan Smuts *see Smuts, Jan Christiaan*

Jan Hofmeyer *see Hofmeyer*

Japan 165, 209

J.B.M. Hertzog *see Hertzog, J.B.M*

Jesuit College of the Immaculate Conception 188

Jingoism 17

Johannesburg 6; *Uitlander rising in*, 9; *headquarters in*, 38; *miners' strike in*, 98-99; *chief of police*, 128; *Gandhi to*, 130

John Wilson *see Wilson, John*

Joseph Chamberlain *see Chamberlain, Joseph*

Judd, Denis *see endnotes*

Juin, Alphonso 190

K

kaiser 34

Kerr, Philip 38 *see also Balliol Kindergarten*

Kestell, Reverend 41

Kimberley 4, 9-12; *Cronwrights settle in*, 8; *Smuts in*, 10; *Smuts' speech in*, 10

Kimberley Town Hall 10

kindergarten 38-39, 42-45, 53, 83; *suffer defeat*, 64, 74 *see also Balliol Kindergarten*

King, the 32, 34, 61, 63, 82, 86, 106, 134, 146-150, 153-154, 161-166, 168-183

King Albert 85

King Constantine 172 (photo)

King Edward VII 34

King Edward VIII 169

King George II *of the Hellenes*, 173-175

King George V 76, 142, 168 (photo); *friend of Smuts*, 161-162, 169-170

King George VI 173, 176 (photo); *friend of Smuts*, 169-170, 175 (photo), 176, 180; *visits South Africa*, 175

Kitchener 33-34, 35 (photo), 36, 38, 41; *peace*, 37

Klipfontein 16

Kruger, President Paul 2, 10, 14-15, 23, 28-29, 31, 39, 65, 123;

government, 5, 8, 31, 64; *isolationism*, 6; *claim to leadership*, 7; *at Bloemfontein Conference*, 28; *complete reform bill*, 28; *nephew*, 30; *former attorney general of*, 53; *former lieutenant of*, 82; *of the Transvaal*, 122

L

labour 130; *market*, 4; *organised*, 66 *see also Chinese labour*
Labour government 100
Labour Party 64
labourers *Indian*, 120-121
Lamont, Thomas 207
Lamont, W.T. 220
Law, Bonar 82, 99
Lawlor, Sheila *see endnotes*
Le May *see endnotes*
League of Nations 80, 89, 170, 197, 211, 213
Legentilhomme, General 196
legislation 42, 65, 123-125, 131-132
legislative council 42
Leonard, Charles 10
Liberal government 63; *of Campbell-Bannerman*, 55, 96; *and the Lyttelton Constitution*, 56
Liberal Imperialists 56
Liberal Party 58, 100
Liberal policy 63
liberalism 54
Liberal/s 51, 68, 97; *against "Chinese Slavery"*, 43; *newspapers*, 142
liberation 174
Libertas 173
Limpopo River 41
Lincoln Gaol 145
List of Honorary Fellows 98
Lloyd, A.W. 65
Lloyd George, David 45, 59, 61-62, 72 (photo), 73-74, 77, 80, 82, 84 (photo), 85-86, 89, 97-98, 146, 155, 162, 168, 186, 205; *at Imperial War Conference*, 76-77; *during First World War*, 80; *and the Palestine command*, 81; *appoints Smuts to War Cabinet*, 82-84, 143, 162; *member of War Cabinet*, 82; *rift between Smuts and*, 87, 90-91; *member of Council of Four*, 88, 187; *Coalition government falls (1922)*, 91, 99, 168; *prime minister*, 141, 162, 186; *and the Irish question*, 146-148, 150-151, 153, 163-164
Locarno Treaty 211
Loch, Sir Henry 14; *high commissioner*, 9
Lockhart, J.G. *see endnotes*
London 34, 53, 55, 67, 75-76, 83, 96, 126, 131, 141, 143, 162, 164-165, 174, 193, 207-208, 217, 222; *colonial secretary in*, 9; *political circles in*, 25; *British Cabinet in*, 33; *Milner and Smuts in*, 45, 77 (photo); *Smuts in*, 58, 75-76, 80, 83, 85, 96, 108, 131, 143, 146, 151, 153, 163; *Imperial Conference in*, 73, 76, 78 (photo), 143, 150-151, 163, 166, 168, 170, 197; *Austro-Hungarian ambassador to*, 85; *Botha comes to*, 96, 131; *Attlee in*, 109; *Gandhi in*, 116, 134; *Gandhi leaves*, 117; *secretary of state for colonies in*, 118; *De Valera invited to*, 148-151, 153, 164, 194-195, 204; *high commissioner to*, 155; *Gilletts in*, 163; *King George in*, 173; *King's headquarters in*, 173; *Free National Committee in*, 193; *Hertzog to*, 206
Lord Oliver *see Oliver, Lord*
Loreburn, Lord 62; *lord chancellor*, 57
Louis Botha *see Botha, Louis*
Louw, Eric 152
Loyalists 33

L.S. Amery *see Amery, L.S.*
Luxembourg 192
Lyttelton, Alfred 52
Lyttelton Constitution 53, 55, 58; *implement or amend*, 56-57; *scrap the*, 61

M
Macmillan, Harold *see endnotes*
Madagascar 196
Maginot Line 193
magnates 43
Magnus, Philip *see endnotes*
Mahaderan, K. *see endnotes*
Mahatma Gandhi *see Gandhi, Mahatma*
Maitland, Sir Arthur Steel 75
majority 10-11, 37, 55, 99, 103, 130, 145, 147-148, 154, 189, 212
Malmesbury 17
Manchester 62, 76, 150
Manchester Evening Chronicle 150
Manchester Guardian 62
Manor House 150
Mansergh, Nicholas *see endnotes*
Mansion House 150
Maories 12
Martial Law 99
Massingham 56
Mauritius 120
Maurras, Charles 188
mayor 10
Mediterranean 212-213; *theatre*, 171; *victory in*, 174; *policy*, 175; *threat to*, 213
Mein Kampf 216
Member of Parliament 83
memoirs *of Prince of Wales*, 168-169; *of De Gaulle*, 191
memorandum 30, 53-55; *Smuts'*, 31; *regarding Transvaal*, 53-55, 57-59; *on the Western front*, 85; *on Indian claims*, 122; *on constitutional relations*, 140-141, 143

Mensdorff, Count Albert 85
mentor/s *Smuts'*, 67; *Gandhi's*, 122
Merriman, John X. 2, 17, 87; *withdrew from Cape government*, 3; *conflict with Rhodes*, 15; *prime minister of Cape*, 39; *Smuts writes to*, 39, 64, 74; *writes about Indians*, 127
Middelburg *peace talks Feb 1901 in*, 32-33, 35
Middle Temple, the 204
military 9, 39, 86, 104, 147, 189, 219; *director-general of*, 24; *matters*, 30; *situation*, 85; *forces*, 105; *personnel*, 108; *force*, 142; *occupation of Greece*, 174; *career*, 191; *defeat*, 193
Millin, Gertrude *see endnotes*
Milner, Lord Alfred 16, 23, 25-26, 31, 33-34, 39-40, 42, 44, 53, 63, 65, 74, 123; *high commissioner*, 22 (photo), 23, 38, 51, 123; *landed in Cape Town*, 23, 25; *early life/career of*, 23-24; *an Imperialist*, 24; *Credo of*, 26; *at Bloemfontein Conference*, 28; *and the franchise question*, 28; *"concessions" to*, 28-29; *and Smuts*, 29, 33, 40-41, 45, 77 (photo); *attitude*, 29-30, 32; *policy*, 32, 35; *and Chamberlain*, 34; *denounces Clause II*, 35; *Kitchener and*, 37; *and Balliol Kindergarten*, 38-39, 42-45, 53, 64, 74, 83; *governor of Boer republics*, 38, 51, 53; *political strategies*, 39; *downfall of*, 41, 44, 51-52; *and Round Table*, 45, 139; *Earl Selborne succeeds*, 53, 57; *and Ireland*, 56; *member of War Cabinet*, 82; *administration*, 123 *see also Imperial War Cabinet*
Milnerism 39, 41
mine owners 63
mining 38, 40, 43

minister/s 10, 28, 57-58, 63, 91, 103 (photo), 152, 163; *Cabinet*, 84; *King's first*, 134-135; *South African*, 146; *foreign*, 222 *see also prime minister*
minister of colonies 97
minister of education 65, 103
minister of foreign affairs 208
minister without portfolio 81, 84, 103-104, 173
Ministry of Aircraft Production 109
mobilisation 218
modus operandi 214; *Hofmeyer's political*, 2; *leaders of Transvaal*, 5; *Smuts'*, 42, 65, 104, 122, 193; *Gandhi's political*, 120; *Smuts' and Gandhi's*, 133; *Nazi's*, 214; *Hitler's*, 216
monarch 163, 173-175, 177-178, 180
monarchy *Greek*, 173-175; *British*, 177-178, 180
Montgomery, Field Marshal 109
Moore, Colonel Maurice 143-146
Moran, Lord 95,107-108; *Churchill's personal physician*, 96 *see also endnotes*
Morley, John 58-59
Morning Post 150
Mountbatten 93, 176
Movement *De Gaulle's*, 194, 196-197
Mr Ashworth *Smuts incognito as*, 85, 186
Mr Smith *Smuts incognito as*, 150
Muir, Dr Thomas 6
Munich 206
Murray, General 81
Muslim 118, 131
Mussolini, Benito 211-214; *Italian dictator*, 210; *defiance of League of Nations*, 211; *threat to Mediterranean*, 213; *colonisation of Ethiopia*, 214

N

Natal 121, 132; *troops in*, 31; *national legislature of*, 118; *receives labourers*, 120; *Indian population*, 120, 133; *responsible government to*, 121 *see also Natal Indian Congress*
Natal Indian Congress 118, 121-122; *Gandhi founds*, 118
National Committee *see Free National Committee*
national legislature of Natal 118
National Party 64, 102, 152, 154
National University, Dublin 144
nationalism *Boer*, 6, 44, 79; *colonial*, 39; *Irish*, 80, 144; *Indian*, 122
Nationalist/s 64, 154; *alliance with Botha*, 64; *Purified*, 102; *1930s*, 152; *De Valera*, 144; *Milner*, 26, *government*, 168; *Party*, 176
native policy 13; *Rhodes'*, 8, 12
natives 3, 13, 36, 124
naval 97, 105
navy 97
Nazi/s 214; *health programmes*, 204; *dictatorship*, 212; *propaganda campaign*, 214
Nazi Germany 102, 191, 199, 208, 220 *see also Germany*
Nazi regime 205, 217
Nazism 204, 212, 218
negotiation/s 28, 212; *between Boers and British*, 28-30, 34; *peace*, 33, 187, 213, 222; *team*, 33; *with Austria*, 85, 186; *in House of Commons*, 106; *between Smuts and Gandhi*, 128, 131; *Anglo-Irish*, 143, 146, 148-149, 153, 165
Netherlands 192; *Princess Juliana of the*, 167; *fall of the*, 193
New Zealand 12
Nietzsche 189, 204

Normandy 193
North Africa 214; *French*, 195-196
North Sea 213
Northcliffe, Lord 74, 86
Northern Ireland 149, 153
Northern Ireland Parliament 147
Norway 105, 192
Nuremburg 208
NZDAP 214

O

O'Brien, Art 154
Old Cape Parliament 7
Oliver, Lord 30
Oliver, Frederick Scott 83
Ons Land 6
Oom Paul 14
Operation Overlord 171, 173
oppression 40, 97
Orange Free State 32, 37, 68, 132; *General De Wet for*; 33, 37; *government of*, 34, 37; *Indians in*, 120, 133
Orange River 10
Orange River Colony 38, 41, 53; *governor general for*, 44, 51, 57; *self-government for*, 58, 63-64, 68
Order of Merit 177; *Smuts invested with*, 176 (photo)
Orlando 87; *member of Council of Four*, 88, 187
Oxford 24, 87; *graduates from*, 38

P

Painlevé 85
Pakenham, Thomas *see endnotes*
Palace of Versailles 186
Palestine *command*, 81; *Allied forces in*, 143
Pan-Africanism 1
Paris 72 (photo), 88, 91, 186, 205, 209, 220-221; *Smuts and Lloyd George in*, 87; *De Gaulle's home in*, 189, 191; *German troops in*, 193; *Smuts in*, 204 *see also Paris Peace Conference*
Paris Peace Conference (1919) 72 (photo), 83, 87-89, 91, 144, 187, 204, 208, 221
Parliament 3, 90, 104, 125, 128, 131, 145, 147, 177 *see British Parliament, Houses of Parliament, Imperial Parliament, Irish Parliament, Member of Parliament, Northern Ireland Parliament, Old Cape Parliament, South African Parliament, Union Parliament*
pass laws 124
Patrick Duncan *see Duncan, Patrick*
Paul Kruger *see Kruger, Paul*
peace agreement 34, 37
peace conference 34, 76
Peace Conference *see Paris Peace Conference*
Peace Treaty 205; *of Vereeniging*, 53
Pearce, Patrick 143
Pechkoff, Colonel 193
Pétain 185, 188-190, 193
Philadelphia 17
Phillips, Lionel 10
Pioneers 74
pis aller 33
Pitsani 14
Plenipotentiary 104
Plunkett, Sir Horace 142-145
Plymouth 76
Polak 134
policy of reprisals 142, 163
political 10, 40, 54, 56, 60, 83, 99-100, 120, 124, 126, 142, 144, 147, 161, 163, 176; *figure*, 2; *philosophies*, 2, 25, 122, 147; *ally*, 2, 15; *strategy*, 2, 39; *life*, 2, 6, 60; *advantage*, 3; *factors*, 4; *set-up*, 6, 33,83; *issues*, 6, 11, 67; *venture*, 7; *situation*, 8, 10, 214; *future*, 9; *op-*

ponents, 9; *manipulation*, 9; *principles*, 12; *career*, 14, 40, 65, 119; *ties*, 25; *testament*, 26; *questions*, 28; *action*, 30, 217; *developments*, 39; *conditions*, 44; *settlement*, 55, 68; *circumstances*, 56; *game*, 58; *position*, 82; *strength*, 83; *stature*, 85; *crisis*, 97, 163; *experience*, 107; *arena*, 118; *power*, 123; *leaders*, 141; *journalist*, 144; *Sinn Fein*, 144
politician 13, 155, 190-191; *Cape*, 17; *British*, 41, 82; *South African*, 82; *Labour*, 142
politics 2, 7, 42-43, 64, 116-119, 126, 141, 178, 179, 216; *Cape*, 6, 13; *South African*, 63, 79; *international*, 75, 173; *British*, 80, 83, 90, 98, 162; *Anglo-Irish*, 154; *world*, 162; *European*, 173; *Greek*, 174
population 32, 55, 125, 179; *British*, 38, 176; *Colonial*, 42; *Natal's Indian*, 120; *Transvaal's Indian*, 124
Porbandar 115-116
Portsmouth 169
Potsdam 221
Pottinger, Brian *see endnotes*
poverty 122, 205
premier 64, 68, 82; *of Canada*, 140; *of Northern Ireland*, 149; *of South Africa*, 150, 168; *of France*, 192
president 27, 29, 54, 73; *of the Transvaal*, 6, 28; *of De Beers Mines Political and Debating Society*, 10; *of the Irish Republic*, 144; *of Sinn Fein*, 145; *of Ireland*, 151; *of the senate*, 177 *see Burger, Schalk; Kruger, Paul; Painlevé*
Pretoria 33-34, 105; *Smuts in*, 30, 127, 154; *headquarters in*, 37; *Gandhi travels to*, 118, 128; *Irene near*, 134; *state banquet in*, 179
Pretoria Conference (May 1902) 32

prime minister 25, 54, 57, 61-62, 80-81, 87, 95-97, 103-104, 106, 124, 134, 143, 147, 151, 161-163, 170, 173, 206-208, 218-219; *of the Cape Colony*, 2, 14, 17, 27, 39; *of the Transvaal*, 64-65; *British*, 75, 90, 98, 102, 107, 109, 141, 150, 169, 186, 218, 221; *of Canada*, 77; *South African*, 84; *Commonwealth*, 108; *dominion*, 145, 148, 180; *of France*, 193 *see Botha, Campbell-Bannerman, Chamberlain, Churchill, Rhodes, Smuts*
prince 135, 167, 169, 173-175, 180, 192
Prince Albert 170
Prince of Wales 63, 165, 205; *Smuts and*, 164 (photo), 165, 167-168; *comes to South Africa*, 169
Prince Philip 167
Princess Elizabeth 167, 180
Princess Frederika 172 (photo), 173-175
Princess Katharine 174
Princess Marie 174
Princess Mary 146
Princess Radziwe 174
privileged trio 190, 199 *see Bevin, Ismay, Smuts*
privy councillor 74, 76
Progressive Party 64
Prussianism 90, 187, 204
Purified National Party 102

Q
Quaker 58
Queen 31, 121, 123, 146, 164-165, 177-180; *Mother*, 167
Queen Elizabeth
Queen Mary 161, 166, 168 (photo)
Queen Mother 167, 176, 178
Queen Sophia 172 (photo), 173

R

Raad 27

racial discrimination 121-122

Rand 28, 38; *goldfields*, 3, 5; *Uitlanders*, 8; *capitalist newspaper*, 42

Randfontein 99

Rawlinson, Colonel Henry 32

reconstruction 41, 80, 211; *Milner's program*, 38, 43

Redmond, John 80, 141

reform 38; *social*, 24; *for Transvaal*, 26; *bill*, 28; *constitutional*, 45

refugee camps 36

regime 39, 65; *Boer*, 14; *Nazi*, 205, 217

registration *Indian*, 120, 123, 127-128, 130

Reich *Third*, 218; *German*, 103

Reitz, Colonel F.W. 29; *state secretary*, 28

Reitz, Colonel D. 103 (photo)

Repatriation Department 43

republic 14, 26, 32-33, 36-38, 41, 54, 63, 104, 120, 123, 151-155, 178, 217; *Afrikaner*, 31; *independent*, 146 *see Boer republics, French Republic, Irish Republic, South African Republic*

Republic of Ireland 144

Republican 144, 152, 188; *Afrikaner*, 53

Republican government 142

Reynaud, Paul 190; *new French premier*, 192-193

Rhineland 206, 211

Rhodes, Cecil John 1-9, 11-17, 39, 41, 74; *visits Stellenbosch*, 1-2; *prime minister of Cape Colony*, 2, 17; *dealings with Hofmeyer*, 2-5, 11, 14-15, 17; *and the Bond*, 4, 7, 11; *language issues*, 4; *very sick*, 5; *and Smuts*, 5-6, 9, 16-17, 27, 41, 74; *and the Cronwright- Schreiners*, 7-8, 13,

27-28; *native policy*, 8; *Hofmeyer alliance*, 9; *strikes at Kruger*, 14; *character of*, 15; *involvement in Jameson Raid*, 8, 15-16, 31; *and John X. Merriman*, 15; *Redivivus*, 16; *policy*, 25

Rhodes Redivivus 16

Rhoodie, Denys *see endnotes*

Riddell, Lord 62, 83

Riebeeck West 116

Ripon 62; *member of Cabinet committee*, 57

Robertson, Sir William *chief of Imperial General Staff*, 81

Robinson, Geoffrey *of The Star*, 53

Robinson, Hercules *high commissioner*, 9

Roman Catholic 149

Rommel, Erwin 195

Roosevelt, Franklin D. 198, 222

Round Table 45, 139, 142

Royal Air Force 84-85, 108

royal family *British*, 160 (photo), 161, 167, 170, 176, 177, 178 (photo), 179, 181; *Smuts relationship with British*, 166-167, 170, 176-179, 181; *Greek*, 172 (photo), 173 *see also Smuts*

Royalist 188

Royalty Monthly 169, 182

Russell, Arthur Oliver 131; *second Baron of Ampthill*, 131; *former viceroy of India*, 131; *member House of Lords*, 131

Russell, George 143

Russia 86, 198, 208, 220-221

Russians 171, 221

S

Salisbury 25, 35

Sandringham 166

Satyagraha (non-violence) 117, 120, 126, 130, 133

Saudi Arabia 95

Schacht, Hjalmar *German banker*, 214

Schiller 203-204

Schlesin, Miss 134

Schreiner, Olive 7, 8 (photo), 9, 13-14

Schreiner, William 14, 15, 27

Second World War (Sept 1939) 88, 101, *Smuts and the War Cabinet during*, 107 (photo), 134, 170-171, 190, 192, 204, 206; *Ireland's neutrality in*, 152

Secret Session 196

secretary of state 118; *L.S. Amery*, 45, 140; *Churchill*, 96-97, 126; *De Gaulle*, 192

self-government 55-56, 60, 79; *regarding Boer republics*, 53, 64, 68, 96; *for Transvaal*, 57-58, 63, 68

settlers 38

Shipley, A.E. 98

Simpson, Wallis 169

Sinn Fein 144-146; *prisoners*, 145

Smith, Mr *see Mr Smith*

Smith, Sir F.E. 86

Smuts, Isie 42, 86, 178 (photo), 203, 215 (photo)

Smuts, Jan Christiaan 1, 6, 21 (photo), 27, 29, 36, 49, 54, 57, 66-67 (photo), 72-73 (photo), 75 (photo), 77-78 (photo), 84 (photo), 94 (photo), 102-103 (photo), 105 (photo), 108 (photo), 109, 160 (photo), 161, 202 (photo), 205-206 (photo), 215 (photo), 222, 225 (photo); *dealings with Rhodes*, 1, 9, 13, 16-17, 41; *as a student*, 1-2, 10, 30, 116, 119, 191, 203-204; *member of the Afrikaner Bond*, 6, 9; *and the Cronwright-Schreiners*, 7, 13-14; *at headquarters of the Bond*, 7, 9; *in Kimberley*, 9-14; *to neutalise criticism of Rhodes*, 9-10; *as advocate*, 10, 34; *Kimberley speech*, 10-13; *speech, letters, and* telegrams from, 11-13, 30, 42, 44, 54, 56, 58-59, 78, 86, 99, 101, 109, 126, 131, 140, 147, 152, 165, 177, 179, 187, 198, 207-210, 212, 216, 219-220; *an empiricist*, 13; *treatment of non-whites*, 13, 37, 123-126, 129, 131-132; *and the Jameson Raid*, 16; *Rhodes' Redivivus*, 16; *settles in the Transvaal*, 17; *as state attorney*, 27 (photo), 33, 43, 96; *at Bloemfontein Conference*, 28-29; *Kruger's chief minister*, 28; *as state secretary*, 28; *draws up a complete reform bill*, 28; *views on the Uitlanders*, 29; *and Milner*, 28-30, 34, 39-45, 77 (photo), 82; *eagerness for peace*, 30, 87, 89, 147, 187, 197, 213; *and Chamberlain*, 30, 218; *ultimatum to Britain*, 31; *and the War (Anglo-Boer)*, 31, 86, 96; *and the Vereeniging peace negotiations*, 33, 37; *and Isie Smuts*, 37, 42, 86, 146, 177, 203, 219; *correspondence with Emily Hobhouse*, 39-40, 56, 76; *and Botha*, 41, 45, 64-65, 67, 73, 81-82, 84, 131, 187, 205; *for a united South Africa*, 41-42, 67-68; *in the Imperial War Cabinet*, 45, 77-78, 82-83, 87, 98, 143, 162, 178 (photo), 215 (photo); *in England*, 45, 53, 58, 75-76, 79-80, 96, 108, 143, 146, 151, 153, 163, 197, 204; *in meeting of Houses of Parliament*, 45, 80; *a Commonwealth man*, 45, 153; *General*, 51, 65, 77, 103 (photo), 104, 129, 145, 148-149, 168, 219; *memorandums of*, 55, 58-59, 140; *and self-government*, 55, 58, 79, 96, 140-141; *and Churchill*, 58-59, 83, 95-101, 104, 106 (photo), 107-108, 110, 113 (photo), 134-135, 171, 174,

190-191, 194-195, 197, 199, 219; *and Campbell-Bannerman*, 59-60, 67-68, 96; *and Gandhi*, 66, 115-116, 119, 122, 126-128, 131, 133-135; *conversion to British imperialism*, 68; *and Lloyd George*, 72 (photo), 74, 77, 80-83, 85-87, 89-91, 98, 147-148, 151, 153; *at Imperial War Conference*, 73, 78 (photo), 79,143, 146; *and the 'Commonwealth'*, 80, 140-141, 145-147, 149-155, 162-163, 175; *and the Irish question*, 80-81, 141, 143, 145-147, 149-155, 162-163, 175; *turns down Palestine command*, 81; *involved in war effort*, 84, 102, 108, 162; *government*, 98; *sent to Western Front*, 85; *as Mr Ashworth*, 85, 186; *to Switzerland*, 85, 186; *at Paris Peace Conference*, 87-89, 91, 144, 186-187, 204-205, 208, 221; *insights concerning Germany*, 88-90, 102-104, 171, 187-188, 191, 203-205, 208-209, 213-214, 216, 220-221; *and Treaty of Versailles*, 91; *as a minister*, 91; *delegate of Transvaal government*, 96; *and the miners' strike*, 98-99; *loses general election 1924*, 100; *Field Marshal*, 101, 109 (photo), 170, 180; *prime minister*, 101-102, 219; *War Cabinet*, 104, 107 (photo), 219; *early life of*, 116, 119, 191; *and the Indian problem*, 124-126, 129, 131-133; *and the Union*, 131; *-Gandhi Agreement*, 135; *contributes to Gandhi memorial volume*, 135; *opposes "Federate or Disintegrate" policy*, 139; *and De Valera*, 144, 146, 149-153, 155, 164, 186; *and the King*, 147, 154, 165; *goes to Dublin*, 149-150, 153, 164, 186; *contact with House of Windsor*, 161-162; *relations with King George V*, 161-166, 168 (photo), 169; *relations with Queen Mary*, 161, 166-168 (photo); *and the royal family*, 163, 166-167, 170, 176-177, 178 (photo), 180; *and the Prince of Wales*, 164 (photo), 167-169; *and King George VI*, 169-171, 175, 176 (photo), 177, 179-180; *and the Greek royal family*, 172 (photo), 173-175; *invested with the Order of Merit*, 175 (photo), 176; *dies 11 Sept 1950*, 180-181; *and France/ French*, 185-188, 191, 194-195, 197-198, 209-210, 212; *and Clemenceau*, 187-188; *and De Gaulle*, 190-195, 197-199; *part of privileged trio*, 190; *and Hitler*, 205, 208-209, 211, 213-214, 216-217, 219-220; *as deputy prime minister*, 206; *conflict with Hertzog*, 66, 207-208, 212, 219; *appeasement*, 209; *and Mussolini/ Italy*, 210-213; *and SWA*, 216

Smuts-Gandhi Agreement 133
Soames, Mary *see endnotes*
social security 204
Solomon, Sir Richard 126, 129; *attorney general of Cape*, 34; *leader of Progressive Party*, 64
Somerset 58
Sophia, Queen *see Queen Sophia*
South Africa 2-3, 5-9, 11-12, 14, 17, 23-27, 30, 32, 35, 37-38, 40-42, 44-45, 54, 56, 59, 63-66, 68, 73-76, 81-83, 86, 88, 90-91, 97, 99-100, 104, 115, 117-120, 122, 124-125, 130-132, 134, 141, 144-146, 152-154, 160 (photo), 162, 164-165, 168-170, 173-176, 178, 180, 187, 191, 193, 203, 205-207, 210, 218-219; *policies of*, 4, 5, 6; *united*, 5-6, 15, 31, 41-42, 65, 67; *politics of*, 6, 8, 28, 32, 55, 79, 118; *racial*

conditions in, 13, 118, 120; *high commissioner for*, 23-24, 38, 44, 51, 109, 123-124, 155, 221; *commander-in-chief*, 28; *British*, 31, 39-40; *governor general of*, 38; *prime minister of*, 102 *see also Botha, Kruger, Milner, Smuts*
South African 7-8, 25, 60, 63, 68, 73, 80, 105, 118, 141, 143, 154-155, 176-177, 179-181, 197; *affairs*, 11; *racial conditions*, 12; *political set-up*, 33, 79, 124; *nationality*, 42; *nationalism*, 44; *history*, 55, 154; *constitution*, 62; *politician*, 82; *prime minister*, 84, 150, 168; *government*, 88, 132, 214, 216; *Parliament*, 102, 162, 218; *states*, 121; *Indians*, 131, 133; *leaders*, 135, 146, 181
South African Republic 11, 18, 34
South West Africa 11, 214
Southern Ireland 148, 153
Spain 172-173, 182
Spears 190
Spender, J.A. 62
Spies, S.B. *see endnotes*
St Cyr 188, 190-191
staats procureur 96
Stalin, Joseph 171, 173, 190, 198, 220, 222
Stamfordham, Lord 149-150, 165; *King's private secretary*, 147, 164; *letters to Smuts*, 149, 166
Stanley Baldwin *see Baldwin, Stanley*
Star of the Order of the Garter 180
state attorney 23, 27, 30, 33, 43; *British*, 27; *secretary of*, 28, 45
statesman 40, 54, 107, 135, 145, 155, 162, 199; *international*, 41, 141, 143; *Commonwealth*, 185
statesmen *British*, 61, 174, 207; *of the Empire*, 76; *European*, 213
Statute of Westminster 79

Stellenbosch 9, 30; *Rhodes visited*, 1; *Victoria College*, 10, 191; *Smuts at*, 116, 119, 203
Steyn, C.F. 34-35, 41, 54
Stoffberg, Mr 116
Strasbourg 204
Stropp Bill 8
superintendent of education 6
SWA 214, 216
Swan, Maureen *see endnotes*
Switzerland 85, 186
Syria 193-194

T
Tanganyika 214
tax *export*, 3; *discriminatory*, 121-122, 133
Taxation Bill 121
Taylor, A.J.P. *see endnotes*
telegram *to Smuts*, 99, 104, 154, 165, 219, 221; *to Attlee*, 109; *Smuts and Gandhi exchange*, 131; *to Churchill*, 171
The European Idea 191
The Mole 2
The Speech from the Throne 177
The Star 53
The Times 40, 56, 142, 201
The World Crisis 101
Third Reich 218
Tories 97
totalitarians 217
Transvaal 5, 14, 17, 25-30, 32-33, 36-39, 41-42, 53-54, 57, 63, 65, 117, 119-120, 122-124, 129, 133; *independence*, 4; *government*, 6, 8, 14, 30-31, 37, 39, 43, 96, 124; *president of*, 28; *governor general of*, 44, 51; *self-government to*, 5758, 63-64, 68; *general election in*, 64; *prime minister of*, 64; *Black Act*, 132; *Republic*, 152
Transvaal Constitution 54
Transvaal Leader 127

treaty 32; *Anglo-Irish*, 148, 154
Treaty of Versailles 91, 204 *see also Peace Treaty*
Trinidad 120
Trinity College 144
Trowbridge, Anthony 200
Truman, Harry S. 222
Tunis 195
Turks 81

U

Uitlanders 15; *Rand*, 8; *leaders of*, 10; *problem*, 28; *of the Transvaal*
Ulster 151
ultimatum 31, 218
under-secretary *Lord Selborne*, 53; *Winston Churchill*, 57, 126; *De Gaulle*, 192
unemployment 88, 204-205
Union 103-104, 131-132, 165, 169, 195; *Cabinet*, 81, 103 (photo); *governor general of*, 170
Union of South Africa (1910) 63, 130, 177
Union Parliament 132-133
Unionist government 51, 53, 132-133
united 38 *see South Africa*
United Kingdom 84, 142 *see also Britain*
United Party 102, 142
United States 12, 190, 194, 196, 198, 217; *president of*, 73; *De Valera born in*, 144; *citizen of*, 145
University College 144

V

Vaal River 10
Van der Byl, Major P.V.G. 103 (photo) *see endnotes*
Vers l'Armée de Métier 191
Verwoerd, Dr H.F. 152
viceroy 121; *of India*, 131, 177; *of Ireland*, 149

Vichy *French government at*, 193; *France*, 195-196
Victoria College 1, 9-10, 191
victory 37, 44, 52, 88, 107, 128-129, 173, 221
villa 100, 212
volk 30
Von Bismarck, Otto 186
Von Lossnitser, Erich 214
Voortrekkers 74

W

Wales 75 (photo), 183 *see also Prince of Wales*
Walker, Eric A. 15, 20
Wanstead 100
War *reference to Anglo-Boer*, 30-2, 35, 41, 51, 53, 60, 96, 122-123, 143, 220-221; *reference to First World*, 45, 79, 81, 84, 86-88, 97, 100, 104, 140, 143, 145, 162-163, 168, 170, 185-189, 204, 209, 220; *reference to Second World*, 101-102, 104, 134, 152, 170-171, 173, 190-194, 198-199, 204, 206, 220-221 *see also Anglo-Boer War, First World War, Second World War*
War Memoirs 85, 91
War Office 81
Washington 194
Weigel, Major Heinrich 214
Weiner-Beit 38
Welsh, David *see endnotes*
Werth, Alexander *see endnotes*
West Epping 100
West Essex 100
Western Front 85
Westminster Gazette 150
Wheeler-Bennett, Sir John 144, 156
White Hall 26, 31, 208
Whitehall 24
Wilhelm I *German Emperor*, 186
William Schreiner *see Schreiner, William*

Williams, Hanbury 38
Wilson, Sir Henry 85, 88, 186-187
Windsor Castle 146, 161, 163
Windsors 161, 163, 165-167, 169, 171, 173, 175, 177, 179-181, 183
Winston, Churchill *see Churchill, Winston*

Wolstenholme, John 81, 119-120
Woodford Division 100

X
Xenophon 188

Y
Yalta 221